The IMF and Stabilization

Developing Country Experiences

The IMF and Stabilization:
Developing Country Experiences

Directed and edited by
Tony Killick

Contributors:
Graham Bird
Tony Killick
Jennifer Sharpley
Mary Sutton

St. Martin's Press · New York

© Overseas Development Institute 1984

St. Martin's Press, Inc., 175 Fifth Avenue, New York, NY 10010
Printed in Great Britain
First published in the United States of America in 1984

ISBN 0-312-40229-5

Library of Congress Cataloging in Publication Data
Main entry under title:

The IMF and stabilization.

   Includes indexes.
      1. International Monetary Fund.   2. Economic
stabilization—Developing countries.   3. Developing countries—
Economic policy.   4. Balance of payments—Developing
countries.   I. Killick, Tony.   II. Sutton, Mary.
III. Sharpley, Jennifer.   IV. Title: The I.M.F. and
stabilization.
HG3881.5.I58I39 1984   332.1′52   83-40190
ISBN 0-312-40229-5

Contents

Contents of Companion Volume

The Quest for Economic Stabilisation:
The IMF and the Third World

1 Introduction and summary of companion volume (*Mary Sutton*)

I. Desequilibria and Policy Antidotes
2 Extent, causes and consequences of disequilibria (*Tony Killick and Jennifer Sharpley*); 3 The potential of domestic stabilisation measures (*Jennifer Sharpley*); 4 Balance of payments policy (*Graham Bird*)

II. The Role of the IMF
An introduction to the IMF (*Tony Killick*); 5 Relationships, resource uses and the conditionality debate (*Graham Bird*); 6 IMF stabilisation programme (*Tony Killick*); 7 The impact of Fund stabilisation programmes (*Tony Killick*)

III. Conclusions
8 Towards a real economy approach (*Tony Killick, Graham Bird, Jennifer Sharpley, Mary Sutton*)

Bibliography
Index

Preface

Controversies about the policies of the International Monetary Fund in its dealings with developing countries have a venerable history. During the nearly three years in which work has been under way on this project the topic has, however, increased in topicality. The newspapers (or anyway their business sections!) are nowadays full of items discussing the work and future of the Fund, and there is widespread questioning about the future of the Bretton Woods institutions. But while interest has heightened, the issues have remained unresolved; the various steps that have been taken to strengthen 'the system' have been largely in the nature of ad hoc fire-fighting. So, more by luck than foresight, we have found ourselves preparing a study which, whatever its defects, is certainly timely.

What impelled us to undertake it was a belief that there was a dearth of serious research not only on the policies of the IMF but also on the whole question of the role of stabilisation in economic development. In the initial description of this project we thus defined our objectives as follows:

> to contribute to a remedying of this neglect; to form an evaluation of the role of the Fund in relation to the attempts of its ldc members to reconcile the need for long-term development with reasonable stability; and to suggest constructive policy improvements. It will be conducted with as much objectivity as is humanly possible, and will not start from any strongly-held ideological or economic-theoretical viewpoint.

In what follows we have thus set an examination of the IMF in the general context of economic stabilisation in developing countries, and our policy recommendations are addressed as much to ldc governments as they are to the IMF and those who control it.

The Overseas Development Institute (ODI) has a long-standing tradition of policy-oriented research in such areas as trade between developed and developing countries; the volume and effectiveness of development assistance; and other ways in which developed-country policies impinge upon Third World development. To move into questions of international finance was a logical extension of its work, particularly since non-concessional flows of capital have assumed so much greater importance during the past decade. It is, moreover, intended to continue this expansion, with plans for future research at ODI into the distributional consequences of alternative responses to balance of payments crises and into the design of developing-country adjustment strategies for the later 1980s.

We have incurred many debts of gratitude in the course of this study. The project was greatly assisted 'w an Advisory Committee made up of people with special knowledgt ·ı our area of study. This met three times: to consider the design cī the project; to review interim results; and to discuss our conclusions. We would like to record our deep appreciation of the assistance provided by committee members. Their role was, however, purely an advisory one and they do not necessarily agree with the views presented here, responsibility for which rests solely with the authors. Those who attended meetings of the committee were:

> Just Faaland (then Chr. Michelsen Institute, now OECD Development Centre)
> John Healey (then Overseas Development Administration, now Department of Trade)
> David Henderson (University College, London)
> Pendarell Kent (Bank of England)
> John King (Department of Inland Revenue)
> Ole David Norbye (Chr. Michelsen Institute)
> Bahram Nowzad (then IMF, now Editor, *Finance and Development*)
> Richard O'Brien (Amex Bank)
> Rosemary Thorp (St Anthony's College, Oxford)

We would also like to record our indebtedness to the staff of the International Monetary Fund and especially to Mr Bahram Nowzad, who was responsible for liaison between the Fund and ODI. Within the proper limits of the confidentiality of its dealings with member-governments, the Fund could not have been more helpful to us and we had many frank discussions with Fund staff at all levels, who also made extensive comments on earlier drafts. Inevitably, we have had to agree to disagree about various results and it goes without saying that the IMF staff is in no way committed to the views we express. The same caveat applies to the many others who have helped us financially, by commenting on drafts and in other ways. These are too many to list fully here (although some are acknowledged at the beginning of individual chapters) but we must especially mention Sidney Dell, G.K. Helleiner and John Williamson who were especially generous in taking time out from their busy lives to comment on a large proportion of our drafts. Grateful acknowledgement is also due to those whose financial support made our work possible. The bulk of this project was funded by a major grant awarded by the Overseas Development Administration, London. The Chr. Michelsen Institute, Bergen, also made a large contribution, for it was under their auspices that Jennifer Sharpley prepared her chapters on domestic policies and Jamaica. We were also assisted by valuable grants from the Amex Bank and the Government of Indonesia.

Many hands have been involved in the typing of successive drafts of these volumes and we would like to set down our great appreciation of the efficiency and dedication of those who have helped us in this way, in particular Margaret Beringer, Ramila Mistry and Catharine Perry. Christine Palmer gave us similarly valuable assistance on the editorial side. Finally, we would like to place on record the large contribution of Robert Wood, who was Director of ODI throughout most of the life of the project. Without his encouragement and advice from the earliest stages of designing our work it would have been impossible even to make a beginning.

T.K., G.B., J.S., M.S.
March 1983

Abbreviations

BoP	balance of payments
BSFF	Buffer Stock Financing Facility
C-20	Committee of Twenty
CCs	credit ceilings
CFF	Compensatory Financing Facility
dcs	developed countries
EAP	Extended Access Policy
EFF	Extended Financing Facility
G-10	Group of Ten
G-24	Group of Twenty-four
IMF	International Monetary Fund
ldcs	less developed countries
OF	Oil Facility
OPEC	Organisation of Petroleum Exporting Countries
PCs	performance criteria
SALs	structural adjustment loans (of the World Bank)
SDRs	Special Drawing Rights
SFF	Supplementary Financing Facility
UNCTAD	United Nations Conference on Trade and Development

'Billion' is used to refer to a thousand million

1 Introduction and Summary of Companion Volume
Mary Sutton

This volume is part of a two-volume study of the IMF and economic stabilisation in developing countries. The present volume presents the results of a series of country case studies, while the companion volume deals with the subject in a more aggregative and general manner. This introduction attempts to build a bridge between the two volumes, first by stating the problem with which the study as a whole is concerned and, second, by briefly summarising the contents of the companion volume.

A statement of the problem

When we began this study in 1980 the world economy was in turmoil and the appropriateness of the policies of the International Monetary Fund (IMF) in developing countries (ldcs) was the subject of fierce debate. Since then the turmoil and the controversy have intensified further. We live now in a world of huge and rapidly changing payments imbalances; of a network of international banking flows which shows signs of outgrowing its capabilities; of uncertainties about the role of the Fund in a situation of large disequilibria and flexible exchange rates. It is a world which appears to thrust much of the burden of payments adjustment upon the oil-importing ldcs, having no effective leverage to exert upon those who earn the counterpart surpluses, and this is a burden which gravely threatens the material aspirations of many of the poorer nations of the world.

In terms both of human welfare and the efficient operation of the world economy, it is thus centrally important to seek improved policies and stronger institutional supports. This study seeks to make at least a small contribution in this direction. It focuses particularly on the stabilisation programmes favoured by the IMF in ldcs but sets these in the general context of economic management in these countries. Its policy suggestions are thus addressed equally to those who govern these countries and to the IMF, especially to those on its councils who determine policy. Our focus is primarily developmental, concerned with reconciling the design of stabilisation programmes with the broader thrust of development strategies.

Stabilisation programmes are designed to deal with macroeconomic disequilibria. These can broadly be defined as the result of an imbalance between aggregate demand and aggregate supply capacity. Such an imbalance will typically result in undesired trends in both prices and the balance of payments (BoP). However, it is usually the emergence of a persistent payments deficit that precipitates corrective action. For while undesired levels of inflation may be tolerated over relatively long periods, a payments deficit can persist only as long as it can be financed by running down reserves or by borrowing. Failing corrective action, once the limits of financing have been reached, balance will be enforced by involuntary dislocations in import supplies. The alternative is a planned adjustment designed to restore equilibrium while minimising any negative impact on development objectives.

Planned adjustment will also necessitate reducing domestic absorption relative to income. However, in this case, the total burden of adjustment need not fall on the side of demand. Reductions in aggregate demand – and consequently in the demand for imports – can be combined with supply-side measures designed to promote the production of exports and import substitutes. The availability of financing will be a main determinant of the speed of adjustment and the feasible combination of demand- and supply-side measures. This is because, in general, aggregate demand can be cut more quickly than production can be increased.

Developing countries are more susceptible than industrial countries to payments imbalances and crises. Instability of export earnings and commodity terms of trade make ldcs more vulnerable to *temporary* disequilibria. However, over the last decade, the payments position of the non-oil ldcs, and particularly the poorest of these countries, has deteriorated sharply, with large and *persistent* deficits on current account becoming commonplace. Thus, during 1974–82, the terms of trade of non-oil ldcs deteriorated by 15% and their current account deficits averaged 20% of exports. While in some countries domestic mismanagement has aggravated the problem, for non-oil ldcs as a group higher oil and other import prices plus sluggish demand for exports due to world recession have been major external causes of their deficits.

In the wake of the first oil shock in 1973–74 commercial bank recycling of OPEC surpluses enabled some non-oil ldcs to finance a large part of their current deficits, but at the cost of a massive increase in external indebtedness. The second oil shock of 1979–80 recreated large global payments imbalances, with the oil-exporters running huge current surpluses and with a large proportion of the counterpart deficits appearing in the payments accounts of the non-oil ldcs. While these surpluses began to diminish rapidly in 1982, the counterpart improvement in the rest of the world was, and was expected to continue to be, concentrated in the Western industrial countries.

The scope for financing ldc deficits from either commercial or concessional sources is more limited now than it was after the first oil shock. While gross commercial lending to non-oil ldcs recovered in 1981, having declined sharply in 1980, the current higher exposure levels of the commercial banks in ldcs relative to the mid-1970s, combined with the sharply deterioring debt and debt service ratios of the non-oil ldcs, their weaker net reserve position, and the well-publicised difficulties of Mexico, Argentina and Brazil, suggest that the post-1973 expansion in lending is unlikely to be repeated. In any case, commercial lending has been heavily skewed in favour of the richer non-oil ldcs.

The prospects for increased concessional aid flows are also bleak. Having increased at an annual average rate of 4% in real terms during 1975 to 1980, aid from the OECD countries declined by 4% in real terms in 1981 and a return to the growth rates of the late 1970s is not expected.[1] In addition, the spectacular growth of aid from the OPEC countries in the wake of the first oil shock (48% p.a. in real terms in 1973–76) gave way to annual average declines of 8% p.a. in 1976–79 and while growth subsequently resumed (4.6% in 1979–80) the expansion of the mid-1970s is unlikely to be repeated.[2] The more hostile world environment has contributed to slower growth in the non-oil ldcs: growth rates have slowed by about one-third since the first oil shock compared with the preceding seven years and it is likely that foreign exchange shortages will increasingly form a binding constraint in the 1980s.

The role of the IMF

One of the principal functions of the IMF is to assist member countries experiencing serious payments disequilibria. The chief means by which it has provided support in the past is through Stand-by arrangements, by which the Fund can assure a member that it will be able to borrow foreign exchange during a specified period and up to a specified amount, provided the member abides by the terms of the arrangement. Developing countries are overwhelmingly the main users of Stand-by arrangments; of the 114 new Stand-bys approved by the Fund in 1976/77 – 1981/82, 108 were with developing countries.

However, the relationship between the Fund and its developing country members is not always an easy one. The central contentious issue relates to the conditionality attaching to the use of some Fund credits. A member's access to Fund resources is expressed in terms of tranches, equal to 25% of its quota to the Fund. The first of these (the 'reserve tranche') is available automatically on request and without conditions, and the next (the 'first credit tranche') is subject to minimal conditions. The Fund also has other low conditionality facilities such as the Compensatory Financing Facility. However, for borrowing in the so-called 'upper credit tranches' finance is conditional on the member government satisfying the Fund that the credit is in support of an adequate programme of domestic policies designed to remedy the payments deficits. The core of an agreed programme comprises a number of 'performance criteria' which are written into a 'letter of intent' from the member and continuing access to the credit is conditional upon adequate progress in the fulfilment of these criteria. Performance criteria vary from case to case but typically include quarterly ceilings on total domestic credit expansion and on credit to the public sector, and ceilings on certain foreign borrowing. Exchange rate depreciations may also be included in programmes, most frequently as pre-conditions for an agreement. The letter of intent will also include other measures which, however, are not performance criteria insofar as continued access to credit is not conditional on their implementation.

While the principle of conditionality is, by and large, not contested, there are strong misgivings about the design and application of conditionality. In particular country cases these misgivings relate to the specifics of the performance criteria. Frequently, Fund credits are negotiated in the midst of an economic crisis, with reserves plummeting, foreign debts accumulating, accelerating inflation and serious dislocations to domestic production. While this increases the value of access to the Fund, as a lender of last resort, it also gives Stand-by negotiations an unwanted flavour, with the member government feeling it is rushing into actions it would rather avoid and believing that it is in a weak negotiating position *vis-à-vis* the Fund. The Fund, for its part, sees itself as forced into imposing harsher conditions than would have been necessary had the member requested assistance at an earlier stage. The policy conditions laid down may be resented, both because of the loss of sovereignty implied and because of a belief that the Fund's objectives do not necessarily coincide with those of the national government. The Fund, on the other hand, often sees itself made a scapegoat for unpopular measures made inescapable by poor economic management.

At a more general level, the payments deficits of ldcs following the two oil shocks presented a major challenge to the Fund. Traditionally, IMF-supported programmes were short-term, designed typically to deal with disequilibria resulting from excess aggregate demand. Increasingly after 1974 the source of payments deficits could be traced primarily to exogenous factors rather than to domestic mismanagement. The distinction between these sources of disequilibria is admittedly not clear-cut, since failure to take corrective action even when the cause is primarily external must be classified as mismanagement. However, after the oil shocks the nature of the payments problem confronted by deficit countries and the Fund was changed. The magnitude of the disequilibria, the limited financing available, and the non-temporary nature of the deterioration in the terms of trade all suggested that the time horizon over which adjustment could be realistically expected was longer than heretofore, and that cost-effective adjustment would necessitate structural adaptation to the changed international environment. Much of this study concentrates on the implications of these changes for both the non-oil ldcs and the IMF.

Structure of this volume

The remainder of this volume comprises four chapters. There are individual case studies dealing with economic management and the role of the IMF in, respectively, Indonesia (1966–70); Jamaica (1972–80); and Kenya (1975–81). These are preceded by a chapter dealing with Latin American experiences and the structuralist school's approach to short-run economic management.

For cross-referencing purposes the chapters in the companion volume are prefixed with the letter M. Thus 'chapter M7' refers to the chapter in the other volume which studies the impact of IMF programmes. Chapter references here which have no alphabetical prefix relate to the contents of this volume.

SUMMARY OF THE COMPANION VOLUME

The main volume is divided into three parts. Part I, 'Disequilibria and Policy Antidotes', comprises three chapters.

Chapter M2 – Extent, causes and consequences of disequilibria

The first of these, Chapter M2, by Tony Killick and Jennifer Sharpley, begins by exploring the complexities of the notion of a BoP 'equilibrium' and offers a definition. Various indicators of the extent of BoP disequilibria are then examined. It is shown that ldcs, taken as a group, experience larger disequilibria than dcs, and that they are more vulnerable to instability in export earnings, commodity terms of trade and international reserves. Relative to imports, ldc reserves are smaller than those of dcs, even though greater export instability argues for a proportionately larger cushion of reserves. The growing magnitude of external debt difficulties is also noted, with the debt-servicing payments of non-oil ldcs far exceeding the cost of their oil imports.

While the larger fluctuations in their BoPs create large difficulties for ldcs, it is the trend towards large persistent deficits which is the more damaging. Even here, it is important to keep the extent of the harm in perspective, for the evidence suggests that the adverse consequences of deficits has often only been moderate. There was much diversity of experience among ldcs and the nature of the policy response itself was a prime determinant of the extent to which foreign exchange shortages impeded development. It is likely, however, that the strength of the BoP constraint greatly increased for many ldcs during the early 1980s.

The chapter then proceeds to examine the causes of BoP difficulties. Data on the relative importance of external and domestic factors suggest that prior to 1973 BoP difficulties were often due to domestic policy mistakes and excess demand. Thereafter, however, external factors assumed the greater importance, particularly in explaining the *deterioration* that occurred in the payments positions of ldcs. The analysis thus provides support both to those who stress the importance of domestic policies and those who emphasise the malign influence of the global environment, with the latter assuming greater relevance in later years.

More briefly, the chapter also examines inflation as another symptom of macroeconomic instability. It is noted that, even if it were desirable, the complete elimination of inflation is almost certainly beyond the power of national governments. Developing countries are shown to have experienced more price instability than the industrial world, both in terms of the price trend and of fluctuations around the trend. Both elements tended to worsen in the decade beginning in 1973.

The next step is to consider the effects of price instability on economic development. While there is shown to be fairly solid evidence of a negative association between inflation and growth, at least above moderate inflation rates, one cannot infer the direction of causality from this. While it is easy to think of ways in which low inflation could promote growth, it is also plausible to hold that rapid growth will assist in holding down inflation. It is suggested that there is a good case for policies which maintain a moderate pressure of aggregate demand on resources and that stabilisation programmes which severely reduce the growth of the economy make it all the harder to achieve the desired reduction in inflation.

The effects of inflation on the productive system, poverty and the distribution of income are also examined. While there are likely to be substantial effects in all three respects, it is difficult to generalise the nature of these. However, there is a general presumption that rapid inflation will tend to increase income inequalities and worsen the position of poverty groups.

The chapter proceeds to discuss the causes of inflation, about which there has been much controversy. The evidence suggests that imported inflation explains only a small part of ldc inflation, since the domestic price level has risen more rapidly than import prices. While the effect of increasing import prices could be magnified by the attempts of income earners to protect their living standards, wage pressures are not a major source of persistent inflation in the circumstances of most ldcs. It is doubtful whether strong propagation mechanisms exist in more than a minority of ldcs to transform rising import prices into a rapid inflationary spiral.

In-depth country studies point to the importance of domestic monetary factors as the major cause of inflation. Numerous investigations have shown monetary aggregates to be highly significant explanatory variables. There is also evidence that government spending is quite commonly more elastic with respect to rising prices than is tax revenue, so that the budget tends automatically to have a destabilising influence, reinforcing any ongoing inflation through deficit financing. These considerations reinforce the case of those, like the IMF, who look to conventional fiscal and monetary demand management measures in the pursuit of stabilisation, and implicitly reject suggestions that such measures are in some sense irrelevant to ldc circumstances.

However, the chapter concludes by pointing out an element of superficiality in monetarist explanations which stop short of examining the political impulses behind over-expansionary fiscal and monetary policies. To some extent, governments tolerate unwanted inflation and BoP deficits because their technical ability to control the relevant variables is limited. But the management of the economy is not just a technical matter of choosing optimum policy instruments. Governments are often unwilling to undertake effective stabilisation programmes because these are feared to result in larger net political costs than the problems which they address. Governments have to weigh the diffused and ambiguous unpopularity of allowing rising prices and foreign exchange shortages against the often more sharply focused unpopularity of counter-measures. A technically sound stabilisation programme will be of no use if it imposes such economic burdens that political upheaval causes it to be abandoned. The speed with which the programme must be executed (which will be largely determined by the volume of supporting finance) is likely to be crucial in determining its social acceptability.

Chapter M3 – The potential of domestic stabilisation measures

Jennifer Sharpley's chapter examines the scope of the authorities in developing countries to control aggregate demand and supply using domestic stabilisation measures. It deals first with the scope of fiscal policy, concentrating on control over budget deficits and excess aggregate demand from the public, private and trade sectors.

The main issue of fiscal policy in ldcs is the trend in the overall government deficit rather than its fluctuations around this trend. Whether or not growing fiscal deficits and inflation reinforce each other in a two-way relationship and are destabilising depends upon the structure of government expenditures and reserves; the government's discretionary response to inflation, and whether real public expenditures are adjusted more rapidly than reserves. To curb the size of government deficits there may be more room for the authorities to reduce real expenditures than to collect higher real revenues in the short run but political considerations make it unlikely that the authorities will welcome a reduction in their planned expenditures and quickly undertake unpopular measures. The priorities the authorities consistently attach to stabilisation goals compared with other goals, such as commitment to social welfare programmes and public investment, will influence their deficit finance requirements and hence the scope for effective fiscal policy.

It is suggested that the ability of the authorities in ldcs to control rapid inflation and payments deficits by fiscal policy might be improved in several ways. A more income-elastic tax structure would increase the built-in automatic stabilising effect of fiscal policy and help to ease the fluctuations in income. A more effective collection of tax revenues will help to slow down the growth of fiscal deficits, money creation and self-generating inflation. Adhering to structural budget planning over four to five years would make it less difficult for the authorities to increase rates of taxation, widen the tax base, improve revenue collection, and index the nominal value of certain taxes for inflation so as to expand real tax revenues and enhance the buoyancy of the tax system in investment when revenues are raised.

Turning to monetary policy, a major task identified in chapter M3 is selecting those financial aggregates whose demand function is the most stable, over whose supply the authorities have considerable control and which best 'explain' the behaviour of the economy. So that the demand for money may be predicted with reasonable accuracy, it is important that the demand-for-money function is both well defined and stable over time. In recent years, an increasing number of studies have explored alternative forms of the demand function in developing countries. In general, these studies include income and the opportunity cost of holding money as the key variables, and real income (nominally adjusted for actual or expected inflation) appears to be a far more important determinant than interest rates in the organised market. Although the key determinants are often well defined and useful for predicting the total demand for money, the stability of the demand-for-money function in developing countries is difficult to demonstrate statistically, because of the lack of consistent time-series data for a sufficient span of years.

The chapter argues that the domestic potential for stabilising the money supply in developing countries depends upon the controllability and predictability of the monetary base and the money multiplier. In general, the authorities must use their limited control over the level of central bank credit to commercial banks, including parastatal banks, to offset the other two components of the monetary base – the instability caused by fluctuations in international reserves and from fiscal deficits financed by printing money. The main instruments of monetary policy are open market operations; variations in reserve requirements; official regulation of interest rates; and direct ceilings on credit. The under-developed nature of financial institutions and markets in developing countries imposes technical limitations on the use of these instruments for stabilisation purposes, and the choice between a fixed or flexible exchange rate and between a domestic credit or money supply target will also influence the efficacy of monetary policy.

The scope of domestic stabilisation measures can be improved in the medium term by the adoption of a more flexible interest rate policy that would allow nominal interest rates in the organised money market to be raised so as to make them positive in real terms. It is suggested that higher real interest rates may encourage the use of open market operations, which are a less expansionary method of financing fiscal deficits than printing money. If more savings are institutionalised in response to higher interest rates, these deposits will expand that component of the monetary base over which the authorities have most control – namely central bank credit to commercial banks. In the private sector, financial reform may produce a savings surplus unless there are sufficient profitable investment opportunities to absorb the increased amount of mobilised savings. While the public sector deficit still has to be stabilised by fiscal policies that reconcile the surpluses and deficits of the private, public and trade sectors, it is argued that financial liberalisation policies may make this reconciliation somewhat easier without curbing total investment.

In addition to fiscal, financial and monetary policies that seek to restore the balance of aggregate demand and supply, it is suggested that a wider range of supporting policies are needed to ease inflationary pressures in key sectors, alter the country's import and export coefficients, and encourage investment during a recession. When demand exceeds supply in the aggregate or in key sectors, the mix of domestic policies will be constrained by the period over which stability is to be achieved; the priority the authorities place on stabilisation; the availability of foreign credit; and by political conditions.

Chapter M4 – Balance of payments policy
In this chapter, Graham Bird reviews the basic theoretical approaches to balance of payments management and alternative policy instruments. Approaches are investigated which stress internal monetary

factors; others which stress the importance of the exchange rate; and finally approaches which highlight structural factors. He also considers the related policy prescriptions, including demand restraint, devaluation, exchange controls and structural adaptation.

The factors affecting the basic policy choice between financing and adjustment are discussed and it is pointed out that unless domestic output can be increased adjustment inevitably entails reducing domestic absorption. This is achieved either by expenditure-reducing or expenditure-switching policies, with the choice of policy reflecting an analysis of the causes of the payments problem. The major supply-side causes of ldc payments problems are reviewed. It is argued that export instability is a problem for many ldcs and that many ldcs have experienced adverse movements in their commodity terms of trade.

Turning to demand-side factors, the discussion focuses on the monetary approach to the BoP which explains payments disequilibria exclusively in terms of domestic monetary disequilibria. An implication of this approach is that control of credit creation is both a necessary and sufficient BoP policy. The only purpose of other policies such as devaluation is to speed up the adjustment. The monetary approach has long been associated with the Fund. In this chapter it is argued that although the policies supported by the Fund do fit within the broad tradition of the monetary philosophy, the Fund's approach is more eclectic than this.

The author argues that the empirical evidence on the causes of payments problems does not unambiguously support any one explanation. He concludes that although it is generally accepted that rapid credit expansion is likely to result in payments deficits and that sound financial policy is necessary for the avoidance of such problems, credit control may not offer the least-cost means of correcting them.

Turning to specific policy instruments, the chapter first considers devaluation. It is argued that, in general, relative price changes do result from devaluation such that domestic output becomes cheaper relative to foreign output. The success of the devaluation in strengthening the BoP then depends on the response to these price changes, particularly the price elasticity of the demand for imports and the domestic currency price elasticity supply of exports. The chapter suggests that, particularly with regard to the former elasticity, pessimism may be misplaced. However, it is also suggested that export supply elasticity is correlated with the level of development and may, in the least developed countries, constitute an impediment to the efficacy of devaluation.

The effect of devaluation on the level of real expenditure is also discussed. It is suggested that generally devaluation will produce a deflationary effect on domestic demand. However, it may have an expansionary effect on output and employment, and therefore contrast with a policy based on credit control.

The chapter concludes that in many cases devaluation is a useful BoP instrument in ldc conditions but that inefficiency and structural immobility, as well as failure to adopt supporting fiscal and monetary measures, may reduce its beneficial impact. Alternative expenditure-switching instruments such as tariffs, multiple exchange rates, foreign trade taxes and subsidies are considered briefly. It is suggested that while such measures have theoretical appeal the associated administrative problems are great.

Having discussed the relative merits of expenditure-switching policies and credit controls, the chapter goes on to examine the merits and demerits of exchange controls. It is argued that while these may exert a significant short-term impact on the BoP they do little to resolve the underlying causes of payments deficits and often militate against export expansion. Finally, the chapter considers structuralist prescriptions. Although in theory not irreconcilable with the monetary approach, in practice structural programmes typically involve additional government expenditure, a larger fiscal deficit and more rapid credit expansion. Further, structural policies seem likely to require more time to take effect than is available.

Part II of the companion volume commences with a brief factual introduction to those aspects of the Fund's work most relevant to this study. After first sketching the history and objectives, it then describes the membership, governance and resources of the Fund. This is followed by summary descriptions of the various facilities and other types of support available from the Fund, leading on to an account of the formalities and modalities of IMF conditionality and, finally, to a selected bibliography. The remainder of Section B comprises three chapters.

Chapter M5 – Relationships, resource uses and the conditionality debate

Taking the period from the Bretton Woods conference to the present, chapter M5 shows how relations between the Fund and developing countries have evolved both in terms of the range of facilities under which ldc member countries may draw Fund financing, and the type of conditionality attached to it. In the 1960s, and particularly in the 1970s, there was a considerable proliferation in the number of Fund facilities – the Compensatory Financing Facility, the Buffer Stock Financing Facility, the Extended Financing Facility, the Trust Fund, and the Subsidy Accounts – that were of primary or exclusive relevance to developing countries, or sub-sets of them. However, there was somewhat greater reluctance to change the basic nature of conditionality, even though the balance moved sharply from low to high conditionality in the late 1970s. Further, recent changes in the conduct of conditionality, the move towards a rather more relaxed approach from 1979 to mid-1981 and the subsequent reversal, are also investigated in this chapter. The importance of political changes and changing views on the appropriate role of the Fund are seen to have an important bearing in this context. The changes in conditionality charted provide evidence that there is considerable scope for modification even under existing statements of Fund policy.

The second part of the chapter provides detailed information on the use of Fund resources by developing countries, and attempts to give some explanation of the trends that are identified. Changing BoP performance, institutional changes, variations in the nature and perception of Fund conditionality are all seen to have a bearing. The examination of the use of Fund resources also investigates the relative importance of the various facilities; for instance it identifies the significance of the CFF and the TF in the mid-1970s, and the general insignificance of the BSFF over the entire period. Perhaps of particular interest in the light of proposals for reform made in Chapter M8 is the discussion of the EFF, which became increasingly relevant as a channel for Fund assistance to ldcs from the late 1970s to 1981, and was in some ways effectively side-stepped after 1981, as part of the retreat from multi-year programmes, and the re-assertion of the more conventional Fund approach. This part of the chapter also contains an examination of the complex relationship between the Fund and the private international banks.

Building on the supposed catalytic effect of IMF programmes on commercial inflows, it is noted that while there is some overall empirical and anecdotal support for this, the banks are placing increasing emphasis on their own independent analyses of country risk. Also it is observed that the relationship is two-way. Not only do the banks look to the Fund to negotiate a programme but the Fund looks to the banks to provide finance. What emerges is concurrent activity involving both the Fund and the banks. However, the Fund and the banks will not always both be involved. Although they are likely to be so in the case of certain middle- and high-income ldcs – the NICs or the major exporters of manufactures – in low-income countries the Fund will largely be on its own. This suggests that the Fund's role may well be different in the two groups of countries, being a lender of last resort for normally creditworthy countries, but a lender of first, or only resort, in the case of most low-income countries. The chapter notes that it was the somewhat ambiguous position of India as a creditworthy low-income country that made its large EFF loan from the Fund contentious. In discussing the role of the Fund, the chapter examines the possible purposes of conditionality; to guarantee repayment; to encourage alignment; to maximise private inflows: to ration scarce resources; or as a tool of world macroeconomic management. The examination concludes that Fund conditionality should be used primarily as a means of encouraging cost-effective payments adjustment in countries where deficits are not merely a short-term phenomenon. While the scope for world macroeconomic management via Fund conditionality may be somewhat limited, the changes that occurred in the early 1980s appear to have been pro- rather than counter-cyclical.

Although the purpose of subsequent chapters is to undertake a more systematic investigation, the final part of M5 presents the arguments raised in the debate over Fund conditionality and attempts to make some preliminary assessment. Is the Fund a doctrinaire, inflexible, monetarist, pro-market, anti-socialist, and anti-development institution? One conclusion reached is that the confidentiality with which the Fund treats its dealings with countries makes objective assessment difficult. However, on the basis of the available evidence it is also concluded that there is considerable scope for flexibility within the Fund's activities, though this may not be exercised; that even though credit ceilings invariably feature as performance criteria this does not reflect a dogmatically monetarist stance; that the Fund has put insufficient weight on the causes of deficits in determining the most appropriate cures; that the Fund does favour market-related solutions but is not ideologically anti-socialist; and that, in the light of the above, there is room for improvement in the way in which the Fund conducts its affairs. It is to the nature of such improvement that chapter M8 is addressed.

Chapter M6 – IMF stabilisation programmes

The following chapter is concerned with the content of IMF conditionality, the degree of flexibility and adaptability which has been displayed in applying conditionality and the underlying rationale for its concentration on domestic credit ceilings as key elements in its programmes. So far as the objectives of Fund-supported stabilisation programmes are concerned, it is shown that it is in the nature of the IMF that these programmes should be in response to balance of payments deficits. Analysis of the objectives of 30 programmes supported by upper-tranche credits in 1964–79 shows that a strengthening of the payments situation was invariably the primary aim. Objectives concerning inflation and growth were secondary, while the distribution of income and wealth scarcely featured at all among the stated aims. Analysis of the same sample showed that Fund staff diagnoses of the causes of payments difficulties placed a heavy emphasis on the effects of expansionary demand policies and other aspects of domestic management. Exogenous factors were generally considered of less importance and this was true – although to reduced extent – even for the post-1973 years.

Turning to the content of Fund-supported programmes, the chapter identifies three components: preconditions (present in only some cases), performance criteria and other elements. The performance criteria form the hard core of the programmes and invariably include ceilings on domestic bank credit both overall and to the government or public sector. 'Other' programme elements may be numerous and wide-ranging (including statements about fiscal and monetary policy, wages and prices, public sector efficiency, etc.) but these are not binding. Exchange rate adjustments appear to have formed part of up to half of programmes in recent years. Liberalisation of trade and payments more generally defined is also included in a minority of cases but there are standard clauses obligating borrowing members to desist from introducing new, or intensifying existing, exchange controls.

The Fund's stated policy is to adapt conditionality to country conditions while retaining uniformity of treatment across countries. On the evidence of chapter M6 the allegation that there is a stereotyped IMF package which is applied in all countries is not sustained. On the other hand, it is argued that there are fairly severe limits to the degree of flexbility achieved in Fund programmes during the 1970s. In particular, the Fund usually prescribed a programme of demand management, even in cases where its staff had not found excess demand to be a principal cause of payments deficits. It is suggested that its record is best described as one of 'constrained flexibility'.

So far as uniformity of treatment across countries is concerned, it is argued that the Fund is unable to achieve this largely because of effective lobbying on behalf of some countries in the Executive Board. However, it is suggested that the resulting distortions are not best described as anti-socialist and that countries lacking in geo-political importance are the chief sufferers. With regard to the problems posed by the two oil shocks, it is argued that the Fund recognised the implications of the huge global payments disequilibria for the deficit countries and for its own role. It responded by increasing its lending power; creating new facilities or enlarging existing ones; and allowing some apparent softening of conditionality. However, it is argued that it found it difficult to alter the content of its programmes to accommodate the changed forms of adjustment required in response to exogenously generated payments deficits. The type of payments disequilibria faced by the typical oil importing ldc in the early 1980s placed severe limitations on the degree of domestic adjustment that could reasonably be expected in the short-to-medium run, and pointed to the necessity for changes in the structure of production and demand. However, the

Fund found it difficult to shift the substantive content of its conditionality in this direction. Moreover, the chapter records that a clear and sharp hardening in conditionality occurred in 1981, returning the Fund to a stance not dissimilar to its pre-oil crisis policy.

Thus, short-term credit ceilings continue to be the central element in IMF programmes. Three reasons are adduced for this: credit ceilings are considered to be a useful monitoring device to indicate the extent to which the stabilisation programme as a whole is being implemented; historically monetary and banking data were among the few accurate and up-to-date statistical series; they are an expression of a monetary approach to the balance of payments. It is suggested, however, that it is improbable that credit ceilings can shoulder the monitoring burden which is placed upon them, and that the data shortage explanation cannot provide a long-term basis for a continuing concentration on credit ceilings. The monetary approach to the balance of payments, while it has made a valuable contribution to understanding, is subject to a variety of limitations and criticisms, and the evidence concerning its validity is inconclusive. There are considerable elements of eclecticism in the Fund's approach and it is not purely monetarist. Nevertheless, it is argued that its underlying policy model may have contributed to a neglect of concern with minimising the costs of adjustment.

Chapter M7 – The impact of Fund programmes

Chapter M7 surveys the evidence on the impact of Fund-supported stabilisation programmes on the balance of payments and other target variables. On the basis of statistical tests carried out as part of this study, other independent analyses and successive in-house IMF reviews of upper-tranche Stand-by and extended facility credits, it is concluded that the programmes are somewhat ineffective. While there is a tendency for them to move payments indicators in the desired directions, and to affect other variables in certain ways, these tendencies rarely pass standard tests of statistical significance. Even when they do pass such tests the results suggest that the programmes have a limited impact.

With regard to the balance of payments, the test results suggest that programmes are associated with a modest short-term improvement in the current account (but this is of low statistical significance). There is a slightly stronger tendency for the basic or overall balances to be improved (but again the statistical significance was found to be low). The tests indicated that Fund programmes do result in inflows of capital from other sources but that the effect is not large. Finally, no systematic association was found to exist between Fund programmes and sustained liberalisation.

Turning to the impact on other target variables, it was found that programmes do not generally have any strong deflationary impact. In fact, there was some evidence of a positive effect on GDP growth but again the statistical significances were generally low. With regard to the rate of inflation, the results suggested that programmes probably result in a net short-run increase rather than the desired reduction. While income distribution is not typically a target variable, it is argued that programmes have a significant distributional impact. Systematic evidence is not available and it is not a variable amenable to testing. Nonetheless, it appears likely that the effects would be rather complex and are unlikely to have any *systematic* tendency to increase or reduce income concentration. In practice, a large proportion of programmes has probably had little impact on inequality one way or the other.

The chapter then goes on to suggest reasons why the impact of Fund-supported programmes is so limited. One possible reason is poor programme implementation, for the Fund has experienced large difficulties in securing governmental compliance with a number of its key performance criteria, with fiscal measures being a major source of difficulty. Compliance with external debt criteria has been good but much less success has been achieved with exchange rate and liberalisation measures. On examining the extent to which programmes influence the policy instruments to which they are directed, it was found that the effect was muted. In particular, while programmes have some tendency to bring about a deceleration in domestic credit this has slight claims to statistical significance. It is inferred that if one accepts the basically monetarist premise underlying the Fund's emphasis on the control of domestic credit, it would seem unlikely that programmes could expect to achieve strong balance of payments results from the limited deceleration they achieve in the expansion of domestic credit. However, when the correlation between implementation and results was investigated, it was found that there was no more than a moderate connection between programme execution and the achievement of the desired results, and very little connection at all between results and compliance with credit maxima. Thus, the hypothesis that IMF-supported programmes have little impact because of poor implementation receives only slight support from the available evidence.

Three other possible explanations are presented as likely contributory factors. The first is the strength of exogenous disturbances since 1973. The second is the general apathy often shown by ldc governments towards stabilisation and payments adjustment, related to the political sensitivity of effective policies in this area. The evidence suggests that an imposed programme to which there is limited government commitment is unlikely to be effective. Finally, it was suggested that weaknesses in the design of IMF-supported programmes, related in particularly to their *de facto* neglect of supply measures, are also likely to have lessened programme effectiveness.

Chapter M8 – Towards a real economy approach

Part III of the main volume comprises the conclusions of the study and proposals for change, in chapter M8. This concluding chapter proposes ways of raising the cost-effectiveness of IMF programmes and of strengthening ldc balance of payments policies.

After a brief re-statement of some of the chief conclusions of earlier chapters, Part II goes on to describe the 'real economy' approach which is the main proposal of the chapter. This places greater weight on supply-side measures and production variables, in contrast with approaches which emphasise the control of aggregate demand and monetary variables. Such a strategy of 'adjustment with growth' is presented as often being more cost efficient for ldcs than present IMF programmes. What is necessitated here is an increase in the output of tradeables relative to non-tradeables, utilising a wide range of policy instruments. Broadly, tradeables can be equated with industry and agriculture, and non-tradeables mainly comprise various services, especially government services. Since the approach is growth oriented, it is essential that investment be protected so far as possible, so it is mainly consumption which must be restrained. This is unwelcome but in the absence of much-enlarged, near-permanent international flows of concessionary finance, we see no alternative.

While relative increases in the production of tradeables are at the heart of our approach, through improved capacity utilisation and more investment, fiscal-monetary demand management measures are viewed as essential supporting measures. There follows an account of the World Bank programme of Structural Adjustment Loans which also has a real economy orientation and has influenced our own thinking.

The implications of our approach for IMF policies are considered in Part III of the chapter. This states the case for a change in these policies and divides suggested reforms into two categories: (a) those of fairly general applicability to all Fund programmes (which could be largely implemented with existing IMF resources), and (b) those relating specifically to programmes designed to deal with structural problems. Given the diversity of country situations there is little scope for general-ised solutions. That programmes should be tailor-made to fit the spe-cifics of the particular country is at the heart of what we are urging, in contrast to the somewhat standardised approach of the Fund.

The IMF has, however, conducted a limited experiment with the Extended Facility which went some way towards what we are suggest-ing. Essentially, the chapter argues for the Fund to bring its actual practices more into line with the case which it set out when introducing the EFF – a case which has become stronger subsequently. The real economy approach can be viewed as a re-design of the type of programme that would be supported, in appropriate cases, by an EFF-type credit. If Fund lending were to shift in this direction, however, it would require more resources and the chapter surveys possible sources of such increases: further increases in quotas; borrowing on the private capital market; and from member-countries; gold sales; and an SDR link.

Part IV of the chapter turns to consider ways in which ldc BoP management could be strengthened. It is suggested that some ldc governments have been slow in coming to terms with the, at least partly irreversible, deterioration in their terms of trade resulting from the two oil shocks and the world recession of the early 1980s. Some responded inadequately to these adverse external shocks, partly because of a reluctance to place sufficient weight upon economic stabilisation as a policy objective. The external causality of BoP difficulties does not remove the need for domestic adjustment. Once shortages of foreign exchange are recognised as the binding constraint upon economic development then it follows that policies designed to deal with this constraint are part of the development effort. The implications of this for development planning are discussed. The importance of avoiding fiscal and monetary excesses is urged, as is the greater use of the price mechanism and the desirability of an active exchange rate policy.

Part V of the chapter considers some of objections that have been raised against our proposals and offers rebuttals, in order to safeguard against a misunderstanding of the changes we are suggesting. Part VI then briefly considers the path by which reforms might be achieved. Confrontationalist attitudes and the advocacy of 'delinking' are rejected as unhelpful. The scope for effective unilateral action within ldcs and the IMF is limited; adequate reforms will perforce have to be secured through international consensus.

Finally, in an appendix but as an integral part of the chapter a concrete illustration is provided of the real economy approach as applied to Kenya. Among its chief features are that it is set in a cost-minimising framework; it is medium-term; it emphasises procedures for achieving a consensus on programme content; it includes a wide range of measures, including many directed at the productive system; quantified performance criteria are replaced by 'review indicators'; there is an agreed timetable of programme execution; and concrete efforts are built in to attract additional supporting finance from non-IMF sources.

2 Structuralism: The Latin American Record and the New Critique
Mary Sutton

I. INTRODUCTION

While the three single-country case studies in this volume relate to African, Caribbean and Asian cases, the debate about stabilisation policy in developing countries has in the past concentrated heavily on Latin American experience. Since the late 1950s there has developed an extensive literature questioning the appropriateness of orthodox stabilisation theory and practice to the Latin American context. Previous chapters have discussed briefly the theoretical content of the structuralist critique of orthodoxy and of the emergent neo-structuralist critique (see chapters M2 and M3). In this chapter we return to the structuralist critique but focus less on its theoretical development than on the empirical record of attempts to respond to disequilibria by implementing programmes that were influenced by the structuralist analysis. Responses to disequilibria vary greatly across countries in conception and outcome reflecting country circumstances, the causes of the disequilibria, the economic constraints and the political predilections of the authorities. The responses describe a continuum rather than a set of discrete approaches and it would be impossible to identify a pure 'structuralist' programme. Nevertheless, it is possible to distinguish programmes that fall broadly within the structuralist tradition. In the first part of this chapter we discuss three: the programme implemented by the Frei administration in Chile (1965–70); the succeeding programme of the Allende administration (1970–73); and the programme of the Velasco administration in Peru (1968–75).

The empirical record of 'structuralist' programmes in the sphere of short run financial management, coupled with the weight of theoretical evidence on the relative importance of 'monetary' and 'structural' factors in explaining inflation (see chapter M2), has left the 'monetarists' ahead in the 'structuralist/monetarist controversy'. The debate has continued, however, and since the mid-1970s there have emerged more refined versions of the 'old' structuralist arguments and new elements in the critique addressing the implications of developments within orthodoxy. While some of the 'new structuralists' have proposed detailed alternatives to orthodox stabilisation instruments, by and large they have been concerned with questioning the efficacy and cost-effectiveness of orthodox stabilisation programmes rather than proposing an alternative. The purpose of the discussion is to elucidate the nature of the neo-structuralist critique by reference to particular country cases. In this section we again take up the cases of Chile and Peru. Clearly, the onus of demonstrating empirically that there is a viable, less costly, means of averting or dealing with a payments constraint, than that associated with orthodoxy, rests with the 'new structuralists'.

The remainder of the chapter is in three sections. Part II deals with the structuralist critique of orthodoxy in theory and in practice, while Part III considers some elements of the critique advanced by the new structuralists. Part IV summarises the chapter and offers some conclusions.

II. THE 'STRUCTURALIST' CRITIQUE – THEORY AND EMPIRICAL RECORD

In this section we begin by considering the historical development of the 'structuralist' critique of orthodox stabilisation programmes; the alternative analysis of the causes of inflation which the 'structuralists' proposed; and the implications of this analysis for stabilisation policy. We then go on to consider three 'structuralist' programmes, evaluating them on their record in relation to short-term financial management.

The 'structuralist' critique of orthodox stabilisation programmes

The 'structuralist' critique of orthodox stabilisation policy emerged in the late 1950s and was associated in particular with the economists of the United Nations Economic Commission for Latin Amercia (ECLA).[1] The elaboration of the critique was stimulated by misgivings about the stabilisation programme designed for the Chilian government in 1955 by the Klein-Saks team of private consultants, and more widely about the stabilisation programmes, supported by IMF credits, initiated in the later 1950s in a number of Latin American countries.[2] The nature of orthodox stabilisation programmes has been dealt with exhaustively in the companion volume (see especially chapter M6). For the purposes of this chapter the typical features to note are three: First, the objectives of the programmes – especially the pre-oil crisis ones – were perceived as essentially short-term, comprising the resolution of an immediate balance of payments problem and/or a reduction of the rate of inflation to tolerable levels. Secondly, the source of the disequilibrium was usually identified as excess aggregate demand. Thirdly, given the diagnosis, the policy instruments were usually the conventional demand management techniques of fiscal and monetary policy combined with exhange rate adjustments.

The structuralists faulted orthodox programmes for addressing only the symptoms of disequilibria. They argued that such programmes could not make a lasting impact on the rate of inflation, because of their failure to recognise that the causes of inflation in Latin America were not adequately explained by reference to the level of aggregate demand, since the fundamental causes were typically rooted in the structures of those economies. They argued that the historical and institutional contexts in which stabilisation programmes were implemented in Latin America differed in important respects from those implicitly assumed in the theories underlying the orthodox approach and that these differences had major implications for the efficacy of orthodox stabilisation programmes.

The historical development of the Latin American economies had resulted in structures of production and trade and institutional features that inhibited smooth alterations in supply in response to the changes in the composition of aggregate demand that would be expected to occur as growth proceeded. Up to the Great Depression of the 1930s the development of many Latin American economies had been based on export-led growth supported by foreign capital. These economies shared a number of important features such as heavy reliance on primary product exports for foreign exchange and fiscal revenues; weak domestic financial structures; large urban populations employed in export-related commerce and service activities; infrastructure geared to exporting; land tenure systems that inhibited full exploitation of the land's potential; very unequal distribution of income; and small industrial sectors. The collapse of export markets in the 1930s had precipitated a change in development strategies away from export-led growth towards import-substitution. However, the transition was not a smooth one because of the magnitude of the structural changes involved and the presence of widespread factor immobility. Price signals did not result in appropriate supply responses because of bottlenecks, particularly in the food-producing and foreign exchange earning sectors (Thorp, 1971).

Institutional factors such as land tenure arrangements, characterised by landowners who were not involved directly in agricultural production and tenants who had neither the motivation nor the resources to fully exploit the land's potential, were viewed as a principal reason for the bottleneck in the supply of agricultural commodities. Rising urban populations and increased incomes in the industrial sector deriving from the import substitution activities increased the demand for food. Given inelastic supply, inflationary pressure was inevitable. Secondly, low and unstable rates of growth of export earnings due to sluggish and variable demand for primary commodity exports, coupled with rapidly rising demand for imports, such as intermediate inputs, as import substitution proceeded, gave rise to a foreign exchange bottleneck. This constituted another major source of inflationary pressure as measures such as tariffs on imports or devaluation were likely to be inflationary.

Devaluation, the critics continued, was likely to be an ineffective response to a payments problem because as primary commodity exporters the Latin American economies were price takers on world markets. Thus, devaluation would leave the foreign exchange price of their exports unchanged while the increased local currency price would not in the short run call forth a supply response for the institutional reasons mentioned above. Thus, foreign exchange revenue would be largely unaffected. Meanwhile, inelastic demand for imports would result in higher costs which would be passed on by monopolistic producers to consumers and would then be reflected in higher wage demands.

A third structural source of inflationary pressure arose in the area of government finance. Latin American administrations were typically heavily reliant on export taxes for revenue. The inadequacy of this tax base and the variability it occasioned for government revenue was viewed as a structural bottleneck. Given that the very unequal distribution of income and the accompanying concentration of political power tended to make significant tax reform impossible, resort to inflationary deficit financing was viewed as a structural problem.[3]

These, then, were identified as the three major structural sources of inflationary pressure in the economy. Superimposed on these were cumulative pressures which develop once inflation is underway. For example, the initial cause of the inflation might be related to a downturn in the export sector. Price controls imposed in response to inflation might tend to aggravate the initial problem by discouraging investment. The structuralists also identified propagation mechanisms which would evolve primarily out of the efforts of wage and profit earners to protect themselves from inflation.

In the long running 'structuralist/monetarist' controversy in the literature both sides were at pains to point out their recognition of the importance of both monetary and structural factors in explaining inflation. However, while the 'monetarists' regarded expansion of the money supply as the principal cause of inflation the structuralists viewed 'some expansion in the supply of money (as) a necessary condition' for the continuation of the inflationary process they described (Seers, 1962, p. 180). The fundamental causes of inflation however were considered to be structural and the money supply was seen as passively responding to, rather than creating inflationary pressures. In the structuralist view inflation is best regarded as an inevitable by-product of development, being an expression of 'the pressure of economic growth on an underdeveloped social and economic structure'. (Wachter, 1979). It could be successfully combated only by removing the supply bottlenecks that were its fundamental cause. This could not be achieved rapidly since it would involve re-allocating investment and initiating far-reaching institutional changes such as land reform or alterations in the structure of taxation. Bringing inflation under control would therefore be a gradual process and 'an integral part of development policy' (Prebisch, 1964).

The structuralists questioned the efficacy of orthodox stabilisation instruments, particularly devaluation. Their main concern, however, was with the impact on economic growth of programmes of demand restraint. They argued that in Latin American circumstances stabilisation programmes that aimed to reduce the budget deficit, the supply of credit and the level of real wages would precipitate a severe recession, which, given the lack of flexibility in the economy, would fail to lay the foundation for resumed growth. Orthodox stabilisation programmes might even accentuate inflation – through increased public utility charges, removal of price controls and increased import duties – while aggravating the underlying structural problems by necessitating reduced government investment in the bottleneck sectors (Thorp, 1971).

Given this critique of the orthodox approach to stabilisation policy, what did the structuralists propose as an alternative? They concentrated on the prerequisites for growth and development given the structural constraints faced by the Latin American economies. They did not ennunciate an alternative approach to short-run economic management, but rather suggested that 'the essence of a fundamental stabilisation policy is a long-term development programme to achieve the structural changes which are needed' (Seers, 1962, p. 192). The outlines of the kind of programme they would be likely to favour were suggested by Grunwald (1964). The major objectives would be to lessen the vulnerability of the economy to fluctuations in foreign exchange earnings and consequently in public revenues, increase the elasticity of supply by increasing the mobility of resources; and increase or at least protect the real incomes of the masses. Measures might include a multiple exchange rate system designed to stimulate non-traditional exports; land reforms; tax reform, notably increasing property taxes in agriculture to encourage expansion of production; and public investment in transportation, marketing and irrigation. Income redistribution was advocated as a means of directing resources towards high-productivity activities. With a view to reducing the instability of fiscal revenues due to fluctuations in earnings from foreign trade the establishment of official stabilisation funds was advocated. Tax revenue above the normal levels accruing in years when earnings were relatively high would be placed in this fund for use in years when revenue was depressed. Simultaneously efforts would be made to reduce dependence on foreign trade taxes for revenue. A passive monetary policy would be pursued but qualitative credit controls would be employed and credit to the private sector would be restricted whenever government borrowing had to be increased.

Such a programme is clearly not designed to deal with an immediate pressing balance of payments problem. It is rather an approach to removing fundamental disequilibria over the medium to long term. In turning now to consider empirical examples of 'structuralist' programmes, we will therefore be particularly concerned to find evidence of a distinctly 'structuralist' approach to stabilisation in circumstances where the room for manoeuvre has been substantially constrained by the need to deal urgently with a payments problem. The three programmes considered below were strongly influenced by structuralist thinking. The first Chilean programme (1965–70) and the Peruvian one (1968–1975) differ greatly from the second Chilean programme discussed (1970–73). The last named was a programme designed to radically transform the Chilean economy from a market to a socialist basis of operation while the others were essentially reformist. However, both types of programme can legitimately be described as 'structuralist' in some sense since, as Seers (1962, p. 192) noted, this school embraced members who interpreted the word 'structure' to include structures of 'income, demand, output, industry, exports, imports, administration, politics, society . . .', as well as members who understood it to refer mainly, if not exclusively, to structures of production and trade. The first Chilean programme and the Peruvian programme belong to the latter tradition while the second Chilean one belongs to the former.

We begin with the Chilean programme of 1965–70. Selected economic indicators for the years since 1969 are presented in Table 2.1 while Table 2.2 shows developments in the balance of payments over the same period.

Chile 1965–70

One of the first economic programmes heavily influenced by 'structuralist' thinking was that implemented by the Christian Democrat administration headed by Eduardo Frei which was elected to office at the end of 1964. It was a programme designed to address the structural weaknesses in the Chilean economy and thereby to eliminate gradually the inflation which had persisted in Chile for almost 100 years. The programme included reforms related to copper production and land ownership. Chile depended for roughly three-quarters of its export earnings on copper. A major objective of the Frei government's programme was to increase native Chilean involvement in copper production by entering into joint ventures with the foreign companies who controlled the industry; to increase the amount of copper refined in Chile and to integrate the industry into the economy. As part of its policy of 'nationalisation by agreement' the government purchased 51% of the shares in the two largest mines in Chile (Anaconda and Kennecott) which between them produced roughly 80% of Chile's copper.

The pace of land reform was accelerated with a view to stimulating agricultural production. Between 1965 and 1969 some 2.9m hectares of land came within the reform programme compared with 20,000 hectares in the previous two years. Substantial reform of the taxation system also took place, notably the introduction of more progressive personal income taxes. Income redistribution was an explicit policy goal. It was to be achieved through real wage increases biased in favour of the weakest groups and increased government expenditure on social services, as well as through the impact of the land reform programme. (The government influenced the level of real wages in a number of ways. For example, in the context of a well organised urban labour force the outcome of wage bargaining in the public sector affected adjustments in the private sector while adjustments to legal minimum wage levels and mandatory wage adjustments were other important channels.) Between 1964 and 1970, the share of salaried income in national income increased from 44.8% to 52.3% (Foxley, 1981).

The increase in the Consumer Price Index in the year to December 1964 was 40.4%. The Frei administration, in keeping with the structuralist approach, viewed inflation as '. . . the alternative to production and employment fluctuations arising from (structural) weaknesses' (Cauas, 1970, p. 816). The implication was that if substantial unemployment was to be avoided inflation would have to be reduced gradually. The objective was to reduce the December to December increase to 25% in 1965, 15% in 1966, around 10% in 1967 and so on. Achieving these reductions while redistributing income in favour of labour implied that the share of capital would fall, except to the extent that productivity increased and the gains accrued to capital rather than labour. The increase in labour's share was to be achieved by means of a wages policy based on nationwide increases equal to 100% of the previous year's rate of inflation.

The failure to keep wage increases within the programmed ceilings was the chief reason for the failure to reduce the inflation rate to the planned extent. Cauas (1970) records that the programme was off target in this respect from the first year. The anti-inflation programme anticipated an average wage increase of 35% in 1965. This target was based on

Table 2.1 Chile: selected economic indicators 1964–80

	(1) Real GDP Growth Rate %	(2) Consumer Price Index annual average (% Change)		(3) Index of real wages and salaries (April figures, 1969 = 100)	(4) Unemployment (Greater Santiago) % of labour force December figures	(5) Terms of Trade (1975 = 100)	(6) Debt Service Ratio	(7) Net International Reserves ($ mn)
		(a) Official	(b) IBRD adjusted*					
1964	4.7	50.0	—	57.5	5.3	125	...	...
1965	5.0	22.2	—	68.7	5.4	138	12.4	-92.7
1966	6.9	27.3	—	76.0	...	198	10.5	...
1967	2.5	21.4	—	91.5	...	180	12.6	...
1968	2.9	23.5	—	87.0	...	201	19.9	...
1969	3.3	28.6	—	100.0	4.6	240	18.3	...
1970	3.7	33.3	—	113.4	4.1	237	18.9	409.3
1971	7.5	19.4	34.9	144.4	4.2	167	21.2	109.5
1972	0.0	79.1	145.6	146.3	3.3	153	9.9	-119.5
1973	-3.7	351.9	461.9	137.0	4.8	192	10.9	-231.4
1974	6.0	506.0	339.4	104.7	8.3	155	11.5	-276.5
1975	-11.2	374.2	375.0	108.3	15.0	100	28.6	-551.1
1976	3.6	211.8	212.0	117.7	17.1	104	31.3	-95.6
1977	8.7	91.9	91.7	152.2	13.9	91	33.2	-102.5
1978	9.2	40.1	40.1	175.5	13.7	87	38.2	514.8
1979	8.3	33.4	—	...	13.4	89	26.2	...
1980	6.5	35.1	—	...	12.0	...	...	...

Sources: For cols.(1) and (2) (a) IFS Yearbook 1981; for (2) (b), (3), and (7) IBRD (1980) Tables 1.19(a); 3; 7; 9.3a, 9.3c and 9.21; for col (4) ILO, Yearbook of Labour Statistics, various issues; for col (5) UNCTAD (1980) Table 7.2; for col (6) IBRD, World Debt Tables, Vols EC-167/74 (Table 6), EC-167/78 (Table II–12).

* The IBRD adjusted series attempts to correct for the deficiencies of the official series which is considered to have underestimated the extent of inflation and inaccurately represented its temporal distribution over the period from 1970–73 since it recorded official prices at their controlled level at a time when a progressively larger proportion of the goods in the index were either traded in the black market or became unavailable.

the assumption that inflation would decline over the course of the year from 40% to 25%, taking account of the fact that wage adjustments were made at different points during the year in different sectors, and of the objective of improving the relative position of agricultural workers. In the event the average increase during 1965 was 45%. This produced estimated real increase in workers' per capita income of 10–12% rather than the 6–8% that had been programmed (Cauas, 1970). This larger than programmed increase in wages was mitigated somewhat on the cost side by a lower than anticipated increase in import costs. The rate of inflation decelerated markedly in 1965 (see Table 2.1) This satisfactory outcome was attributable to three factors: first, while consumption increased by more than the programmed rate (6.4% rather than the programmed 4%), investment spending grew by less than half the anticipated figure (4% rather than the programmed 9%); secondly, excess industrial capacity; and thirdly, the favourable foreign trade situation. Real GDP grew by 5%. However, the money supply expanded by 65% rather than the programmed 47% as a result of unplanned increases in government expenditure (Cauas, 1970).

During 1966 real GDP grew by almost 7% facilitated by a major improvement in the terms of trade (see Table 2.1). However, consumption increased by 10.5%, with private consumption growing slightly more rapidly than government consumption (IBRD, 1980). The rate of inflation increased from 22% in 1965 to 27% in 1966. The budget for 1967 proposed a sharp deceleration in the rate of growth of government expenditure in line with a proposed change in wage policy to take account of the fact that real increases in both 1965 and 1966 had been higher than planned. Wage increases in the public sector were to be limited to 15%, or less than the rate of inflation in 1966 (ECLA, 1968). These contractionary measures were inadequate to deal with demand pressures and, as the figures in Table 2.1 illustrate, failed to slow down the rate of growth of real wages. Consumer prices increased by 21% in 1967 while the real GDP growth rate declined sharply (see Table 2.1). The loss of momentum in 1967 was partly due to a downturn in the foreign trade sector as copper prices declined. The terms of trade recovered in 1968 but the rate of growth remained sluggish and although the index of real wages slowed a decline of 5% inflation increased to 23.5%. In late 1969 the government introduced restrictive fiscal and monetary measures in an attempt to curb inflation which was still accelerating. Price controls were tightened and limits were placed on the expansion of money and credit and on government current expenditure, while wage increases were to be strictly controlled. (In fact, as Table 2.1 illustrates the index of real wages and salaries rose sharply in 1969.) These measures failed to prevent a further increase in the rate of inflation which had reached 35% per

Table 2.2   Chile: balance of payments 1965–80 ($USm)

	1965	1966	1967	1968	1969	1970	1971	1972	1973	1974	1975	1976	1977	1978	1979	1980
Exports (fob)	692	860	878	914	1173	1135	984	858	1316	2152	1591	2116	2145	2460	3836	4706
Imports (cif)	-625	-780	-777	-802	-927	-848	-920	-1090	-1329	-1901	-1520	-1472	-2152	-2886	-4190	-5331
TRADE BALANCE	67	80	101	112	246	287	64	-231	-13	250	70	644	35	-426	-354	-625
Invisibles and Transfers	-109	-183	-238	-357	-256	-313	-255	-227	-275	-551	-567	-488	-579	-662	-836	-1160
BALANCE ON CURRENT ACCOUNT	-42	-103	-137	-145	-10	-26	-191	-458	-288	-301	-497	156	-544	-1088	-1189	-1784
Direct Investment and Other Long-term Capital	115	177	151	299	189	232	35	291	287	307	181	48	54	1511	1788	2053
of which exceptional financing	...	...	...	...	...	...	...	...	(349)	(560)	(254)	—	—	—	—	—
BASIC BALANCE	73	74	14	154	179	206	-156	-167	-1	6	-316	204	-490	423	598	268

Source: Balance of Payments Yearbook, International Monetary Fund, Vols. 22, 27 and 32.

Note: (1) The current account is defined here to include goods, services and private unrequited transfers. Official unrequited transfers are included in Direct Investment and other Long-Term Capital.
(2) Due to rounding error in converting from SDRs to $US from 1971 the basic balance figure may not always be exactly the sum of its components.

annum by the time the Frei administration left office in late 1970.

Some 'structuralist' commentators attribute the failure of the Frei programme to achieve a permanent decline in the rate of inflation simply to the level of wage adjustments permitted. For example, Foxley (1981) commenting on the Frei programme, argues that to be successful programmes of this kind need to advance consistently on the three fronts of price stability, structural reform and income redistribution. In the Frei case, he suggests, the precarious balance was upset by organised labour's success in winning larger than programmed increases, leading inevitably to higher than programmed rates of inflation. This line of argument suggests that the major shortcoming of the Frei programme was the absence of an incomes policy. Others, however, reject as inadequate the kind of 'reformist-structuralist' approach adopted by the Frei administration, advocating a much more radical approach to the structural disequilibria of the Chilean economy. Such an approach was to be adopted by the succeeding Allende administration. However, it is worthy of note that while failure to control one of the propagating mechanisms resulted in a higher than programmed inflation level, at the end of the Frei period the actual inflation rate was only slightly above the historical level. Further, the balance of payments position was healthy, some structural changes had occurred and a degree of functional income redistribution had been achieved. Thus, the Frei administration bequeathed to its successor an economy not facing a balance of payments constraint but experiencing low growth (3.7% in 1970), and persistent inflation.

Chile 1970–73

The Popular Unity condition government of Salvador Allende took office in November 1970 committed to transforming Chile into a socialist state. It held that the economy's problems could be overcome only by a radical transformation of economic and social structures which would counteract, in the words of the Minister of Economic Affairs, Pedro Vuskovic, 'an increasing subordination of the Chilean economy to foreign interests; an increasing concentration in the ownership of the means of production and, accordingly, increasing concentration of control of the basic sectors of the Chilean economy by foreign interests or powerful national monopolistic interests; and an increasing concentration of national income' (Zammit, 1973, p. 49). The government's principal objectives were to restructure the economy into three property sectors, one of which would be socially owned, one privately owned and the third jointly owned; to increase the wage earners' share of national income and to begin the socialist transformation of the economy.

On the economic front the Popular Unity government had, as we have seen, some room for manoeuvre when it took office. As Table 2.2 illustrates the balance of payments position was reasonably healthy. The level of international reserves was at an historically high level ($409m) as a result of a policy of reserve accumulation followed during the later years of the Frei administration's term. On the other hand, foreign debt had also grown considerably over these years, and was equivalent to 19% of export earnings. The room for manoeuvre was also circumscribed by the fact that while, following the presidential election, Popular Unity controlled the executive branch of the legislature, it was in a minority position in the Congress. This meant that Congress was in a position to veto Popular Unity proposals, including revenue – raising changes in the structure of taxation.

Popular Unity's immediate priority was to reactivate the economy while 'dampening . . . inflation through direct price controls . . . the maintenance of a fixed exchange rate, special financial assistance for the elimination of supply bottlenecks, and proper programming of the fiscal deficit and the expansion of money and credit' (IBRD, 1980, para. 116). During its first year in office the Allende administration brought into production the ample spare capacity existing throughout the economy following the previous four years of slow growth and the impact of the contractionary policies introduced during 1969. During 1971 domestic production was stimulated by expansionary wage, fiscal and monetary policies, involving general nominal wage increases averaging 55% and biased in favour of lower paid workers; an increase in central government expenditure of 32% in real terms and a more than doubling of the money supply (see Tables 2.3 and 2.4).

Several macroeconomic indicators for 1971 were impressive. Real GDP increased by 7.5%; industrial output increased by 11%; the share of national income received by wage and salary earners increased from 52% in 1970 to 62% in 1971. The official Consumer Price Index showed the rate of inflation to have decreased to 19%. The official CPI is however generally believed to understate the rate of inflation during the Allende years as prices were strictly controlled and black market sales became progressively more important. An alternative series compiled by the World Bank for the years from 1970 and included in Table 2.1 suggests that the true rate of inflation in 1971 was 35% (IBRD, 1980). State control over key sectors of the economy was also extended during 1971, with over 80 enterprises being taken over. Land reform was greatly accelerated, with almost as many hectares being taken over during 1971 as in the previous six years.

Less positively, gross domestic investment declined by 7.7% in 1971 while the foreign sector experienced difficulties due to both a very sharp deterioration in the terms of trade and a marked reduction in

Table 2.3   Chile: central government revenue and expenditure 1969–75 (m pesos at constant December 1969 prices)

	1969	1970	1971	1972	1973	1974	1975
Current Revenue	15.6	17.0	17.0	15.7	9.9	19.3	18.6
Current Expenditure	11.3	13.7	18.3	19.8	11.1	16.9	14.4
Current Account Surplus or Deficit	4.3	3.3	−1.4	−4.2	−1.2	2.4	4.2
Capital Revenues	0.4	0.4	0.1	0.2	0.2	—	—
Capital Expenditures	4.1	4.4	5.6	5.1	3.4	8.5	3.9
Expenditures Financed Directly by the Banking System	—	—	—	1.5	7.5	—	—
Overall Surplus or Deficit	0.6	−0.8	−6.8	−10.6	−11.8	−6.1	0.3
Memorandum Item							
Overall Surplus or Deficit as % of GDP	0.9	1.3	7.8	11.9	21.7	6.9	0.4

Source: IBRD, 1980, Tables 5.2 and 5.9.

Table 2.4   Chile: monetary survey 1970–74 (m pesos)

	1970	1971	1972	1973	1974
Foreign Assets (Net)	4	—	−10	−220	−1,344
Domestic Credit	18	39	101	726	4,008
Claims on Government (net)	10	27	78	637	3,425
Claims on Private Sector	8	12	23	89	583
Money	10	21	54	225	837
Quasi-money	7	11	30	256	1,269
Other Items (net)	5	7	7	26	558

Source: IFS Yearbook, 1981.

loans from Chile's traditional creditors. The value of copper exports declined by 16.5% – a combination of a 3.5% fall in volume and a 13.5% decline in unit value. There was a net capital outflow of $52m in 1971 compared to a net inflow of $156m in 1970 (IBRD, 1980). The balance of payments basic balance swung from a surplus of US$206m in 1970 to a deficit of $156m in 1971. As reserves fell to the equivalent of only one month's imports, the government suspended debt service payments in November 1971. It negotiated a rescheduling agreement with private US banks in early 1972 and later that year the Paris Club Group of

Creditors rescheduled debt service falling due between November 1971 and the end of 1972. The escudo was devalued in December 1971, at which time net foreign exchange reserves were roughly one-quarter the level of the previous December (see Table 2.1).

The apparent progress achieved during 1971 depended crucially on the existence of widespread idle productive capacity throughout the economy. By the end of 1971 serious supply shortages were becoming evident as inventories and foreign exchange reserves were run down and capacity limits were reached in a number of sectors. Increases in wages, government spending, credit expansion and the money supply exceeded programmed levels during 1971; average income per employed person increased by 55% compared to the 40% originally foreseen by the government; the deficit of the state sector increased by 145% in real terms and was double the programmed level; credit to the public sector was six times the level at 1969–70; money held by the private sector increased by 119% compared with a programmed increase of 54% (Griffith-Jones, 1981). Minister Vuskovic acknowledged in March 1972 that there had been 'much faster progress in income redistribution, than in adjusting supply to this new structure of income distribution, resulting in more or less appreciable imbalances between supply and demand' (Zammit, 1973, p. 53).

Nonetheless, expansionary policies were continued in 1972. While domestic production stagnated, government expenditure increased by 85% in nominal terms. The central government deficit had been equivalent to 1% of GDP in 1970. During Popular Unity's first year in office it had increased to 7.8% of GDP. In 1972 it increased further to 11.9% (see Table 2.3). The money supply, which had more than doubled in 1971, rose by a further 157% in 1972. In both years more than four-fifths of the expansion in domestic credit (of 117% and 159% respectively) went to the government sector (see Table 2.4). The official CPI showed a December 1971 to December 1972 increase of 163% while unofficial indices suggested increases of over 200%.

By the end of 1972 Chile's net foreign exchange reserves were negative (−$120m). The difficult payments position was exacerbated by a further deterioration in the terms of trade in 1972 (see Table 2.1). Copper prices declined by a further 10% while the volume of copper exports was unchanged. Total export earnings declined by 13%. However, while the trade balance deteriorated, the balance on capital account improved. Loans from Chile's traditional creditors declined sharply during the Popular Unity period. For example, official lending from US government agencies which had amounted to $236m between 1968 and 1970 fell to $44m between 1971 and 1973 (Whitehead, 1979). However, in 1972 credits from Latin American and socialist countries resulted in foreign loan commitments recovering to their 1970 level.

During 1972 Popular Unity's minority position in Congress limited the scope for effective economic management. For example, Congress rejected Popular Unity proposals to enact legislation curbing black market activities, reforming the taxation structure, nationalising industrial monopolies, and restructuring the banking system. Popular Unity was restricted to using the instruments controlled by the Executive, such as the exchange rate, public sector pricing, wage setting and allocation of credit. The economy became 'a battlefield for political struggle' between Popular Unity and the opposition parties. The economic deterioration continued during 1973. Real GDP declined by 3.7%. The official CPI recorded an inflation rate of 352%. Money supply expanded by a further 317% while domestic credit increased more than seven-fold. The government sector absorbed 89% of this credit expansion and the central government deficit was equivalent to 22% of GDP. In 1973 copper prices recovered, increasing by 55%. Combined with a 6% volume increase, this contributed to an improvement in the current account balance. However, by the end of 1973 net foreign exchange reserves had declined further to minus $23.1m. The Popular Unity government had, like the Frei administration, pursued a wage policy of full compensation for loss of purchasing power due to inflation, with larger increases being awarded to the lowest paid groups. Thus in January 1972 the minimum wage was increased by 22% (the rise in the official CPI in the year to December 1971) and the minimum wage for blue collar workers was increased by 50%. Further adjustments were announced in October 1972 (100%) and May 1973 (61%). However, the redistributive gains of 1971 were rapidly eroded as inflation accelerated. It is estimated that by the third quarter of 1972 the real minimum wage had fallen below the average level of 1970 and that by the third quarter of 1973 it had fallen to or below the levels of the mid-1960s (IBRD, 1980). Employment expanded up to 1973 as workers were absorbed into the central government and the expanded state and mixed sectors. Unemployment in the Greater Santiago area had fallen to 3.3% of the labour force by 1972 but increased during 1973 to almost 5%.

Popular Unity's short term economic strategy had relied on the existence of significant excess capacity in the economy. When this situation no longer obtained the Government was unable to curb the demand pressures set in motion in 1971. The imperative of increasing its popular support in order to enable fuller implementation of its programme of radical structural transformation led Popular Unity into populist policies that proved self-defeating.[4]

In a sympathetic analysis of the reasons for the failure of the Popular Unity experiment in Chile, Griffith-Jones (1981) stresses the extent to which emphasis on the structural causes of Chile's inflation – low growth, and underutilised productive capacity – led Popular Unity to concentrate on structural reform and to relegate short-run financial management to a secondary role. Popular Unity proceeded on the assumption that its programme of structural reform would complement short-run economic management. In fact structural reforms often exacerbated economic problems in the short-run with land reform and changes in the ownership and management of industries tending to depress output.

The role of exogenous factors, such as the deterioration in the terms of trade and the decline in capital inflows from private and official sources, was significant. However, as Grifftih-Jones stresses, unfavourable developments in the external environment might have been anticipated and planned for in designing short-run economic policy. The starting position in the Chilean case was favourable: there were not large inherited financial disequilibria and the economy initially had high foreign exchange reserves, plentiful industrial stocks and much idle productive capacity. She argues that maintaining a high level of foreign exchange reserves should have been a priority as this 'will act as a protective cushion against probable net capital outflows (or reduction in net capital inflows) as well as for unexpected changes in the international environment, such as a deterioration in the . . . terms of trade' (Griffith-Jones 1981, p. 7). Such a strategy was not followed in the Chilean case and the very rapid depletion of foreign exchange reserves increased the economy's vulnerability to exogenous shock.

Popular Unity's failure to control the level of aggregate demand led to hyperinflation and a payments crisis. The planned large increases in wages were exceeded and this combined with a pricing policy which kept prices in both the nationalised and the private sectors artificially low, resulted in demand pressures which, after existing space capacity was brought into production, manifested themselves in inflation and increased imports. Price controls failed to limit inflation and resulted in scarcities and the proliferation of black markets. Attempts to introduce rationing systems had very limited success and alienated large segments of the business community and consumers. While there were major political and social constraints on its room for manoeuvre, Popular Unity compounded the difficulties by neglecting short-run economic management and concentrating on its distributional and structural goals. Hyperinflation reversed the distributional gains of the first eighteen months while the economic crisis contributed to Popular Unity's violent overthrow in September 1973 and the subsequent reversal of its ownership reforms.

Peru 1968–75

The third example of a structuralist-influenced economic programme is, like the first, of the reformist rather than radical type. The military government headed by President Velasco which assumed power in Peru in October 1968 continued the import substitution strategy begun in the early 1960s, but allied it to a programme of wide-ranging reforms designed to bring about a structural transformation of the Peruvian economy. Major ownership reforms including nationalisation of the petroleum industry, mineral production and fish processing, as well as limited land reform and re-organisation of industry to provide for worker participation, were introduced with a view to reducing Peru's historical dependence on foreign capital and control and directing the economy towards a more autonomous development path. The programme was strongly nationalistic and derived from the view that 'the weakness of export production and general lack of dynamism in the economy during the 1960s could be remedied by the assertion of national control over the economic surplus' (Thorp and Bertram, 1978, p. 303). This would be done by adopting a tougher stance towards foreign investors operating in Peru and by reducing the monopoly power of the local 'oligarchy' in both industry and agriculture. The government, indigenous investors, and agricultural producers would then have greater scope and their increased activity would reduce the vulnerability of the economy and pressure on the balance of payments by increasing value added in exporting sectors, increasing domestic food supply, and domestic production of intermediate inputs (Thorp, 1979). Selected economic indicators for 1967–80 are presented in Table 2.5 while developments in the balance of payments are recorded in Table 2.6.

When the Velasco government assumed office the Peruvian economy was recovering from a payments crisis which had led the preceding Bélaunde government to devalue the sol by 42%, and to introduce new taxes and tighter import controls during 1967. While inflation in 1968 was high by historical levels (18.9%), the balance of payments was relatively healthy. The trade balance was in surplus, while the current account deficit had been reduced to one-sixth of its 1967 level (see Table 2.6). Foreign borrowing had increased rapidly in 1965–67 and the debt service ratio was in the region of 15% in 1968. The central government deficit was equivalent to less than 3% of GDP in 1968 and fell to less than 1% the following year (IBRD, 1973). The initially favourable balance of payments situation allowed the Velasco regime considerable room for manoeuvre when it took office. Added to that, Peru's terms of trade followed a favourable trend from 1967 to 1970 (improving by 29%). Following a decline (of 22%) between 1970 and 1972, the index improved by 40% in 1973.

Helped by the favourable starting position and the terms of trade, Peru's growth, inflation and balance of payments indicators were

Table 2.5 Peru: selected economic indicators 1967–80

Year	(1) Real growth rate of GDP %	(2) Increase in Consumer Price Index %	(3) Unemployment (% of labour force)	(4) Terms of Trade Index (1975=100)	(5) Investment GDP Ratio	(6) Debt Outstanding (disbursed US$m)	(7) Debt Service Ratio	(8) Net International Reserves ($m)
1967	3.5	9.8	....	109	14.9	634.5	11.1	....
1968	0.0	18.9	....	117	13.0	743.6	14.6	109.9
1969	4.1	6.3	....	133	12.4	853.8	12.0	151.6
1970	7.3	4.9	4.7	141	12.4	898.0	13.9	423.2
1971	5.1	6.9	4.4	119	12.6	1016.5	19.6	331.8
1972	6.0	7.1	4.2	110	12.8	1159.0	18.5	397.3
1973	6.2	9.5	4.2	154	12.7	1431.1	30.4	410.6
1974	6.9	16.9	4.0	134	15.2	2213.0	22.9	692.5
1975	3.5	23.6	4.9	100	17.4	2980.1	25.0	111.8
1976	3.1	33.5	5.2	126	16.6	3672.5	26.9	-751.7
1977	-1.0	38.5	5.8	120	14.6	4706.4	30.4	-1100.9
1978	-1.8	57.8	6.5	103	14.0	5367.4	31.1	-1025.0
1979	3.8	66.7	7.1	97	14.2	6050.4	31.6	553.9
1980	3.1	59.2	7.0	....	16.6	....	....	1285.1

Sources: For cols (1), (2), (5), IMF, IFS Yearbook 1981; for col. (3) ILO, Yearbook of Labour Statistics, 1981, Table 9; for col (4) UNCTAD, Handbook of International Trade Statistics 1980, Table 7.2; for col (6) & (7) IBRD, World Debt Tables, Docs. EC-167/80 (table x), EC-167/75 (Table 9) and EC-167/80 (Table I-A); for col (8) IBRD (1973) and (1981).

Table 2.6   Peru: The balance of payments 1967–80 ($USm)

	1967	1968	1969	1970	1971	1972	1973	1974	1975	1976	1977	1978	1979	1980 (first half)
Exports (fob)	742	850	880	1034	890	944	1112	1506	1291	1361	1726	1933	3469	1942
Imports (cif)	-810	-673	-653	-687	-721	-812	-1097	-1909	-2389	-2100	-2164	-1600	-2088	-1251
TRADE BALANCE	-68	177	227	347	169	132	16	-403	-1099	-739	-439	333	1381	691
Invisibles and transfers	-237	-230	-254	-201	-238	-197	-316	-349	-475	-509	-541	-585	-885	-553
BALANCE ON CURRENT ACCOUNT	-305	-53	-27	146	-69	-65	-300	-752	-1573	-1248	-980	-252	496	138
Direct Investment and other long term capital	157	-123	157	39	44	139	446	747	1326	862	1006	318	873	-271
– of which exceptional financing	—	—	—	—	—	—	—	—	—	(165)	(280)	(252)	(539)	(139)
BASIC BALANCE	148	70	130	185	-25	75	145	5	248	-386	27	66	1369	-133

Source: International Monetary Fund, *Balance of Payments Statistics,* Vols 27 (August 1976) and 32 (Yearbook 1981, Part I).
Notes: As for Table 2.2.

satisfactory during the early years of the Velasco regime. Between 1969 and 1973 real annual GDP growth averaged 6%, the rate of inflation averaged 7%, the basic balance was in surplus (except in 1971) and the level of net foreign exchange reserves increased (see Tables 2.5 and 2.6). Some income redistribution occurred, although it appears that it was confined to within the top quintile of the distribution (Schydlowsky and Wicht, 1979).

However, even during these years investment and production trends gave cause for concern. The Government had anticipated an upsurge in investment in the wake of the ownership reforms it had introduced. This did not materialise. The investment ratio had already declined from 21% in 1962 to 13% by 1968. For the next five years it ranged between 12.4% and 12.8%. The sluggishness of domestic private investment and the unwillingness of foreign concerns to enter into partnership arrangements with Government (particularly in the case of mining) forced the Government to take over more of the investment function than it had anticipated and more than the management personnel available to the Government could efficiently administer. Further, most of the enterprises taken over were unable to generate a surplus for investment. The increased costs associated with the Government's expanded role, coupled with its unwillingness to risk alienating its civilian political constituency by introducing major tax reform contributed to rapid expansion of the fiscal deficit. From its very low level in 1969 the deficit increased by 83% in constant terms in 1970 and more than doubled the following year. The government resorted to foreign borrowing to finance the expansion in public investment. Peru's foreign debt almost doubled in nominal terms between 1969 and 1973 (see Table 2.5). Further, the volume of exports declined by 38% between 1968 and 1973 due to reductions in fishmeal, copper, cotton and sugar output. The growth in foreign debt combined with the poor export performance and a downturn in the terms of trade resulted in the ratio of debt service payments to export earnings reaching almost 20% in 1971.

Between 1973 and 1977 a number of factors conspired to precipitate a payments crisis. Chief among these were the decline in copper prices from the very high levels of 1972–74 – the fall between 1974 and 1975 being 45% and coinciding with a decline in production in Peru; the disappearance of anchovies from the coastal waters in 1973 leading to a decline in the volume of fishmeal exports of 78% in that year; and the disappointing outcome of oil exploration in the Amazon Basin, coupled with the increase in the world price from 1974 while Peru was still an importer. An attempt to quantify the impact of these largely exogenous factors together with that of military imports (which are estimated to have represented approximately 10% of imports in 1976 and 20% in

1977) concluded that 'the four factors together represent a cost of over half a billion dollars annually in the period 1974–77, representing more than one-third of actual export earnings and nearly one-half of the average current account deficit' (Cline, 1981, p. 304). In 1975 the current account deficit was equivalent to 119% of export receipts, the debt service ratio was 25% and net international reserves were declining rapidly. The rate of inflation was 23.6% in 1975 having accelerated steadily from 1971.

As the crisis grew, the controlled prices of food and petrol were increased in June 1975; in August President Velasco was replaced by President Bermudez (his former Finance Minister); the following month there was a moderate devaluation of the Sol followed in January 1976 by budget cuts, tax increases and further price rises. In March 1976, President Bermudez, facing urgent debt repayment problems, began negotiations with the major US banks[5] for a loan to support the balance of payments. The banks, less sanguine now about Peru's growth prospects, particularly in the light of the oil exploration results, agreed to roll-over Peru's debt conditional on Peru's agreeing to a stabilisation programme designed by the banks. This programme involved a devaluation of the sol by 31% in June 1976, increased excise taxes, further increases in the controlled prices of petrol, electricity and transportation, more favourable treatment of foreign investment and a reversal of many of the anti-private sector policies of the Velasco regime (for example, the fishing fleet was sold back to private enterprise). The agreement brought to Peru an initial $200m in loans with a second $200m to follow contingent on adherence to the agreed package of measures. Agreement by 75% of the lenders (by $ participation) that Peru was making satisfactory economic progress would ensure the release of the second tranche of the loan.

For the first six months of the agreement (June to December 1976) Peru fulfilled its commitments and the banks released the second instalment of the loan. By the first quarter of 1977 however, government spending far exceeded the agreed bounds. The banks refused to negotiate further loans without IMF participation.[6] When the Peruvian authorities then began negotiations with the Fund the situation was critical. Real GDP growth had slowed down from 1974 and was negative in 1977. Net foreign exchange reserves were negative from 1976. The foreign debt had more than doubled from 1974 to reach $4.7bn, and the debt service ratio was 30%. The consumer price index increased by 38.5% in 1977. There followed a series of stabilisation attempts with IMF involvement, which we shall consider in Part III of this chapter.

Why did the Velasco programme fail? Cline (1981) suggests a mixture of bad luck and bad management, the former related to the exogenous changes noted above and the latter to misguided policies.

The import substitution strategy was put in jeopardy by the decline in export volume, although the impact was delayed by the favourable terms of trade in most years up to and including 1974 (see Table 2.5). The problem posed by the dearth of new foreign investment in mining and the long gestation period of government initiated projects was superimposed on the existing anti-export bias deriving from high levels of protection and an overvalued exchange rate (for example, the exchange rate was fixed from the devaluation of 1967 until 1975 despite a 140% increase in the price index over the intervening years), as well as natural resource constraints in fishing, sugar and cotton. This, added to the decline in private investment, deterioration in the management of nationalised enterprises and expanded government expenditure supported by foreign borrowing rather than increased domestic revenue, is sufficient to explain the appearance of a payments crisis as soon as export prices declined and the international banks reduced their unconditional lending.

Structuralist analysts, looking beyond these proximate causes, find the fundamental cause of the failure to create a restructured and more autonomous economy in an inadequate appreciation on the part of the Velasco regime of the nature and functioning of the economic structure they sought to transform. Thorp and Bertram (1978) suggest that the military correctly identified many of the structural impediments to sustained autonomous development, the chief of which being the dualistic nature of the economy. The government chose not to address this problem directly but to concentrate on trying to revive growth in the modern sector. Their confidence in the potential dynamism of indigenous investors proved unwarranted, while their traditional-sector policies (amounting to a redistribution of one-third of the land to the benefit of one-third to one-quarter of the rural labour force) were carried out without a transfer of resources into agriculture and without an improvement in the rural/urban terms of trade, which reflected the perceived need to keep down urban food prices.

In the Thorp and Bertram view, it was the failure to tackle structural problems from a political stance compatible with the declared aims that undid the Peruvian experiment: 'By refusing to move to the Left the Military lost their opportunity to mobilise mass support among the traditional sector labour force, and to use major re-distributive policies to promote a more inward-directed development strategy. At the same time, by attacking business interests and the Right, the Military lost the confidence and support of local capitalists and alienated foreign interests' (Thorp and Bertram, 1978, p. 319).

Schydlowsky and Wicht (1979) also stress the dualistic structure of the economy and the continued neglect of agriculture. However, they view the payments problems of 1967 as a manifestation of the problems associated with policies of import substitution. The strategy involves a faster rate of growth in the industrial sector than in the agricultural sector. Since the former, at least in the earlier stages of import substitution, tends to be foreign exchange demanding (for raw materials and intermediate inputs), and the latter is foreign exchange supplying, a payments problem is likely to arise. In the Schydlowsky and Wicht view, the Velasco Government, by implementing a thorough-going policy of import substitution, caused the inevitable payments problem to occur earlier than it might otherwise have done, while aggravating the already-present distortions in prices and costs. The bias against agriculture in the internal terms of trade continued, while in industry tariff protection led to high cost industrial output which was uncompetitive internationally and investment incentives continued to favour capital intensive production despite the growth in unemployment and underemployment. This fundamental error was compounded by poor macroeconomic management wherein no effort was made to sum the impact of the individual policies in order to assess their likely effect on the balance of payments. In their view many of the Velasco regime's goals could have been achieved via a strategy based on increasing production for export. In Part III we return to the Thorp and Bertram and Schydlowsky and Wicht analyses as they relate to the later Peruvian stabilisation attempts.

Structuralism in practice – the record

With respect to short-run economic management the empirical records of the three structuralist-influenced economic programmes considered above were poor. The Velasco period in Peru and the Allende period in Chile both ended with the economies in major payment crisis. The record of the Frei programme in Chile was comparatively much better but the programme failed to effect the planned reduction in the rate of inflation. Obviously, the excessively rapid expansion of aggregate demand which featured in each of these programmes is not by any means exclusive to structuralist programmes. However, the broadly structuralist approach as demonstrated in practice in the late 1960s and early 1970s appeared to contain a bias towards neglect of short-run financial constraints. The structuralists' insistence on the need to remove supply bottlenecks in the medium to long-run appeared to be seen as justifying this neglect. Structuralism in practice came to be associated with populism. It typically involved two stages. The characteristic features of the first stage were expansion of public expenditure and the money supply, increased government intervention, tighter price and import controls and extensive wage increases. The second stage typically witnessed a reluctant retreat into orthodox contractionary policies when a payments crisis arose or inflation reached intolerable levels.

Thus, although they differed greatly from each other and particular circumstances attended their failures, the three programmes discussed above serve to illustrate a central weakness of the structuralist approach, that is, the failure to ally to the longer term objectives a coherent, consistent approach to short-run economic management. Structuralists have tended to reject the traditional demand management techniques of fiscal and monetary policy without replacing them with alternative effective instruments. As Thorp and Whitehead (1979, p. 15) concede, 'it was commonly found that at the moment of crisis the structuralists lacked a coherent and practicable alternative package to monetarist measures'. Thus, not only at the level of academic debate but also in the light of the empirical results of attempts to operationalise the approach, structuralism lost the first round in the debate with orthodoxy. Many of the 'old structuralists' extended their analysis of the structure and functioning of the Latin American economies to create dependency theory. Others concentrated on refining the structuralist critique in the light of experience and of the new problems of the 1970s. The old structuralists were concerned primarily with long-run economic development. Their interest in stabilisation policy arose out of a fear that orthodox programmes entailed avoidable costs in terms of reduced output and employment. The 'new structuralist' critique focuses on the costs of adjustment, their distribution across social groups, and the impact of the speed of adjustment sought and the phasing of policies on the magnitude of these costs. We next consider this critique taking up once again the cases of Chile and Peru.

III. THE NEW STRUCTURALIST CRITIQUE

Since the mid-1970s there has been emerging a 'new' structuralist critique of orthodoxy. There are within this critique major elements of continuity with 'old' structuralism. There is also a number of new dimensions and emphases reflecting recent developments in the Latin American and the world economies.

During the 1970s a number of Latin American countries (Chile, Argentina, Uruguay) implemented stabilisation programmes that were broadly within the orthodox tradition but differed in major respects from programmes of the late 1950s. The attempts at programmes influenced by structuralism (notably in Chile under Allende in 1970–73, and less so under Frei in 1965–70 and Velasco in Peru in 1968–75) had been carried out by administrations to the left of the political spectrum. The ultra-orthodox programmes initiated in the mid-1970s were implemented by right-wing administrations. There was much greater emphasis than before on the need for long-term transformation of the economy – by means, for example, of a reduction in the size of the public sector, strengthening of private capital markets, opening up the economy to freer trade – as a condition of price stability. Stabilisation objectives went hand in hand with the longer term aim of creating a laissez-faire economy. In this second round, the monetarism of the earlier period became in a sense a 'new form of structuralism' (Foxley, 1982). A major part of the new structuralist critique is a critique of these ultra-orthodox programmes. However, the critique of old-style ortho- doxy has also been refined and is applied to countries such as Peru which has experienced successive attempts to implement orthodox stabilisation programmes since the mid-1970s.

Between phases one and two the ground of the debate has shifted somewhat. In the 1960s the 'structuralist–monetarist controversy' con- cerned the causes of inflation. In the 1970s and 1980s in line with the changes in the external environment for developing countries since the first oil price rises, and the breakdown of the system of international trade and payments in place since Bretton Woods, balance of payments problems have come to occupy centre-stage. Secondly, the emphasis in the case put by many new structuralists is less on efficacy and more on cost-efficiency. New arguments on efficacy grounds continue to be adduced, including those that, in some circumstances, devaluation can be recessionary and that money and credit restrictions can, by increas- ing the costs of working capital exercise an upward pressure on prices. (These arguments are discussed in chapters 3 and 4 of the main volume.) However, partly reflecting the weight of empirical evidence on the efficacy of orthodox measures, the new structuralists – at least when commenting on country experiences – focus their attention on the costs (in terms of reduced output, unemployment, etc.) incurred during the transition to equilibrium and especially on the distribution of these costs among social groups.

Below, we consider some of these strands in the new structuralist approach as they apply to Peru from 1977 and Chile from 1975. We begin with Peru. Selected macroeconomic indicators and balance of payments magnitudes for these years are included in Tables 2.1 and 2.2 for Chile (pp. 26 and 29) and Tables 2.5 and 2.6 for Peru (pp. 36 and 37).

Peru 1977–80

In a report prepared in 1977, the IMF identified the endogenous causes of the Peruvian payments crisis as the expansion of public sector spending without adequate taxation measures and a passive monetary policy which had led by 1975 to demand pressures which were mani- fested in the acceleration in the rate of inflation and the widening of the current account deficit. The deterioration in the current account was also due, in the Fund's view, to the increase in domestic costs of production relative to those abroad which had been nurtured by import prohibitions, licensing and tariffs.[7] The appropriate instruments for dealing with the crisis were therefore compression of aggregate demand and exchange rate reforms.

In March and again in July of 1977 there were unsuccessful attempts to negotiate Stand-by arrangements with the Fund. Disagreements between the Peruvian authorities and the Fund on the quantitative ceilings and targets, as well as disagreements within the Peruvian administration concerning the degree of demand contraction, led to the failure of the negotiations. As part of the second attempt to negotiate a Stand-by the Peruvian authorities increased the subsidised prices of food and fuel. The wave of strikes and riots which ensued contributed to the Peruvians' decision to break off negotiations with the Fund. Thorp and Angell (1980) record that there followed renewed attempts by the Peruvians to by-pass the Fund by negotiating directly with their creditors. They, however, lacking confidence in the proposed economic policies, insisted that Peru work out an agreement with the Fund.

A Stand-by arrangement was finally agreed in November 1977. The arrangement was in support of a programme designed to reduce the public sector deficit by, on the one hand, reducing expenditure and, on the other, increasing revenue via increased taxes and improved collection. Import controls were to be liberalised and the exchange rate allowed to float. Diz (1982) reports that, with the exception of the ceilings on short and medium-term foreign debt, the quantitative targets specified in the agreement (relating to total domestic credit, credit to the public sector and the level of net foreign exchange reserves) were complied with for only a three-week period in December 1977. Fund credits were suspended in early 1978 and foreign banks halted plans to provide $260m in rollover loans. By mid-1978 the crisis had reached its peak. Net foreign exchange reserves had declined to minus $1.2bn, while debt service of approximately $1bn was due during 1978. Real GDP was continuing to decline and inflation was approaching an annual rate of 100% (IBRD, 1981).

In May 1978 the Peruvian authorities launched a major stabilisation programme involving a devaluation followed by a crawling peg system; increasing the controlled prices of food and fuel and removing most subsidies; introducing new tax measures; raising interest rates; and imposing new controls on government spending. Following the introduction of this programme the international banks agreed to roll over $200m in amortisation due to them during the remainder of 1978, conditional on the signing of a new agreement with the Fund.

A Stand-by arrangement in support of the programme introduced in the previous May was approved in September 1978, whereupon a complete rescheduling of Peru's foreign debt was begun. The aims of the programme supported by the Stand-by were to restore balance of payments equilibrium, bring about a deceleration of inflation and revive production in strategic sectors of the economy. Once again, the central instrument was a reduction in the public sector deficit; the public sector's current account was to shift from a deficit of 1% of GDP in 1978 to a surplus of 5.75% in 1979, while the overall deficit was to decline from 7% of GDP in 1978 to less than 2% in 1979 (Diz, 1982).

From mid-1978 to mid-1979 the Peruvian authorities adhered strictly to the programme's conditions, remaining well within the ceilings on net domestic assets of the Central Reserve Bank, credit to the public sector and new foreign debt, and exceeding the target for net international reserves. The balance of payments position showed some improvement during the second half of 1978 and the rate of inflation declined between the first and second halves of the year, resulting in an annual increase of 57.8%

There was a marked improvement in most indicators during 1979 as illustrated by Tables 2.5 and 2.6. Growth resumed and net foreign exchange reserves were positive for the first time since 1975. However, the rate of inflation accelerated in 1979 (to 66.7%) despite a marked improvement in public sector finances. (Diz (1982) records that the public sector current account showed a surplus of 4.1% of GDP in 1979 – somewhat less than the 6% programmed in the second Stand-By arrangement – while the overall deficit was reduced to 1.9% of GDP in line with the target reduction).

The second (1978) Stand-by arrangement had been due to run until December 1980 but was replaced in August 1979 by a third in order to allow Peru to avail of the newly-ratified Supplementary Financing Facility (see chapter M5). This third arrangement was also in support of the programme launched in May 1978. Again, the performance criteria were fully complied with and the programme ran its full course.

Peru's payments position weakened again during 1981 with deficits on current account and overall balance replacing the surpluses of the previous year. The rate of inflation accelerated to 70%. In June 1982 Peru negotiated an extended arrangement with the Fund. A central objective of the three year programme is to reduce the public sector deficit which having fallen to 2% of GDP in 1979 had expanded to 8% of GDP by 1981 (IMF, 1982).

The payments crisis and the failure to adjust to it between 1975 and 1978 involved very high costs to the Peruvian economy. Real per capita GDP declined by 8.1% in this period, the investment ratio declined from 17% to 14%; open unemployment increased from 4.9% to 6.5% of the labour force while underemployment increased from 42% to 52%

of the labour force.[8] During the period of recovery real per capita GDP growth resumed slowly with a 1.2% increase between 1978 and 1980; the investment ratio recovered to 16.6%; unemployment continued to increase in 1979 before declining slightly in 1980.

In evaluating the Peruvian experience in 1975–80 neo-structuralists adduce the difficulties encountered between 1975 and 1978 in implementing a stabilisation programme as evidence of the inappropriateness of the orthodox instruments employed, and question the sustainability of the improvement ultimately achieved on the balance of payments front. There are however, within the critique a number of conflicting interpretations of why the policies were inappropriate. For example Thorp *et al*. (see Thorp (1979), Angell and Thorp (1980), Thorp, Buchdahl and Behr (1979)) argue that between 1975 and 1978 the Peruvian problem appeared intractable because the orthodox policies being applied were bound to be costly, inefficient and unsuccessful in the Peruvian context. The analysis on which the measures were based ignored, in their view, important features of Peruvian economic and political reality. The balance of payments crisis was part of a long-term structural crisis in export supply. This supply problem was evident since the 1960s and was due in the case of sugar, cotton and anchovies to natural resource constraints. The problem was compounded by the fact that the multinational corporations who controlled much of Peru's mining industry had been slow to carry out major investments during the 1960s because of the increasingly aggressive Peruvian tax legislation. In these circumstances export sales would be expected to be insensitive to the exchange rate in the short run. Further, in an atmosphere of credit squeeze, depression and political instability, exchange rate policy was not likely to prevent capital flight. Further, the effect of higher import prices would be to fuel cost-push inflation. This was because, apart from those of the state sector, imports comprised intermediate inputs and capital goods which could not be substituted in the short-run. While state sector imports might in the abstract appear more amenable to compression the political will to comply with strict fiscal controls was lacking. Therefore, in the Thorp *et al*. view, the instrument of relative prices could be expected to contribute little to closing the external gap and the burden of the stabilisation policies would have to fall on demand contraction. The realities of the Peruvian economic and political situation placed severe limits on the potential effectiveness of this approach. Debt repayments and defence commitments were large and growing, and internal consumption of exportables was low. Contraction of import demand was a costly strategy since it would be achieved at the cost of a decline in investment.

Thorp *et al*. see in the economic developments in Peru between 1975 and 1978 proof of the ineffectiveness of the policy measures employed.

They point out that after the emergence of the crisis in 1975 the payments position deteriorated further in 1976 before showing some improvement in 1977. In both years export earnings increased and export volume increased significantly in 1977, due primarily, they argue, to new copper production coming on stream. Imports declined slightly in 1976 and remained constant in dollar terms in 1977. In 1978 imports were finally compressed. Angell and Thorp (1980) estimate that almost half the reduction was due to import substitution in fuel, 44% to the fall in defence imports and only 4% each to declines in items directly affected by the stabilisation measures, that is, consumer goods and intermediate inputs. The loss of reserves continued in 1976 and both long-term and short-term debt continued to rise until 1977. Thorp *et al.* concede that non-traditional exports responded strongly to the exchange rate reforms and export subsidies but they attribute the turnaround in the economy in 1979 not to a sudden responsiveness of the internal economy to the stabilisation policies, but to an abrupt upturn due in large part to buoyant mineral prices. They predicted that the upturn in 1979 would be a temporary phenomenon and after it had been reversed the long-term crisis in export supply would manifest itself once again.

In the longer term historical perspective the events of 1968 to 1980 resemble the later stages in two preceding cycles when Peru's export-led growth model ran into crises of export supply – circa 1880 when the export sector was virtually destroyed by war and during the Great Depression of the 1930s. On all three occasions the chief manifestation of the looming payments crisis was 'rapid increase of the public foreign debt, as governments sought to sustain the growth rate of the economy at a level above that which the export sectors could by themselves support' (Thorp and Bertram, 1978, p. 6). Thorp and Bertram suggest that a breakdown of the export-led model tends to occur every fifty years and to last roughly twenty years. The export-led model has in their view kept Peru a dualistic dependent capitalist economy without the basis for self-sustaining autonomous growth and development. Thus, the major misgiving of the Thorp *et al.* school is that the stabilisation policies of the last five years have succeeded only in suppressing the fundamental structural problem confronting Peru.

The adoption of an import substituting industrialisation strategy in the early 1960s was an attempt to provide a new basis for growth. In contrast to Thorp *et al.*, Schydlowsky and Wicht (1979) consider that it was this option that ultimately precipitated the crisis of 1975–78. During the 1960s structural problems aggravated by government policies perpetuated the dualistic structure of the economy. Agriculture continued to be neglected while industries, protected behind tariff walls, increased their output but lost competitiveness. In addition to this anti-export bias in the industrial sector there was an anti-labour bias, as the price of capital was kept artifically low. The foreign exchange producing sectors (agriculture, fishing and mining) were growing more slowly than the foreign exchange demanding sector (manufacturing), leading to the classical payments crisis that inevitably results from a strategy whose success depends on a faster rate of industrial than primary sector growth.

In the Schydlowsky and Wicht view, the reforms of the Velasco regime and its reliance on exchange and import controls aggravated this inherent tendency, while imprudent foreign borrowing postponed the crisis but also exacerbated it. When the crisis finally arose in 1975 its causes were misdiagnosed by the policy makers. In their view there was no general problem of excess demand and stabilisation policies addressing the demand side were inevitably counter-productive. The general devaluation which formed part of the programme negotiated with the private banks and the later Fund-supported programmes could have only a minimal effect in promoting exports of manufactures because import costs rose with the exchange rate while in the traditional sector short-run supply elasticity was low. Similarly, price responsiveness of imports was low and they were reduced in response to recession rather than relative price changes. But recession was accompanied by inflation as food and input prices rose. The ensuing efforts of wage earners to maintain their real incomes fed the inflationary process. The government deficit failed to narrow because the recession reduced tax revenue, while the credit restraint fed the recession.

Schydlowsky has argued (see for example 1979 and 1982) that in semi-industrialised ldcs generalised devaluation and demand restraint involve unnecessarily high costs. This is because they fail to elicit potential supply-side responses that could bear fruit in the short run and could contribute to containing the costs of stabilisation. The principal features of these economies that inhibit the operation of the traditional prescriptions *vis-à-vis* the balance of payments are first, low price elasticities of export supply and import demand, and secondly, excessively large non-traded goods sectors. The price elasticity of export supply is low, typically because the aggregate supply curve for products which could be exported is S-shaped. It has a fairly inelastic portion corresponding to activities such as mining and industrial agriculture, an intermediate segment for food agriculture and a very elastic segment for industry. These differing supply elasticities reflect the varying cost structures of the activities – structures which differ for a variety of reasons, including as a result of economic policies which discriminate between them. While its supply curve is relatively elastic the industrial sector depends, more than any other, on imported inputs. For this reason devaluation will tend to increase the profitability of industrial production much less than that of primary production. Since the elasticity of mining and industrial agriculture with respect to the exchange rate will tend to be low, the aggregate elasticity of exports to devaluation will be low. The elasticity of demand for imports with respect to the exchange rate may be lower than the price elasticity of demand, if the import components of goods offered on the domestic market are similar, or if domestic factor remunerations are very responsive to changes in the exchange rate, such that devaluation does not significantly change relative prices. The non-traded goods sector typically comprises both non-tradeable goods and 'tradeable non-traded' goods rendered thus by policies which, as part of an import substituting industrialisation strategy, impose duties on imports and offer a low exchange rate for exports.

The objective of the alternative stabilisation strategy suggested by Schydlowsky is to operate on the elastic upper section of the supply curve of exports, and to transform tradeable non-traded goods into traded goods. The mechanism for accomplishing these aims is a differential devaluation. Such a policy would, by setting the rate for each product at a level at least comparable to the total exchange rate affecting industrial costs, raise the local currency revenue from the export of industrial goods. This would bring the structure of exchange rates on the sales side into line with the implicit structure created by trade restrictions and other policies on the cost side. Thus 'the cost differences that cause the export supply curve to be S-shaped would be offset and the kink in the export supply curve would disappear . . .' (1982, p. 119). The same mechanism would transform tradeable non-traded goods into traded goods by raising the export point. Such a policy would, in addition to offsetting existing implicit multiple exchange rate structures on the cost side, complement import restrictions with export promotion; provide an outlet for excess capacity typically built up over the years of an ISI policy; and allow existing idle capital and labour to be employed as the economy grew out of its balance of payments problem.[9]

In the Peruvian case, Schydlowsky and Wicht (1979) argued that a strategy based on industrial production for export rather than for the domestic market could have achieved many of the Velasco regime's goals if applied in 1968 and that even in 1975 there was still scope for implementing such a strategy as a means of overcoming the payments crisis. They point out that, largely as a result of factor cost distortions favouring capital, Peru had in 1968 a large capital stock that was underutilised, as well as high un- and underemployment of labour. Policies directed towards increasing capacity utilisation could have substantially increased output, export earnings, fiscal revenue, employment and growth. These policies might have included export subsidies or compensated devaluation, removal of restrictions on raw material imports, production incentives, and more flexible labour practices associated with a move towards generalised triple-shift production.

Even if such policies had not been adopted until 1975, the costs of stabilisation could, they argue, have been contained by focusing on the 'constrained supply' capacity of the economy. Had the move towards full capacity utilisation been phased over a five year period (to allow time to establish markets), Schydlowsky and Wicht's estimates suggest that current account deficits would have persisted in 1975 and 1976, necessitating new borrowing of $800m, but that by 1977 surpluses would have appeared out of which the debt could have been repaid. They argue that such stabilisation through growth was feasible in 1975. It would have been a low-cost strategy and would also have overcome the fundamental cause of the payments problem – sectoral imbalances – by curing rather than repressing it.

In response to the structuralist critique, defenders of the Peruvian stabilisation programmes argue that the policies were appropriate and that they were successful as soon as they were fully implemented. Cline (1981), for example, argues that the programme launched in 1976 would have worked had not the government shattered it with an excessive budget in 1977. In Cline's view the government's pursuance of excess demand policies for two years after the disequilibrium had reached crisis proportions, coupled with an inappropriate exchange rate, was responsible for the loss of output in 1977 and 1978. The shock of corrective adjustment became much greater than it would have been had it been undertaken earlier. He hypothesises that, had the government introduced its 1978 stabilisation measures in 1975, the external imbalance would have been corrected in 1976 and 1977, Peru would not have approached bankruptcy, and . . . the total sacrifice in growth would have been much smaller' (Cline, 1981, p. 322).

Which of these conflicting interpretations does the empirical evidence appear to support? A key contention in both the Thorp *et al.* and Schydlowsky and Wicht arguments is that Peruvian imports and exports are not responsive to exchange rate changes. The empirical evidence casts doubt on this contention. For example, Cline (1981) reports results of a simple regression analysis of the responsiveness of Peruvian imports and exports to changes in the real exchange rate based on data for 1959–78. The results suggest that a one per cent depreciation in the real exchange rate causes a one per cent fall in imports. Similarly with regard to exports, these statistical tests indicate that a one per cent depreciation in the real exchange rate calls forth about a one half of one per cent rise in exports. The Cline tests are based on data for a relatively short period and cannot be taken as conclusive.[10] However, data compiled by UNCTAD on import and export volumes and the real effective exchange rate contained in Table 2.7 appear to corroborate the Cline findings. Cline himself quotes the developments in Peru's trade balance between 1977 and 1978 when stabilisation measures including devaluation were being applied. He notes the decline in the value of imports and the rise in the value of exports between 1975 and 1978 (see Table 2.6).

Table 2.7   Peru: exports, imports and the real effective exchange rate 1975–1979

	1975	1976	1977	1978	1979
Quantum Index of Exports	100	77	91	118	181
Quantum Index of Imports	100	77	64	61	50
Real Exchange Rate	100	92	80	59	59*

Source: Import and Export series UNCTAD, *Handbook of International Trade Statistics*, 1980, Table 7.2; Real Effective Exchange Rate Series from unpublished UNCTAD data.

* First six months only.

As noted above however, Thorp *et al.* contend that the year to year developments in Peru's payments position were largely unrelated to the stabilisation measures. They point to the continuing deterioration in 1976. While the basic balance did deteriorate in 1976, the implications for the efficacy of the stabilisation measures are not clear. The trade balance improved in 1976, although the volume of exports declined. As Thorp *et al.* emphasise, a considerable part of the increase in the volume of exports in 1977 was due to increased copper production which was unrelated to developments in the exchange rate, reflecting rather investment decisions made many years earlier. Copper exports increased by 70% in volume terms in 1977. Of the total increase in export earnings in 1977 of $365m, 45% was accounted for by increased earnings from copper. Similarly, the expansion in petroleum exports (which more than trebled in volume terms between 1977 and 1978 and increased by 70% in 1979) is largely unrelated to exchange rate movements. The Cline tests had predicted an increase of 15% in the quantum of exports between 1975 and 1978 and Cline attributes the larger than predicted increase to the copper and petroleum volumes. Other traditional exports recording volume increases in 1975–78 included silver, lead and zinc, as well as fish products, coffee and wool. The traditional exports identified by Thorp *et al.* as facing major crises of supply – sugar, cotton, fishmeal and fish-oil – all recorded significant declines in volume.

There is little disagreement about the responsiveness of non-traditional exports (such as textiles and clothing, semi-processed timber, frozen and canned fish, dried flowers, onions, garlic). Tests by

Sheahan (1980) have shown that these exports respond strongly to the exchange rate. In 1975 non-traditional exports accounted for 8% of total export earnings. Following the devaluations of 1976 and 1977 they rose two and a half times in dollar value between 1975 and 1977 accounting for 14% of total exports in the latter year. Earnings from non-traditional exports increased from $330m in 1978 (17% of total export earnings) to $680m in 1979 (20% of total export earnings).

The other central contention of Schydlowsky and Wicht (1979) is that there was no generalised excess demand in 1975 and that the increasing government deficits reflected primarily declines in government revenue brought about by the recession. The data in Table 2.8 below suggest that the expansion in the central government deficit in 1973 did reflect primarily reduced revenue. However, the expansion in the deficit in 1975 resulted from an increase in expenditure of 15% in real terms, exceeding the 10% rise in revenue. The public sector deficit is estimated to have expanded from 6.3% of GDP in 1974 to 10.5% in 1975 (IBRD, 1981). Thorp *et al*. acknowledge the role of fiscal deficits in the payments crisis and the need for demand restraint. While criticising the 1977 Stand-by as unduly harsh in demanding a too rapid pace of adjustment, they regard a major achievement of the 1978 programme to have been the attainment of some degree of control over public spending (as mentioned on page 45 above this did not prove to be a lasting achievement).

Table 2.8   *Peru: central government revenue and expenditure, 1972–80, constant 1975 prices*

	1972	1973	1974	1975	1976	1977	1978	1979	1980
Revenue	83.7	73.1	80.8	88.6	85.2	87.4	94.1	102.6	120.9
Expenditure	89.2	90.4	92.8	106.7	109.3	105.6	96.0	91.9	125.5
Deficit/ Surplus	–5.5	–17.3	–12.1	–18.1	–24.1	–18.2	–1.9	10.7	–4.6

Source: IMF, *Government Finance Statistics Yearbook*, Vol. V, 1981. Nominal figures deflated by implicit GDP deflator, *IFS Yearbook 1981*.

The Schydlowsky and Wicht and Thorp *et al*. analyses of the Peruvian payments crisis highlight one of the central features of structuralism, that is the unwillingness to allow issues of short-run stabilisation on the one hand and longer-run development to be compartmentalised. This emphasis on the need to locate particular episodes of disequilibrium within the historical context of a country's economic development is one of the major contributions of the structuralist critique. However, this approach often leads structuralists to insist on the need for major reorientation of economic policy at precisely those moments when the scope for such change is most circumscribed. Schydlowsky and Wicht do not underestimate the dimensions of the challenge posed by their strategy; it would necessitate '(1) a major break with past policy, (2) a major break with past tradition in management, (3) a virtual revolution in the labour market with the possibility of full employment drastically affecting union power, (4) a major confrontation with GATT and other countries over export supports' (1979, p. III–27). It is difficult to see how changes of this kind could have been implemented between 1975 and 1978 given the dimensions of the payments crisis and the consequent obligation on the Peruvian authorities to concentrate on avoiding external bankruptcy. Thorp *et al.* acknowledge that the scope for innovative action narrows rapidly once a payments problem arises. They consider that the scope for the kind of fundamental structural change which they favour was there in 1968 but that the Velasco regime failed to devise a clear and comprehensive strategy. Nonetheless, Thorp *et al.* consider that even in 1975 the payments crisis could have been managed by instruments such as direct controls and selective taxes but that the Peruvian authorities' realistic assessment of what would be acceptable to the private banks and the Fund, on whom they were now dependent, led them to opt for orthodox demand restraint instruments.

Chile 1975–79

A major part of the neo-structuralist critique addresses issues arising out of recent stabilisation programmes in some of the so-called Southern Cone countries, notably Chile (from 1975), Argentina (from 1976) and Uruguay (from 1974). In each of these cases stabilisation programmes were adopted coincident with major reorientations of economic policy in a laissez-faire direction under military regimes. These programmes have been labelled 'new orthodoxy' (Diaz-Alejandro, 1981) and 'neo-conservative' (Foxley, forthcoming). What distinguishes them from the conventional approach is their emphasis on the need to supplement traditional demand management policies by trade and financial reforms which extend the role of the price mechanism as the allocative instrument. Such reforms are viewed as essential to prevent the continual recurrence of inflation and payments problems. Thus, like structuralist programmes, these southern cone programmes have adopted a longer time horizon and a broader approach than conventional programmes wherein the objective is perceived as essentially short-term and confined to the relaxation of an immediate payments constraint.

The 'southern cone' programmes seek to transform the politico/economic context and to establish a new basis for growth reliant on market economy principles. The programmes in Chile, Argentina and Uruguay are all typically included in the 'southern cone' case. However, for a variety of reasons the Argentine and Uruguayan programmes were not pursued with as much conviction and consistency as the Chilean programme.[11] For this reason and because much of the literature concentrates on the Chilean case we shall confine our attention to this.

We have seen, earlier (pp. 29–34) that when the Popular Unity government of Salvadore Allende was overthrown in September 1973 the Chilean economy was in crisis: inflation was estimated to be over 20% per month, production was falling, net international reserves were negative, debt service payments were in arrears and the central government and public sector enterprises were running large deficits. Negotiations with the IMF began in November 1973 and a Stand-by arrangement in the first (ie low-conditionality) credit tranche was concluded in January 1974. In March 1974 the Paris group of creditors, with the Fund acting as consultant, agreed to roll over 30% of debt repayments outstanding for 1973 and 1974. Further, both the volume and unit value of copper exports increased markedly in 1974. These factors contributed to the improved payments position in 1974 relative to the previous three years (see Table 2.2). While net international reserves remained negative, the loss of reserves was small by comparison with the preceding four years (see Table 2.1). The official Consumer Price Index showed inflation to have increased from 352% in 1973 to 506% in 1974. However, the World Bank series shows a decline from 462% in 1973 to 340% in 1974. Real GDP grew by 6%, having declined steadily from 1971. However, unemployment increased from 4.8% to 8.3% of the labour force. During 1974 also, a number of key economic decisions were implemented, including decontrol of prices, introduction of a very rapid programme of tariff reductions, creation of a capital market, devaluation and unification of the exchange rate, reform of the tax system, introduction of a new foreign investment code, and reversal of the structural changes fostered by the previous regime, by, for example, cessation of land expropriation, settlement of outstanding expropriation claims of foreign investors and return of socialised enterprises to the private sector.

A number of factors combined in early 1975 to provoke the introduction of a severe austerity programme. Chief among them was a collapse in copper prices at the end of 1974. The unit value of copper exports declined by 38% between 1974 and 1975. Combined with a 13% fall in volume, this resulted in a halving of Chile's earnings from copper in 1975. While non-traditional exports had been expanding since 1974 this did not compensate for the decline in copper earnings. The current account deficit tripled in 1975. This, added to a decline in long-term capital inflows attributable to tightness in international capital markets and lack of confidence in Chile's prospects for economic and political stability, resulted in a substantial deficit on basic balance (see Table 2.2). The loss of reserves accelerated, with Chile's negative holding doubling in one year. The looming payments crisis was clearly perceptible by the end of the first quarter of 1975.

Further, inflation began to accelerate in the first quarter of 1975. The CPI rose by 61% in that quarter compared with an increase of 39% in the last quarter of 1974. Griffith-Jones (1981) reports that the Fund had been very critical of demand management during 1974. The continuing high inflation was in the Fund view attributable to excess demand caused primarily by the wage and salary increases granted in January 1974. Griffith-Jones suggests that the authorities were aware that continued Fund support would be contingent on severe demand restraint. These factors strengthened the position of those in the cabinet who argued that stabilisation could be achieved only by applying a programme of 'shock treatment' which however painful in the short run would lay the foundation for sustained growth.

The programme introduced in April 1975 and supported by a Stand-by arrangement in the second and third tranches, aimed to reduce inflation to the world level and remove the foreign exchange constraint. This was to be achieved through monetary policy, supported by fiscal restraint and devaluation. The stabilisation objectives were to be pursued in tandem with a continuation of longer-term policy reforms, i.e. decontrol of prices, trade liberalisation, development of a capital market and privatisation of economic activity designed to transform the economy so that it operated to the maximum possible extent on free market principles.

Fiscal balance was achieved by 1976. The central government deficit had already been reduced during 1974 from 20% of GDP in late 1973 to 7% in 1974 (see Table 2.3). In 1975 central government expenditure was cut by 28% in *real* terms. Combined with increased revenue as a result of tax reforms introduced at the end of 1974 and improved tax collection, this resulted in a surplus in the budget in 1975. The following year, in the wake of increases in public utility prices and credit restrictions, the deficits of the remaining public sector enterprises were also eliminated.

The balance of payments position also improved in 1976. The current account and basic balances showed surpluses while the level of net foreign exchange reserves, although still negative, improved markedly (see Tables 2.1 and 2.2). The exchange rate had been put on a crawling peg in October 1973 and depreciated slowly during 1974. This depreciation was accelerated during 1975. Export earnings from copper recovered in 1976, due primarily to a 25% increase in volume, while non-copper exports continued to expand. The real value of non-copper exports increased by 47% between 1974 and 1976 (IBRD, 1980). This improvement in export performance combined with a reduced volume of imports (the index declined from 155 in 1974 to 104 in 1976) accounted for the improved payments situation in 1976.

The rate of inflation decelerated between 1974 and 1976 but remained at the three digit level. Despite the elimination of the fiscal deficit and efforts to limit credit to the private sector, the money supply continued to grow rapidly, increasing by 258% in 1975 and 194% in 1976. The main source of reserve money creation was the build up of international reserves due to capital repatriation, short-term capital inflows, the growth of non-copper exports and reduced imports. Concern about the impact of the growth in reserves on the money supply provoked a revaluation of the peso in July 1976 and again in March 1977. (From early 1978 until mid-1979 the Chilean peso followed a published schedule of mini-devaluations. In mid-1979 the rate was fixed at P39/US$ which was maintained until mid-1982.) Between 1975 and 1978 the inflow of foreign currency to Chile accounted for 80% of the cumulative change in the monetary base (Zahler, 1980).

The Fund had played a crucial role in 1974 and 1975 in granting credits to Chile and in facilitating Chile's access to other sources of credit especially through the renegotiation of official loans. The Fund's direct influence diminished in 1976. In that year Chile began to obtain access to loans on the private international capital markets. These markets had become more liquid and the 1975 stabilisation strategy had increased Chile's credit-worthiness. Its need of the IMF 'seal of approval' was correspondingly reduced. In 1976 negotiations between Chile and the Fund on the terms of a new Stand-by arrangement failed. Griffith-Jones (1981a) reports two reasons for the failure. In the first place the Fund was critical of what it considered to be excessive adherence by the Chileans to the principles of a free market economy. She states that the Fund counselled the Chileans to increase public investment and fund it by additional direct taxation and hinted in documents prepared in 1976 at the possibility of introducing price guidelines or even some kind of incomes policy. The second and more important area of disagreement was the appropriate level of real wages. A system of wage indexation had been introduced in late 1974. This contributed to a significant improvement in average real wages and salaries relative to late 1973. However, they remained 20–30% below the levels of 1970 (IBRD, 1980). As part of the programme of austerity adopted in 1975, the wage adjustment formula was modified. White-collar salaries increased slightly by 1975 but blue-collar wages fell by 8% on 1974. According to Griffith-Jones the Fund wanted further reductions in real wages in 1976. The Chilean authorities resisted this and maintained the same wage policy in 1976 as had been followed in 1975. With the deceleration of inflation this resulted in a 7% real increase in the level of wages and salaries in 1976. This was followed by a further substantial (25% on average) real increase in 1977, but it was not until 1978 that average real wages and salaries exceeded their level of 1970 (IBRD, 1980).

In 1975–76 Chile suffered 'its worst recession since the 1930s' (IBRD, 1980, p. 96). Industrial production declined by 23% and real GDP by 11.2% while unemployment reached 15% of the labour force. The austerity measures were relaxed somewhat during the second half of 1976. Relaxation of limits on credit to the private sector contributed to a recovery in industrial production of 12%. Real GDP grew by 3.6% but open unemployment continued to increase to over 17% of the Greater Santiago labour force. Fiscal restraint was continued, with central government expenditure increasing by only 2% in real terms. While there was some deterioration in the payments position in 1977, thereafter the basic balance was in surplus as capital inflows were more than sufficient to cover current account deficits. The level of net international reserves was positive in 1978 for the first time since 1971. The real GDP growth rate also recovered to 8.7% in 1977 and remained around this level until 1980. The rate of inflation declined to double digit level in 1977. By 1980 it had been reduced to 35% per annum or roughly the same level as in 1970.

Judged on the performance of the payments, inflation and growth indicators, the Chilean programme achieved its stabilisation objectives. The massive payments imbalance of 1973 was quickly corrected and there was a rapid accumulation of international reserves from 1976. The inflation rate declined steadily and the growth rate recovered strongly from 1977. However, the transitional costs were very great. The recession of 1975–76 was extremely severe, entailing a 19% decline in per capita GDP in 1975 alone. Unemployment peaked in 1976 but has remained very high. (In 1980 it was 12%. If persons covered by the Minimum Employment Programme and earning half the minimum wage were included it would be 17.2% according to estimates in Foxley (forthcoming).) The deep recession co-existed in 1975 and 1976 with treble-digit inflation and the rate of increase did not decline to historical levels until 1979 despite the rapid elimination of the fiscal deficits.

Developments in these macro indicators and the record on stabilisation are however inseparable from the fundamental realignment of the economy that was simultaneously put in train. Reforms in the financial and trade spheres achieved the objective of liberalisation and the extension of free market principles. Chilean tariffs were rapidly reduced from an average level of 94% in December 1973 to 52% in January 1975 and 10% in June 1979. Interest rates were freed in May 1975. Price controls were virtually eliminated: O'Brien (1981) records that whereas in 1973 roughly 4,000 products had been subject to price controls, by

1978 the number was eight. A thorough programme of privatisation reduced the number of public enterprises from 507 in 1973 to 15 in 1980 (Foxley, 1982). As the State withdrew from the economy it was expected that Chilean and foreign investors would move in to take its place. However, the transition has been far from smooth. While there are many arguments in favour of freeing interest rates on efficiency grounds (see chapter M3), the Chilean experience illustrates some of the problems that can ensue. Following their freeing, the nominal monthly interest rate jumped from 9.6% in April to 19.0% in May. In the context of declining monthly inflation rates, lags in inflationary expectations and credit restrictions, real interest rates averaged 7% per month for thirty day money during the last six months of 1975, with a 5½% spread between deposits and loans (IBRD, 1980). Thereafter the rates declined but the annual real rate was still 43% in 1978. Real short-term interest rates were considerably higher than rates attached to indexed long-term securities which led to a concentration of capital inflows in the short end of the market. The gross investment rate meanwhile was sluggish. Having declined from 13.3% of GDP in 1975 it fell further to 9% in 1976 and 1977, before recovering to the historical level of approximately 15% in 1979.

The neo-structuralist critique of the Chilean stabilisation programme is based on the contention that the costs incurred, particularly during 1975–76, were dispropotionate to the size of the problem and owed more to the political objectives of the Chilean authorities than to the need to relax the immediate foreign exchange constraint. Commentators such as Foxley (1981, 1982 and forthcoming), Diaz-Alejandro (1981), O'Brien (1981) and Zahler (1980) have highlighted the interplay of stabilisation measures with reforms born of commitment to a rapid extension of free market principles.

Foxley (1980) for example argues that the Chilean authorities overreacted to the acceleration of inflation at the beginning of 1975 and to the drop in copper prices. Imports were reduced mainly by contraction of internal demand and the contraction was so severe that by the middle of 1975 the accumulation of reserves was having an expansionary effect on the monetary sector. Fiscal policy, involving sharp reductions in public investment, strengthened the recessionary tendencies. He contends that eschewing price controls and relying instead on reducing inflation by restraining aggregate demand lengthened the stabilisation period and accentuated the depression in industrial production. It was not until the middle of 1976 that the authorities decided to attack the problem of expectations through manipulation of a key price, the exchange rate. Zahler (1980) and Foxley (1980) stress that the difficulties involved in controlling the money supply and therefore the rate of inflation were exacerbated by the policy of liberalisation in the financial sector, i.e. freeing interest rates and partial freeing of international capital movements. Because interest rates rose above those prevailing on international markets substantial capital inflows were attracted.[12] As a result inflation did not decline as rapidly as programmed despite the reduction in the fiscal deficit and the restriction in credit to the private sector. The burden of adjustment fell heavily on public sector spending, including capital expenditure, public sector employment and social services.

The severity of the recession in 1975–76 owed much to the deterioration in Chile's terms of trade in 1975. A World Bank study (cited in IBRD, 1980) found that the terms of trade loss suffered by Chile as a result of the world recession was the largest of the 120 countries in the survey. The Bank Report (1980) estimates that the loss of copper revenues in 1975 was equivalent to about 10% of the previous year's GDP and that when the rise in import prices is added, the terms of trade effect equalled about 12% of GDP. Such a huge decline in the capacity to import at a time when Chile was not attracting commercial capital inflows due to uncertainty about its economic and political stability, and was meeting some hostility from official lenders opposed to the curtailment of human rights, made recession unavoidable. However, the Bank Mission concurred in the view that the recession might have been somewhat less severe and prolonged had economic management been different. The Bank staff stressed the contribution of overly-expansionary policies in late 1973 and 1974 in increasing the vulnerability of the economy to the payments crisis but argued that even after the onset of the crisis it might have been possible, through the selective use of price and import controls, to alleviate some of its impact on production and employment and to divert some additional resources to the relief of the greatest hardship. Further, they argued that the government could have acted sooner to restimulate the economy in 1976, given the build-up of international reserves and the evidence of declining inflationary expectations.

Another aspect of the neo-structuralist critique of the 'southern cone' programmes concerns the distribution of the burden of adjustment across social groups. For example, Foxley (1981, 1982 and forthcoming) and Diaz-Alejandro (1981) argue that the 'southern cone' programmes have had a regressive impact on income distribution. The difficulties involved in assessing the impact of stabilisation programmes on income distribution have been discussed in chapter M7. Typically the data are incomplete and open to various interpretations. For example, in the absence of comprehensive data Foxley quotes figures on consumption by quintile for Santiago only for 1969 and 1979. The figures show a fall in the share of the bottom quintile (from 7.6% to 5.2%) and an increase in that of the top quintile (from 44.5% to 51.0%).

However, we do not have details of the year-to-year changes over the decade and so cannot relate them closely to the impact of the stabilisation policy. Thus one has to reply on partial indicators.

The most obvious distributional indicator in the case of Chile is the increase in unemployment in 1975 and the continuing high levels thereafter. The greatest burden of adjustment undoubtedly fell on the unemployed who were concentrated in the lowest income groups. While the real wages of those in employment declined in 1975, data compiled by the World Bank (1981) suggests that the decline was less than the fall in national income leading to an increase in labour's share of income. Developments in agricultural prices and output suggest a substantial shift towards that sector, but there is no evidence on how the gain was distributed within the agricultural sector. Other policies likely to have had major distributive consequences include the decline in public expenditure involving reductions in capital investment such as public works and housing, and in social services. On the revenue side, the introduction of a value added tax in 1975, which by 1977 covered even basic food items (such as wheat, flour and milk), was likely to have been regressive. Further, the rapid privatisation of large numbers of previously state-owned companies facilitated a concentration of assets in the hands of the larger Chilean firms who had access to foreign borrowing (Zahler, 1980).

A final element in the critique of the 'southern cone' programmes postulates a link between the economic policies pursued and political repression. The inclusion of this issue in the critique is clearly within the structuralist tradition which rejects treating stabilisation as a technical problem, and seeks to make explicit the political and social implications of stabilisation policies. The programmes adopted in Chile (from 1975), Argentina (from 1976) and Uruguay (from 1974) were all implemented by authoritarian military regimes. Critics argue that programmes involving such high costs for large sectors of the urban population could be implemented successfully only by authoritarian regimes. In the 'southern cone' cases, the stabilisation programmes followed periods of increased participation by organised labour and efforts to redistribute income and wealth. The succeeding administrations had to deal with economic disequilibria of major proportions. They were also ideologically opposed to the politics of their predecessors.

Commentators such as O'Brien (1981), Whitehead (1979), Lichtenzstejn (1982) and Frenkel and O'Donnell (1979)[13] argue that the policies adopted to deal with the economic crisis were not ideologically neutral but combined alleviating the payments problem with greatly reducing the power of organised labour. Sheahan (1980b) argues that certain features of the 'southern cone' economies, such as extreme concentration of ownership of capital, land and other natural resources, restricted access to education and high levels of unemployment, 'greatly increased the likelihood that emphasis on efficiency criteria would foster repression' (p. 291). Free market principles may dictate on efficiency grounds equating wages to marginal product, freeing interest rates, adjusting overvalued exchange rates, lowering protection, removing subsidies and welcoming foreign investment. In the 'southern cone' context, Sheahan contends, such policies are likely to imply, or to be perceived to imply, lowering the wages of urban labour while increasing prices paid to owners of capital; increasing the price of imported necessities (usually including food) while paying higher prices to exporters; penalising previously protected local industry while providing incentives to foreign investors; and removing subsidies on basic necessities such as food and fuel.

The distinguishing feature of the 'southern cone' programmes is their simultaneous persuance of short-term stabilisation and longer-term fundamental reforms. An evaluation of the efficacy and cost-effectiveness of the total programme would have to take account of the longer-term impact of the financial and trade liberalisation as well as of the short-run stabilisation impact. However, considering the stabilisation element in isolation, the record of the Chilean programme is mixed. There was a rapid and significant improvement in the payments position. The record on inflation was poor – at least within the time horizon usually associated with orthodox programmes. Inflation did decelerate but after five years had still not declined below historical levels. The growth, output, investment and employment indicators reveal a deep and prolonged recession. The deterioration in the terms of trade in early 1975 superimposed on accumulated excess aggregate demand made major adjustment inevitable. However, the commitment to a rapid and thorough reorientation of the economy led to dislocations in the goods markets due to the very rapid trade liberalisation, and in financial markets due to the behaviour of short-term interest rates, and exacerbated the stabilisation problems. The fact that, as Foxley (1982) points out, when there was a trade-off between short-run stabilisation and long-term reforms, it was the long-term objectives that often prevailed, explains why the limited improvements achieved in the macro indicators appear to have been accomplished at such high cost.

SUMMARY AND CONCLUSIONS

In this chapter the empirical record of three structuralist influenced economic programmes was considered, as was the new structuralist critique of orthodox stabilisation programmes. Both topics were discussed with reference to Peru and Chile.

In Part I the origin and nature of the structuralist critique was briefly discussed. Some of the central tenets of the structuralism that was current in the late 1950s and 1960s were noted. These included the contentions that inflation in Latin America was typically caused not by excess aggregate demand but by structural bottlenecks in the agriculture, foreign trade and government sectors; that the existence of these bottlenecks reduced the efficiency of the price system as an allocative mechanism, rendering devaluation in particular an ineffective instrument; that monetary expansion accompanying inflation was accommodating rather than causal; that combating inflation would of necessity be a gradual process since it would involve removing supply bottlenecks by re-allocating investment; and that stabilisation policy could not therefore be divorced from development policy.

Three economic programmes that were heavily influenced by structuralist thinking were then considered: those of the Frei administration in Chile (1965–70); the Velasco administration in Peru (1969–75); and the Allende administration in Chile (1970–73). It was suggested that the empirical records of these programmes illustrated that, as an approach to short-run economic management structuralism was seriously deficient. While no one of the three programmes discussed epitomised exactly the structuralist approach, they all served to illustrate a crucial weakness. In each of the three cases, underestimation or even disregard of short-term financial constraints undid the programmes. Particularly, in the cases of Chile in 1970–73 and Peru in 1968–75, the authorities' belief in the efficacy of structural change as a stabilisation strategy and their antipathy to restraining the growth of aggregate demand led them to neglect demand-side inflationary pressures and payments imbalances until they had reached crisis proportions.

In Part II the new structuralist critique of the orthodox stabilisation programme ultimately adopted in Peru in 1978 and of the ultra-orthodox programme adopted in Chile in 1975 was considered. The 'old structuralists' interest in stabilisation policy arose out of a conviction that orthodox policies did not work because they were inappropriate to Latin American conditions and that these policies entailed avoidable costs in terms of reduced output and employment. The new structuralist critique also concentrates on questions of efficacy and cost-efficiency.

In the case of Peru (1977–80), efficacy arguments were to the fore. The structuralists' contention that orthodox policies – in particular devaluation – were bound to be ineffective, was noted. However, as discussed elsewhere in this study (see especially chapter M4), the evidence on the efficacy of devaluation does not favour the structuralist view. In the particular case of Peru, it was argued in this chapter that the evidence did not support the export pessimism implied in the new structuralist critique.

The new structuralists are distinguished by the nature of their critique of orthodox approaches to stabilisation rather than by their advocacy of a set of clearly defined alternative policies. They are united in attributing major importance to supply-side constraints on growth. Beyond this however, as the Peru case illustrates, the favoured strategy varies. Confronted with short-term problems related to the need to reduce inflation or relieve a pressing payments constraint, the tendency among structuralists has been to either advocate price and exchange controls or to propose major policy alterations and institutional reforms. The record of controls is poor except over very short periods (see chapter M4) while the opportunity for introducing major changes tends to narrow rapidly once a payments deficit becomes severe. Notwithstanding these caveats however, the thrust of both the Thorp *et al.* and Schydlowsky critiques considered in this chapter echoes a theme running through much of this study: That is, the desirability of moving away from a standard conventional approach to stabilisation to embrace a wider variety of policies and instruments honed to particular country circumstances.

In the second case considered above (Chile 1975–79), the cost-effectiveness element in the new structuralist critique was prominent. A special feature of the post-75 Chilean programme was that short-term stabilisation goals were part and parcel of a longer term strategy designed to transform the workings of the economy to accord more closely with free market principles. The new structuralists contend that this mix of objectives imposed costs that were grossly disproportionate in size and duration to the limited stabilisation achievements. It was argued that combining fiscal and monetary restraint with major reforms in the trade and financial fields did seriously exacerbate the stabilisation problems. The inflow of private capital from abroad attracted by the very high interest rates that prevailed following their freeing in 1975 frustrated anti-inflation policies while the rapidity with which tariffs were lowered contributed to the massive recession. The new structuralists stress that the kind of 'shock treatment' adopted in Chile in 1975 is likely to be a higher-cost strategy. This is partly because in their view orthodox policies such as devaluation and monetary restraint may have perverse effects in the short-run. But, in any case concentrating the necessary reduction in domestic absorption in a very short period is likely to accentuate the costs of adjustment. They would favour a gradual phasing of adjustment policies. The advantages of a gradualist approach have been argued throughout this study (see especially chapter M3) although of course the possibilities are constrained by the availability of financing.

The critique of the Chilean case also focused on the distribution of the burden of adjustment across social groups. While the income distribution data are not adequate to allow categorical statements on the total redistributive impact of the policies pursued it is clear that the major burden of the shock treatment was borne by the unemployed. One fifth of the workforce was unemployed at the depth of the recession and these were drawn primarily from the lowest income groups. It was noted that the new structuralist critique of the Chilean and other 'southern cone' stabilisation programmes of the mid-to-late 1970s postulates a link between the stabilisation policies and political repression. This feature of the critique is in line with the long-standing structuralist approach which does not treat stabilisation as a technical problem only, but seeks to make explicit the political and social implications of stabilisation policies.

Footnotes

1. Among the early exponents of structuralism at ECLA were Juan Noyola, Osvaldo Sunkel, Aribal Pinto and Raul Prebisch. A guide to the major contributions of these and others is contained in Seers (1962).

2. The critique was worked out primarily against the background of Chilean experience but was held to have wider applicability not only within Latin America but in developing countries in general; see for example, Seers (1962, p. 195).

3. Thorp (1971, pp. 189-90) notes that some 'structuralists' disputed the inclusion of this third, taxation, bottleneck in the list of sources of inflationary pressures. She points out, however, that it cannot be excluded on the grounds that it is demand inflation since the structuralists reject the demand pull/cost push categorisation and concentrate on structural factors which usually have elements of both cost and demand, or on the grounds of its being a political rather than an economic explanation as that applies equally to the agricultural supply bottleneck.

4. Griffith-Jones (1978, 1981) points out that when, after 1971, the electoral, gradualist path to socialism had been chosen by Popular Unity, there was a 'dysfunctionality' between the political and economic strategies. The latter exhausted the full range of positive effects during the first year so that by the time the crucial electoral confrontation occurred in the Congress elections of March 1973, all the negative effects of the excessive demand growth had manifested themselves.

5. These were Citibank, Bank of America, Chase Manhattan, Manufacturers Hanover, Morgan Guaranty and Wells Fargo.

6. The decision of the banks in 1977 to make further loans to Peru conditional on the negotiation of a Stand-by arrangement with the Fund, reinforced the dependence of ldcs faced with balance of payments crises on the Fund. The evolution of private bank lending in the 1970s had seen the banks advancing balance of payments loans to ldcs. This trend towards commercial bank involvement in areas previously reserved to the Fund reached its peak in the Peruvian case when the banks not only extended balance of payments loans but, having made the loans conditional on meeting macroeconomic performance tests, monitored the economy to ensure compliance. The negative outcome of the Peruvian experiment led the banks to take the view in later cases that the Fund was the appropriate source of advice for ldcs in balance of payments difficulties. The banks' involvement in Peru 'demonstrated the fraility of such direct intervention by banks; for reasons of data availability,

technical capacity and political sensitivity, it proved impossible for the banks to enforce their lending conditions, and the adverse publicity for the intervention (plus its ineffectiveness) caused the leading bankers involved to resolve that they would not become entangled again in similar packages in the future but would rely on the IMF as the monitoring authority (Cline, 1981 p. 306). For a fuller discussion of the 1967–77 Peruvian experiment with the private banks see Stallings (1979) and on the role of the private banks in Peru since the 1960s see Devlin (1981).

7. International Monetary Fund, 'Peru – Recent Economic Developments', Washington DC, 1977, p. 1, quoted in Thorp, 1979 (p. 123).

8. Underemployment is defined by the Peruvian Ministry of Labour to include working less than 35 hours a week or earning less than the minimum wage.

9. The same mechanism could, Schydlowsky argues, contribute to a more cost-effective price stabilisation strategy. By assuming that output cannot be expanded in the short run, and by proceeding as if inflation were always the result of generalised excess demand, traditional prescriptions close off viable policy options. In Schydlowsky's view there is scope for expanding output within the time frame in which aggregate demand reductions can be achieved. Many LDCs have unused capacity in their existing industrial sectors which could be used to contain price increases. Schydlowsky identifies four types of inflation (demand-pull, cost-push, exchange rate and spiral) and argues that there is a role for differentiated devaluation in combating each of them. In the case of 'low grade inflation' (up to 20–25%) it is possible to try to drown excess demand in increased supply by means of a differentiated devaluation provoking export-led capacity utilisation in the tradeable non-traded sector. In the case of cost-push inflation, the objective of weakening the link between wage increases and cost increases would be facilitated by economies of scale attendant on fuller utilisation of installed capacity and increased X-efficiency as a result of higher and more stable volumes of production. Similarly, differential devaluation is in appropriate policy for forestalling exchange rate inflation by bringing into production the excess capacity in the tradeable non-traded sector to earn foreign exchange and alleviate the scarcity threatening to generate inflation. In the context of virulent spiral inflation, differentiated devaluation, allied to an incomes policy and an active crawling exchange rate, could change the context in which the economic agents are operating from a zero-sum to a positive-sum game by holding out the prospect of expanded real incomes (Schydlowsky, 1982).

10. For example, Cline finds a significant effect of changes in the real exchange rate on import volume only when the equation is specified in annual percentage change form. For exports however the equation is specified in absolute levels. Schydlowsky, in a comment on the Cline paper (Cline and Weintraub 1981) reports that running the regression in percentage change form does not give a significant effect for changes in the real exchange rate on export volume.

11. The Argentine programme is analysed from a broadly structuralist perspective by Frenkel and O'Donnell (1979) and Beccaria and Carciofi (1981), while the Uruguayan programme is discussed in Finch (1979).

12. See Zahler, Table 10.

13. Frenkel and O'Donnell (1979) in their analysis of what they term the 'bureaucratic authoritarian' states stress that the stabilisation policies hurt not only the working class but also penalise many supporters of the preceding coup, particularly the local business community who are penalised by the lowering of tariffs as well as by credit restrictions. They argue that it is only the depth of the preceding crisis and the fear of the business community provoked by the perceived threat to them during the preceding period that enables the economic technicians, the local business community and the nationalistic Armed Forces to maintain a united front and introduce programmes which Frenkel and O'Donnell characterise as benefiting primarily exporters and holders of finance capital.

References

Angell, Alan and Thorp, Rosemary, 'Inflation, stabilisation and attempted re-democratisation in Peru, 1975–1979', *World Development*, Vol.8, No.11, November 1980, pp. 865–886.

Beccaria, Luis and Carciofi, Ricardo, 'Recent Experiences of Stabilisation: Argentina's Economic Policy 1976–81', *IDS Bulletin*, December 1981, Vol. 13, No.1, pp. 51–59.

Cauas, G., 'Stabilisation Policy – the Chilean Case', *Journal of Political Economy*, Vol.78, No.4, 1970.

Cline, William R., and Weintraub, Sidney (eds) *Economic Stabilisation in Developing Countries*, The Brookings Institution, Washington DC, 1981.

Cline, William R, 'Economic Stabilisation in Peru, 1975–78', in William R. Cline and Sidney Weintraub (eds), *Economic Stabilisation in Developing Countries*, The Brookings Institution, Washington DC, 1981.

Crockett, Andrew D., 'Stabilisation Policies in Developing Countries: Some Policy Considerations', *IMF Staff Papers*, Vol. 28, No.1 March 1981, pp. 54–79.

Devlin, Robert, Transnational banks, external debt and Peru, *CEPAL Review*, August 1981, No.14, pp. 153–184.

Diaz-Alejandro, Carlos F., 'Southern Cone Stabilisation Plans' in William R. Cline and Sidney Weintraub (eds) *Economic Stabilisation in Developing Countries*, The Brookings Institution, Washington DC, 1981.

Diz, Adolfo C., 'Economic Performance under Three Stand-By Arrangements. The case of Peru, 1977–1980' in John Williamson (ed), *IMF Conditionality*, London, MIT Press, 1982.

ECLA, *Economic Survey of Latin America 1966*, United Nations, New York, 1968.

Finch, M.H.J., 'Stabilisation policy in Uruguay since the 1950s' in Rosemary Thorp and Lawrence Whitehead (eds), *Inflation and Stabilisation in Latin America*, London 1979.

Foxley, Alejandro, 'Stabilisation policies and their effects on employment and income distribution: a Latin American perspective', in William R. Cline and Sidney Weintraub (eds), *Economic Stabilisation in Developing Countries*, The Brookings Institution, Washington DC, 1981.

Foxley, Alejandro, 'Towards a Free Market Economy Chile 1974–1979', *Journal of Development Economics*, 10(1982) pp. 3–29

Foxley, Alejandro, *Latin American Experiments in Neoconservative Economics*, University of California Press, forthcoming.

Frenkel, Roberto and O'Donnell, Guillermo, 'The Stabilisation Programs of the International Monetary Fund and their Internal Impacts', in Richard R. Fagen (ed) *Capitalism and the State in US – Latin American Relations*, Stanford University Press, Stanford, California, 1979.

Griffith-Jones, Stephany, 'A critical evaluation of Popular Unity's short-term and financial policy', *World Development*, Vol.6, 1978, pp. 1019–1029.

Griffith-Jones, Stephany, *The Role of Finance in the Transition of Socialism*, Frances Pinter, London, 1981.

Griffith-Jones, Stephany, 'The evolution of external finance, economic policy and development in Chile, 1973–1978', *Institute of Development Studies*, Working Paper No.160, April 1981a.

Grunwald, Joseph, 'The "Structuralist" School on Price Stabilisation and Economic Development: The Chilean Case', extract reproduced in Gerald M. Meier, *Leading Issues in Development Economics*, Oxford University Press, New York, 1964, pp. 213–219.

IBRD, The Current Economic Position and Prospects of Peru, Washington, December 1973.

IBRD, *Chile – An Economy in Transition*, A World Bank Country Study, Washington, January 1980.

IBRD, *Peru – Major Development Policy Issues and Recommendations*, a World Bank Country Study, Washington, June 1981.

IMF, *Survey*, June 21, 1982, p. 187.

Lichtenzstejn, Samuel, 'IMF – Developing Countries Conditionality and Strategy', in John Williamson (ed), *IMF Conditionality*, London, MIT Press, 1982.

O'Brien, Philip, 'The New Leviathan: the Chicago School and the Chilean Regime 1973–80', *IDS Bulletin*, December 1981, Vol.13, No.1, pp. 37–50.

Prebisch, Raul, 'Economic Development or Monetary Stability: The False Dilemma', extract reproduced in Gerald M. Meier, *Leading Issues in Development Economics*, Oxford University Press, New York, 1964, pp. 207–210.

Schydlowsky, Daniel M., 'Alternative Approaches to Short Term Economic Management', in Tony Killick (ed), *Adjustment and Financing in the Developing World*, IMF/ODI, Washington, June 1982.

Schydlowsky, Daniel M, *Containing the Costs of Stabilisation in Semi-Industrialised LDCs – A Marshallian Approach*, Centre for Latin American Studies, Boston University, Discussion Paper Series, No.32, December 1979.

Schydlowsky, Daniel M. and Wicht Juan J., *The Anatomy of an Economic Failure : Peru 1968–78*, Centre for Latin American Studies, Boston Univertsity, Discussion Paper Series, No.32, February 1979.

Seers, Dudley, 'A Theory of Inflation and Growth in Under-developed Economies Based on the Experience of Latin America', *Oxford Economic Papers*.Vol.14, June 1962, pp. 173–195.

Sheahan, John, 'Peru: Economic Policies and Structural Change, 1968–1978', *Journal of Economic Studies*, 1980(1) 7(1), pp. 3–27.

Sheahan, John, 'Market-oriented Economic Policies and Political Repression in Latin America', *Economic Development and Cultural Change*, Vol.28, No.2, January 1980(2), pp. 267–291.

Stallings, Barbara, 'Peru and the US banks: privatisation of Financial Relations' in Johnathan D. Aronson (ed), *Debt and the Less Developed Countries*, Boulder, Colorado, Westview Press, 1979, pp. 225–51.

Thorp, Rosemary, 'Inflation and the Financing of Economic Development', in Keith Griffin (ed) *Financial Development in Latin America*, Macmillan, London 1971, pp. 182–224.

Thorp, Rosemary, 'The Stabilisation Crisis in Peru, 1975–1978', in Rosemary Thorp and Laurence Whitehead (eds), *Inflation and Stabilisation in Latin America*, London 1979.

Thorp, Rosemary and Bertram, Geoffrey, *Peru 1890–1977, Growth and Policy in an Open Economy*, Macmillan, 1978.

Thorp, Rosemary, Buchdahl, Claudio Herzko, Balona Behr, Carlos Alberto, 'The Experience of Peru', in *The Balance of Payments Adjustment Process in Developing Countries*, UNCTAD/UNDP Project INT/75/015, mimeo, 1979.

Thorp, Rosemary and Whitehead, Laurence, *Inflation and Stabilisation in Latin America*, Macmillan, London, 1979.

Wachter, Susan M., 'Structuralism vs Monetarism: Inflation in Chile' in Jere Behrman and James Hanson (eds) *Short Term Macroeconomic Policy in Latin America*, NBER, Other Conference Series, No. 14, Ballinger, 1979, pp. 227–255.

Whitehead, Laurence, 'Inflation and Stabilisation in Chile 1970–7' in Rosemary Thorp and Laurence Whitehead (eds), *Inflation and Stabilisation in Latin America*, Macmillan, London, 1979.

Zahler, Roberto, 'The monetary and real effects of the financial opening up of national economies to the exterior, the case of Chile 1975–1978' *CEPAL Review* April 1980, pp. 127–153.

Zammit, J. Ann (ed), *The Chilean Road to Socialism*, Institute of Development Studies, Sussex, England, 1973.

3 Indonesia, 1966–70[1]
Mary Sutton

This case study differs from the others in this volume in that it is an historical study, concluding at approximately the period when the others commence. There are three reasons for its inclusion. First, it provides an intrinsically interesting example of a successful anti-inflation programme and demonstrates that stabilisation can be achieved even when starting from a position of acute disequilibrium. Secondly, it illustrates the close interplay of economic and political factors in stabilisation attempts. Thirdly, since the IMF played an important role in supporting the stabilisation programme, in the negotiations on rescheduling Indonesia's foreign debt, and in securing foreign assistance, it provides an analysis of Fund support in this pre-oil crisis programme.

The study is in five parts. Part I outlines the background to the crisis of 1965–66 and describes the situation immediately prior to the inauguration of the stabilisation programme. Part II analyses the content of the programme implemented between 1966 and 1970. Part III evaluates its impact of the rate of inflation, the balance of payments (BoP), growth and income distribution. It also discusses briefly the weakening of stability in 1973 and the consequent measures adopted in 1974. The study ends at this point as subsequent discussion of macroeconomic policy in Indonesia must focus on the role of oil revenues in the economy—a subject which does not fall within the ambit of our project. Part IV analyses the role of the Fund in relation to the succession of Stand-by arrangements in 1968–74 and the meetings of the Intergovernmental Group on Indonesia. Part V summarises the study and offers some conclusions.

I. THE ECONOMIC AND POLITICAL BACKGROUND

In terms of the macroeconomic performance of the Indonesian economy, the twelve years between 1962 and 1973 divide clearly into three sub-periods. As illustrated by Table 3.1, the first five years (1962–66)

Table 3.1 Indonesia: selected growth, inflation and balance of payments indicators, 1960–74

	(1) Real GDP growth %	(2) Real GDP growth per capita %	(3) Gross fixed capital formation to GDP %	(4) Jakarta cost of living index % increase	(5) Balance on current account (US$m)	(6) Basic balance (US$m)	(7) Net official foreign exchange reserves (US$m)
1960	....	....	....	37.7	–84	98	328
1961	5.1	2.5	20.0	26.9	–526	–169	129
1962	2.4	–0.1	7.7	174.0	–248	–126	117
1963	–2.4	–4.8	9.4	118.7	–227	–104	–6
1964	3.8	1.3	14.3	104.7	–229	–51	–39
1965	0.0	–2.5	8.3	305.5	–247	24	–60
1966	2.3	–0.3	4.4	1044.7	–123	–52	–42
1967	2.3	–0.3	8.0	171.0	–283	–16	–56
1968	11.1	4.3	8.8	12.8	–251	3	–51
1969	7.1	4.8	11.7	15.9	–383	–69	–86
1970	7.5	3.2	13.6	12.3	–376	–20	–34
1971	5.9	6.6	15.8	4.4	–418	5	–91
1972	9.4	8.5	18.8	6.5	–386	–66	285
1973	11.3	4.9	17.9	25.8	–531	45	783
1974	7.6	2.3	16.8	40.7	568	1090	1472

Sources: Cols. (1), (2) and (3) IFS, various issues; col (4) for 1960–66 Newmann, 1974, Table 27 and for 1967–74 IFS – from 1967 the base is September 1966; cols. (5) and (6) IMF, *Balance of Payments Yearbook*, various issues; col (7) unpublished Fund documents, except 1970–72 for which source is *B.I.E.S.*, vol. X, no. 2, July 1973.

were ones of acute disequilibria. The rate of increase of consumer prices rose from 27 in 1961 to over 1000 in 1966; the BoP (basic balance) was, with the exception of 1965, in deficit from 1961, net foreign exchange reserves were negative from 1963, and from the beginning of 1966 Indonesia was unable to service its foreign debt; real per capita GDP declined at an average annual rate of 1.3%; and the gross investment ratio averaged 8.8% per annum, implying a declining capital stock. By contrast, during the last four years of the period (1970–73), real per capita GDP grew at an average annual rate of 5.8%; consumer prices rose at an average annual rate of less than 12% and the investment ratio increased to 17.9%. Although by 1970 foreign debt had been rescheduled and substantial new aid commitments secured, the improvement in the BoP was not so marked during this period, with the basic balance continuing in deficit until 1971 and net foreign exchange reserves remaining negative until 1972 (the major turnaround in the BoP came in the wake of the 1973–74 oil price rises: between 1972 and 1974 the level of net foreign reserves increased five-fold while the surplus on basic balance grew twenty-fold between 1973 and 1974). During the intervening sub-period, Indonesia experienced fundamental political change, in the wake of which economic stabilisation became the primary governmental economic objective. The programme of stabilisation and rehabilitation implemented between October 1966 and April 1970, and the role of the IMF in supporting it, is the prime focus of this study. We begin however, by examining the causes of the disequilibria that manifested themselves in the mid-1960s.

Table 3.2   Indonesia: sectoral origin of changes in the money supply 1962–1966 (bn Rps.)

	1962[a]	1963	1964	1965	1966
Public sector	66.3	. . . .	362	1154	12603
Private sector	5.1	. . . .	122	695	5610
Foreign sector	–9.2	. . . .	–12	20	–256
Miscellaneous	6.1	. . . .	–25	–22	1679
Total change in money supply	68.2	142.1	447.0	1847	19636

Source: Bank of Indonesia, 1968.

Note: [a] The figures for 1962 do not include the activities of the private commercial non-foreign-exchange banks.

The principal cause of the hyperinflation of the 1962 to 1966 period was government budget deficits financed by money creation. The average annual rate of price increase (as measured by the 62-commodity Jakarta cost of living index) was 349% in those years while the rate of growth of the money supply (currency plus demand deposits) averaged

Table 3.3   Indonesia: total central government budget deficit and the money supply, 1960–66 (m new Rp)[a]

	(1) Total government budget deficit	(2) % change	(3) Deficit as % of revenue	(4) Money supply (currency plus demand deposits)	(5) % change	(1) as % of Δ (4)
1960	10.2	–26	20	47.8	37	79
1961	26.3	158	42	67.6	41	133
1962	47.2	79	63	135.9	101	69
1963	167.7	255	97	278.0	105	118
1964	397.9	137	140	725.0	161	89
1965	1602.9	303	173	2572.0	255	87
1966	16700.0	943	128	22208.0	763	85

Source: Bank Indonesia, 1968 and 1974, Tables 13 and 29.
Note: [a] New Rp were introduced in December 1965 (see below, p. 78) with 1 new Rp equivalent to 1000 old.

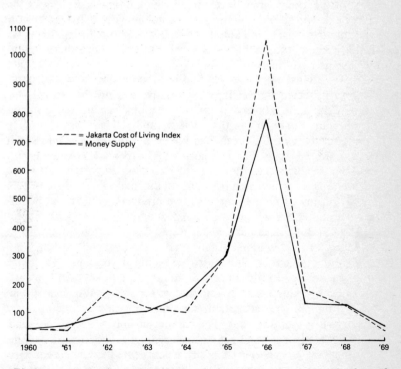

Figure 3.1   Jakarta cost of living index, and money supply (currency plus demand deposits), 1960–69, annual percentage changes

277% per annum (see Tables 3.1 and 3.3 and Figure 3.1).[2] Table 3.2 illustrates that the major factor in the year to year changes in the money supply was advances to the public sector.

In 1962 the central government budget deficit was equivalent to 63% of revenue and to 69% of the year's increase in money supply. By 1966 the deficit was equivalent to 128% of revenue and 85% of the increase in the money supply (see Table 3.3). Central government revenue averaged 4.6% of GDP from 1962 to 1966 while expenditure averaged 9.8% (Sundrum, 1973, Table 1).

As the rate of inflation increased and price expectations adjusted, the income velocity of circulation, which had averaged roughly 9 in the 1958 to 1961 period, increased to over 13 in 1962 and to 25.5 in 1966 (Sundrum, 1973, Table 4). As a result, prices rose faster than the money supply as shown in Figure 3.1.

Despite the size of budget deficits, expenditure as a percentage of GDP declined from 18.7% in 1961 to 10.6% in 1965, while revenue declined from 13.3% to 3.9% (Sundrum, 1973, Table 1). One reason for the decline in government command over resources was the performance of the foreign trade sector upon which it depended heavily for tax revenue (up to 60% of current revenue emanated from taxes on imports and exports). As Table 3.4 indicates, exports earnings declined steadily between 1960 and 1964. A number of factors contributed to the poor export performance.

The traditional export sectors had been in decline from the 1940s. Adversely affected by the Japanese occupation and the struggle for independence, the ratio of exports to net national product had declined from 28% in 1939 to 10% in 1950 (Paauw, 1981). There was a recovery in 1951 fuelled by the Korean War boom, but thereafter the ratio fell back to around 10%. The composition of exports also altered with extractive products becoming progressively more important: the share of mineral exports increased from 26% of the total value in 1950 to 45% in 1965 (Paauw, 1981). From 1958 two products, rubber and petroleum, accounted for about 70% of export earnings. Rubber was produced both on plantations, which were largely Dutch-owned up to 1958, and by smallholders. Estate production declined steadily from 1953 to 1963 and was attributable to the ageing of trees and a reluctance to replant in a politically uncertain climate (see below). In contrast, smallholder production increased but was not sufficient to compensate for both the fall in estate production and the steady decline in world price between 1960 and 1965. The volume of rubber exports increased by 23% between 1960 and 1965 while earnings declined steadily from $307m to $222m. Export earnings from petroleum, however, peaked in 1958. Domestic consumption increased its share of total production of refined petroleum products from 33% in 1959 to 58% in 1964 (Thomas

Table 3·4 Indonesia: year to year changes in balance of payments magnitudes 1960–61 to 1969–70 (US$m)

	1960–61	1961–62	1962–63	1963–64	1964–65	1965–66	1966–67	1967–68	1968–69	1969–70
Exports (fob)	-115	-55	-55	-25	2	81	57	102	122	178
Imports (cif)	-307	319	135	13	-20	13	-210	-25	-164	-121
Invisibles and Transfers	-20	14	-59	10	0	30	-7	-45	-90	-50
Total Current Account	-442	278	21	-2	-18	124	-160	32	-132	7
Long-Term Capital	175	-235	2	55	93	-200	196	-13	60	42
Basic Balance	-267	43	22	53	75	-76	36	19	-72	49
Foreign Reserves	-199	-12	-123	-33	-21	18	-14	5	-35	52

Source: IMF, *Balance of Payments Yearbook*, various issues.

Notes: 1 The current account is here defined to include visible trade plus services and non-governmental transfer payments, while the basic balance includes the current account plus official transfers plus long-term capital flows.

2 A minus sign indicates a change that worsens the BoP.

and Panglaykim, 1973, Table IV-8). Further, from the point of view of government finance, the gross figures for export earnings from petroleum and petroleum products overstate the amount of foreign exchange available to the government since they include foreign exchange used by the foreign companies to purchase imports and to remit abroad. While the volume index of exports showed a 9% increase between 1960 and 1966 the terms of trade index showed a 24% decline over the same period.

Another factor affecting export performance was the overvalued exchange rate which acted as a tax on exports, although detailed estimates of the degree of overvaluation are not available. However, Mackie (1971, p. 64) records that the black market rate for the Rupiah was generally in the region of 300% of the official effective rate until about 1958 and thereafter varied between four and twelve times the official rate. The deterioration of infrastructure and transportation facilities due to lack of maintenance also contributed to the poor performance as did the introduction of progressively more complex bureaucratic procedures and exchange controls in an attempt to ration scarce foreign exchange. The value and volume of imports also declined steadily from 1961 to 1964. In 1965 the foreign exchange constraint was such that imports of rice, Indonesia's staple food, were banned.[3] Net foreign exchange reserves were negative from 1963 and successive BoP deficits were financed by foreign borrowing. By the end of 1965 Indonesia's foreign debt was estimated to be in the region of $2.4bn of which 92% was medium- and long-term debt. Almost 60% of the total was owed to Eastern bloc countries (*B.I.E.S.*, June 1966, Table 1).

What were the reasons for the huge budget deficits of the 1960–65 period? The impact of the poor performance of the foreign trade sector on government revenue has already been noted. Simultaneously with this decline in revenue there was also increasing pressure on expenditure from the government budget because of population growth (2.5% p.a.) and the historical role of the government sector as a major employer. Between 1958 and 1966 Indonesia's population increased from 88.4m to 107.8m. Roughly 10% of the rapidly growing workforce was employed in the services sector which included the civil service and the armed forces. It was estimated that the level of over-staffing in government departments and agencies was up to 30% in the mid-1960s, so that 'government employment, both civil and military . . . constituted a vast system of unemployment relief . . .' (ibid, p. 28). The size of the civil service and armed forces resulted in wages and salaries absorbing a large part of government expenditure, even though in the hyperinflation years the remuneration of civil servants lagged far behind the rate of inflation. For example, in 1965 salaries of civil servants totalled Rp.450bn, or 49% of government revenue (*B.I.E.S.*, February 1966,

p. 7). Additionally, the nationalisation of Dutch enterprises in 1957 had placed virtually all the large-scale industrial enterprises and half the plantations in government hands. Nationalisation of British and American companies in 1963, further increased government owner- ship. Subsidisation of government estates and industries increased rapidly. For example, government credits to state enterprises increased ninefold during 1960–64 (Thomas and Panglaykim, 1973, p. 118). Once deficit financing had begun a self-perpetuating link was estab- lished between government deficits and prices. As the rate of inflation rose government expenditure rose faster than revenue (which tends to be fixed in the short-run) leading the authorities to increase further money creation (Aghevli and Khan, 1977). Thus, unable to finance the desired level of expenditure through taxation the government began to rely more and more heavily on the inflation tax to transfer resources to it from the public (Grenville, 1981). While these economic and social factors contributed, a further major part of the explanation resides in the political sphere.

Politically, the period from Indonesian independence (1949) to the adoption of the Stabilisation and Rehabilitation Programme in October 1966 divides into two sub-periods. The first, usually referred to as the 'liberal' period, was based on a system of parliamentary democracy with a president of limited power. President Sukarno held this office throughout the period. In 1957, a political crisis over widespread revolts in the outer islands, born of dissatisfaction with the concentra- tion of power and resources in Java, precipitated the imposition of martial law and the ending of parliamentary democracy. The prevailing political philosophy now became President Sukarno's concept of 'guided democracy' which he described as a mixture of nationalism, Islam and Marxism. The reintroduction in 1959 of the constitution originally drawn up in 1945 but abandoned a few years later, bestowed wide-ranging powers on the President. Of the previously prominent political parties only the Communist Party (PKI) retained significant influence and it collaborated with Sukarno. Under the new political regime the President shared power with the army. However, there were deep divisions within the army on its attitude towards Sukarno and the army was, by and large, strongly opposed to the PKI. This three-way alliance was therefore insecure and depended critically on President Sukarno's ability to maintain a delicate balance between the interests of the two opposed factions. In economic terms, state seizure of all Dutch property in Indonesia at the end of 1957 marked the beginning of a much more interventionist phase which continued until 1965.

The roots of the hyperinflation of 1962–66 are usually traced to the early years of 'guided democracy'. While the government budget had been in deficit each year from 1952, up to 1957 the deficit was equivalent on average to 15% of revenue. The rate of increase of consumer prices was also relatively modest during these years. In 1957 however, the government deficit was equivalent to 24% of revenue, rising to 51% the following year. The rate of inflation increased from 8% in 1956 to 35% in 1958. Mackie argues that the government decision in December 1956 to put aside budgetary restraint, in the face of political challenge posed by the regional rebellions, represents a more important turning point in Indonesia's economic and political history than the nationalisation of Dutch enterprises in December 1957, which has generally been viewed as the post-war watershed. Thereafter, deficit financing came to be used as a 'political safety valve', allowing the government to 'sidestep awkward questions about how to make ends meet, whenever this might have entailed decisions which would have antagonised elements in the political community whose support (was) essential to the regime' (Mackie, 1967, p. 20).

Two costly military campaigns spearheaded by President Sukarno and the PKI, and opposed by the army, helped to distract attention from internal disunity and economic deterioration. The first was a successful campaign launched in 1962 against the Dutch for West New Guinea which, as West Irian, became part of Indonesia in May 1963. The second was the 'policy of confrontation' with Malaysia which lasted from 1963 to 1966. This resulted from the opposition of President Sukarno and the PKI to the formation of the federation of Malaya, Sarawak, Sabah and (until 1966) Singapore, to become the nation of Malaysia. Sukarno and the PKI denounced Malaya and Singapore as tools of British neo-colonialism and the formation of Malaysia as part of an 'imperialist plot' to encircle Indonesia. These military campaigns contributed to economic decline; it is estimated that during 1960–65 over one-third of the foreign debt accumulated by Indonesia was used for military expenditure. The decision in 1964 to break off all commercial relations with Malaysia as part of the policy of confrontation affected almost half of Indonesia's export trade. Further, Western donors demonstrated their disapproval by reducing their aid commitments. Another significant drain on resources during this period were the prestige projects – national monuments, tourist hotels and mosques – which were intended to inspire national unity and were accorded priority in the government budget. These non-productive investments, known as the President's Special Projects, were continued even when expenditure on development projects was being severely curtailed in the later years of the hyperinflation.

There were attempts to reduce the government deficit on several occasions between 1957 and 1965 but each was abandoned before reaching its objective. Following one attempt in 1959 at budget restraint and a monetary purge – which involved reducing the value of all

Rp.500 and Rp.1000 denomination banknotes to 10% of their face value and 'freezing' 90% of bank deposits over Rp.25,000 – the money supply was reduced by one-third and the rate of inflation moderated in 1959 and 1960.[4] However, a number of factors conspired in late 1961 to provoke a new round of price increases. These included a rice shortage which developed in September 1961 due to drought; increased money creation to finance the military campaign in West Irian which began in early 1962; and speculation brought about by the downward trend in the foreign exchange reserves. From 20% of revenue in 1960 the government deficit widened to 42% in 1961 and 63% in 1962; the money supply almost doubled between 1961 and 1962; and net foreign reserves declined from US\$328m in 1960 to \$117m in 1962. This marked the beginning of the period of acute disequilibria.

There was an attempt to check inflation during 1963. Stabilisation measures adopted at that time included budget austerity, relaxation of the many controls that had been introduced since 1958, an emergency programme of imports made possible by foreign assistance, and a new exchange rate regime designed to promote exports. The latter was the fourth attempt since 1955 to reform the complex multiple exchange rate system.[5] The impact of these reforms – an 86% devaluation in the basic official exchange rate, elimination of existing export taxes, revision of import surcharges and the introduction of a new exchange retention scheme (under which exporters retained 5% of their export proceeds and a further 10–15% was automatically allocated to them for purchasing essential imports) – was estimated to be a depreciation of roughly 40% in the effective export rate and a somewhat larger effective devaluation of the import rate (Kanesa-Thasan, 1966, p. 361).

The stabilisation measures were introduced in May 1963. Assisted by a good rice harvest in April/May, the measures appeared to be having an impact, resulting in a sharp fall in inflation. However, the escalation of confrontation with Malaysia in September 1963 negated any progress that had been made. The planned reduction in the government budget deficit in 1963 and its elimination in 1964 were not achieved – the deficit grew from 63% of revenue in 1962 to 103% in 1963 and 140% in 1964. The new foreign exchange regulations were replaced in 1964 by another system whose main feature was a new export inducement certificate scheme under which exporters were allowed to retain approximately 20% of their foreign exchange earnings. By the end of 1964 there were three effective buying rates and seven effective selling rates (Johnson and Salop, 1979, p. 54).

Thus, the principal cause of hyperinflation resided in the government attitude to economic stabilisation. The Sukarno administration illustrates an extreme case of the neglect of financial discipline which also occurred in some of the other socialist/populist experiments considered in this study (see chapters 2 and 4).[6] During the years of 'Guided Democracy', internal political struggles took precedence over prudent economic management as expansionary fiscal and monetary policies were employed as a means of conflict resoultion. Thomas and Panglaykim (1973, p. 76) sum up the situation thus:

> The outward stability at the top over the . . . years when 'guided democracy' and 'guided economy' gradually became the state ideology, provided the thin veil hiding the deep-seated antagonisms between competing groups centred around the President, the Army and the Communist Party. Until one group succeeded in uniting the various diverse elements under one banner . . . it was futile to expect that much could be done in economic affairs.

The political crisis of 1965–66 paved the way for the introduction of the Rehabilitation and Stabilisation programme of October 1966. On the night of September 30, 1965, there was an attempt by the PKI faction in the ruling alliance to remove forcibly the anti-PKI leaders within the army. The attempt, from which President Sukarno did not dissociate himself, failed and within days the army had carried out a successful counter coup. In an ensuing bloody civil war the army and anti-communist civilian groups took revenge on the PKI. It had been the largest communist party outside the Eastern bloc and China, with an estimated three million members. It was now virtually annihilated. It is estimated that between 300,000 and 500,000 people alleged to be members or sympathisers were killed, and many more were arrested. Simultaneously, opposition to President Sukarno, born of dissatisfaction with his apparently ambivalent attitude to the attempted left-wing coup, grew. It was enunciated in the first instance by student groups and ultimately by the army. In March 1966 Sukarno was effectively replaced by a triumvirate comprising General Suharto (commander of the Armed Forces), Sultan Hamengkubuwono IX (the Sultan of Jogjakarta) and Adam Malik. Sukarno was formally stripped of his remaining powers in February 1967 and General Suharto was appointed acting President. In March 1968, Suharto was appointed President.

In the six months between the coup attempt and the de facto transfer of power, the economic situation continued to deteriorate. Over this period, the Jakarta cost of living index increased by 510% while the money supply grew by 237%.[7] Domestic industrial production stagnated, as, starved of imported inputs, plants operated at only 20–30% of capacity. An ineffectual series of stabilisation measures was introduced in late 1965, which included a planned balanced budget for 1966, abolition of subsidies to public utilities and on petroleum products, new taxes, wage adjustments, devaluation and a currency reform.[8] In December 1965, Bank Indonesia (the central bank) defaulted on letters of credit held by Japanese exporters.

In July a programme of stabilisation and rehabilitation was announced, aimed at controlling inflation and restoring production. However, the major economic policy measures were not announced until October. Between the transfer of power in March and the 'October Regulations' priority was given to consolidating the new political order, ending the confrontation with Malaysia and addressing the debt problem. Repayments due in 1966 amounted to $530m, or $100m more than anticipated foreign exchange earnings in that year (*B.I.E.S.*, June 1966, p. 4). Efforts to reschedule the debt began in May and in July Indonesia's Western creditors met under the chairmanship of the Netherlands. A second meeting in mid-September to which Indonesia was invited, was attended by delegations from Japan, the USA, West Germany, France, Netherlands, Italy, the UK and Australia, as well as by officials from the IMF and observers from New Zealand, Canada and Switzerland. Agreement in principle was reached on a moratorium and rescheduling but drawing up of a timetable was postponed until the next meeting in December. In October 1966 the Soviet government agreed to a moratorium on debts until 1969. Bilateral rescheduling agreements were subsequently negotiated with most of the other communist creditor countries under which repayment was deferred until 1970. In the meantime, emergency relief for 1966 had been obtained (see p. 96).

During this period Indonesia was not formally a member of the IMF. It had joined the Fund in 1954 and had Stand-by arrangements in 1961 and 1963. The latter was in support of the 1963 stabilisation programme but was cancelled when the beginning of the policy of confrontation with Malaysia rendered attainment of the fiscal targets impossible. Indonesia withdrew from the Fund and the World Bank in August 1965 in protest at Malaysia's admission to UN membership.

In June 1966 a Fund mission visited Jakarta to discuss re-entry and Indonesia officially applied for membership in July. The Executive Board agreed the terms for re-entry at the September 1966 Annual Meeting and Indonesia formally rejoined the Fund in February 1967. From the autumn of 1966, however, Fund personnel were assisting in the preparation of the stabilisation programme (Tomasson, 1970, p. 47), and at the September meeting of Indonesia's creditors the Fund was asked to prepare BoP forecasts which would assist the Western creditor countries to organise reschedulings.

II. THE REHABILITATION AND STABILISATION PROGRAMME 1966–1970

At the September 1966 meeting with Western creditor countries, the Indonesian authorities outlined their programme of 'rehabilitation and stabilisation'. Its four interrelated objectives were:

(a) by rendering a more proper role to market forces, (to) create a wider and equal opportunity for participation in the development of our economy by all creative efforts, state and private, domestic and foreign alike;
(b) the achievement of a balanced State Budget;
(c) pursuance of a rigid yet well-directed credit policy of the banking system;
(d) establishment of a proper link between the domestic and the international economy through a realistic exchange rate, and thus creating stimuli to reverse the downward trend of the balance of payments.[9]

As its title suggested, the programme had two elements and was to have two phases. The first phase, 'rehabilitation', would begin with a period of 'resuscitation', lasting from July to December 1966, during which the government would try to ensure an adequate supply of essential commodities. This referred in particular to the so-called nine basic commodities – rice, sugar, salt, kerosene, textiles, rough batik, coconut oil, salted fish and soap. Between January and July 1967, the emphasis would be on improving productivity and increasing the supply of essential commodities. Phase two, 'stabilisation', would last from July 1967 to July 1968 at which time the emphasis would switch from stabilisation to development. The September announcement revealed that the rehabilitation programme would be primarily concerned with four sectors: food, infrastructure, exports and clothing. With hindsight, and employing a yardstick more fashionable now than then, a striking feature of the Indonesian programme was the emphasis on measures addressed to the real economy. The twin goals of the programme – controlling inflation and restoring production – were pursued in tandem with adjustments being made whenever it appeared that the desired balance between the two elements had been lost.

Extensive changes in the rules governing foreign trade announced in October 1966 marked the beginning of the rehabilitation and stabilisation programme, while the unification of the exchange rate in April 1970 can be taken as marking its completion. Below, we consider the thrust of fiscal and credit policy, as well as the financial and exchange rate reforms introduced, during the intervening three and a half years.

Fiscal policy
Since budget deficits had been the principal cause of hyperinflation, their elimination was a prime target of the stabilisation programme. The budget adopted for 1967 showed total revenue and expenditure balanced at Rp.81.3bn. While the realised revenue and expenditure

figures reveal a small deficit, equivalent to 3% of revenue, this was a remarkable contrast to the 1966 result which recorded a deficit equivalent to 128% of revenue. How was this turnabout achieved? The expenditure side of the 1967 budget reflected the adoption of a programme of 'severe austerity' and strict control over spending. Current expenditure accounted for 81% of the realised total and of this salaries of government employees accounted for 45%. The development budget accounted for 19% of total expenditure and within it priority was given to rehabilitating existing productive capacity rather than to launching new projects. Expenditure was concentrated in the four sectors identified as priorities for the rehabilitation programme. Most of President Sukarno's 'special projects' were abandoned and the ending of the war with Malaysia presaged a reduction in military expenditure. Control over government expenditure was tightened in a number of ways. Responsibility for the budget was returned to the Ministry of Finance; all government expenditures were to be recorded in one budget; no supplementary or special budgets were allowed; and budgetary allocations were made on a quarterly basis.

In nominal terms revenue increased more than six-fold between 1966 and 1967 and as a proportion of GDP it increased from 4.1% to 10.0%. This improvement was due to a number of factors in addition to more accurate recording of receipts. During the years of hyperinflation the efficiency of the taxation system had deteriorated but efforts to improve tax collection had begun in mid-1966. The results for 1967 were better than anticipated in the budget. Realised income tax receipts were more than double the budgeted level, while corporation tax realised 154% of the budgeted amount. Tax reforms and changes in the exchange rate used for determining the local currency value of imports on which customs duty was levied also had a positive impact. The import valuation rate was raised from Rp.10 per US$ in October 1966 to Rp.90 in March 1967 and again to Rp.130 in July 1967. (The contribution of direct taxes to government revenue continued to be relatively small; in 1967 only 19.8% of total revenue derived from this area. Similarly, dependence on taxes raised on foreign trade continued to be very high, with 40.6% of total revenue coming from excises, import duties and export taxes.)

A major factor in balancing the 1967 budget was the inclusion of part of the foreign assistance obtained in that year in current budget revenue. In February 1967, Indonesia's western creditors, now known as the Inter-governmental Group on Indonesia (IGGI), agreed to assist with the rehabilitation programme. Fund estimates had indicated a likely BoP deficit of $200m in 1967. The IGGI accepted that this was the level of credits required in 1967 and it was expected that bilateral negotiations with individual IGGI members would result in loans and grants of this amount becoming available early in 1967; in the event commitments in 1967 amounted to $173m. The Indonesians proposed that all the aid committed for 1967 should be made available through the BE (Bonus Ekspor) market. This was a free market in export certificates and as part of the move towards decontrolling trade and payments various steps were taken over the life of the programme to enlarge the coverage of this market. Under the BE system (which is discussed in more detail below) exporters exchanged their earnings for a combination of BE certificates and Rupiah converted at the official rate. The BE certificates could be sold in the open market and used to purchase imports from the BE list of essential commodities and raw materials. As part of the October regulations, it was announced that Bank Indonesia would create BE certificates against foreign aid funds and sell them on the open market. (It also began to sell some of the foreign exchange which exporters were obliged to sell to it. The difference between Rp.10 to the $ rate at which the authorities purchased the foreign exchange and the rate at which they sold it contributed significantly to government revenue in 1967, accounting for 12% of the total.) This procedure, they argued, would assist in increasing the supply of essential imports as well as contributing to government revenue. The IGGI donors initially resisted this use of aid funds since it would reduce the scope for aid-tying.[10] Posthumus (1971, p. 21) argues that two factors explain the eventual acquiescence of the donors to this use of aid. These were 'the strong support of the Indonesian policies, including the specific proposals regarding the forms of aid, by the IMF representatives . . . (and) the fact that the Netherlands had already after intensive bilateral discussions with Indonesia, accepted the BE mechanism as the channel through which both its 1966 aid as well as its 1967 aid to Indonesia should be introduced into the Indonesian economy'. In the event sale of credit BE accounted for 29% of realised budget receipts in 1967. It can be viewed as having financed the entire development budget plus 10% of the current budget.

Thus, relying heavily on foreign assistance, the authorities almost balanced the budget in 1967. However, the official deficit, of Rp. 2.7bn, understates the discrepancy between revenue and expenditure as two items were not included in the expenditure total. These were a salary increase to government employees paid in December 1967 and advances made to the official procurement agency, BUL, for rice imports. The cash deficit in 1967 was Rp.11.7bn, or 14% of revenue, and it was financed by advances from Bank Indonesia. Further, the inclusion of foreign assistance on the revenue side of the Indonesian budget, rather than as a financing item, is unconventional (Glassburner, 1979; Booth and McCawley, 1981). If a narrower definition of revenue, excluding foreign assistance, is employed, the resulting deficit is very substantially larger than the formal deficit. In Table 3.5 budget data for 1967 to 1969–70 are presented. Following Booth and Mc-Cawley (1981) the 'real' or overall budget deficit is defined to be the difference between the total expenditure and routine revenue, that is, revenue excluding foreign assistance. On this definition, the 'real' deficit in 1967 was equivalent to 45% of routine revenue. If an adjustment for the extra-budgetary expenditure mentioned above is also made, the 'real' deficit was approximately 60% of routine revenue.

Table 3.5 Indonesia: central government budget 1967 to 1969–70, formal and 'real' deficits or surpluses (Rp. bn)

	1967	1968	1969 (Q1)	1969–70
Total receipts	84.9	185.3	58.8	334.8
Total expenditure	87.6	185.3	58.6	334.7
Formal surplus (+)/ deficit (−)	−2.7	0	+0.1	+0.1
Routine receipts	60.2	149.8	45.9	243.7
Total expenditure	87.6	185.3	58.6	334.7
'Real' overall deficit	27.3	35.6	12.7	91.0
(as % of routine revenue)	(45)	(24)	(28)	(37)
Foreign assistance	24.7	35.5	12.9	91.1

Source: Bank Negara Indonesia (Unit 1), *Reports for the Financial Years 1966–1967, 1968 and 1969–70.*

During 1967 the rate of inflation was reduced from 635% to 112% (see Table 3.7) although it was still well above the target rate of 65%. This target appeared to be attainable until the final quarter of 1967. The quarterly rate of price increase had fallen from 32% in the first quarter to 10% and 12% in the second and third respectively but it rose to 31% in the final quarter. The reasons for this acceleration are discussed shortly.

This acceleration in inflation in late 1967 necessitated substantial revision of the estimates of government expenditure for 1968. The revised budget showed revenue and expenditure some 30% higher than the original. With a view to increasing government revenue the rate for sales of foreign exchange was raised in January 1968 from Rp.140 to Rp.240 per US$ (see Table 3.10). The valuation rate for import duties was raised from Rp.130 to Rp.240 in January and to Rp.275 in June. Also, in April, the prices of petroleum products, electricity and public transport were raised.

The 'rice crisis' of late 1967 strengthened the authorities in their view that increasing the supply of the nine 'essential commodities' was vital to the success of the anti-inflation programme. In particular, ensuring an adequate supply of rice at stable prices became the priority for 1968. This was to be achieved by increasing domestic production, importing larger quantities and improving the system for distributing rice within Indonesia. In 1967 the new official rice procurement agency (BUL) had been charged with procuring and distributing the rice required for payments in kind to the civil and military services and with intervening in the market in order to stabilise rise prices. When the rice shortage developed in the last quarter of 1967 BUL held inadequate stocks to perform this second function. As a result, provision was made to import 600,000 tons of rice in 1968 compared to the 270,000 in the previous year. By mid-1968 it became clear that purchases on this scale could not be financed within the revised budget estimates. Given the symbolic importance attached to formally balanced budgets it was decided to remove BUL's operations from the budget and to finance them directly from Bank Indonesia's credit.

The formal budget for 1968 was then balanced in line with the revised plan. There was, however, a small cash deficit (Rp.2.9bn) which was financed by Bank Indonesia. Once again, 81% of total expenditure was on the current budget which was entirely financed from domestic resources. The development budget was financed by foreign assistance and within it priority was accorded to financing the production of textiles and sugar, and purchases of fertiliser and pesticides. The contribution of direct taxes to total revenue increased from 19.8% in 1967 to 27.5% but dependence on revenue derived from taxes on foreign trade remained at roughly 40%, the same level as the previous year. Foreign assistance provided 19.2% of total revenue. If foreign assistance is removed from the revenue side of the budget the 'real' deficit in 1968 was equivalent to 24% of routine revenue (or 26% if an additional adjustment is made for the cash deficit). The December-to-December increase in the Jakarta cost of living index was 85%.

In 1969 a new fiscal year, running from April to March was adopted.[11] A budget covering the transitional three-month period showed a small formal surplus of Rp.143m. (The 'real' overall deficit was equivalent to 28% of revenue.) The budget for 1969/70 also showed a small formal surplus. A surplus of Rp.27.2bn on the routine budget plus aid funds financed the development budget. Once again, foreign assistance accounted for one-fifth of total receipts. Taking total expenditure in relation to *routine* receipts only, there was a 'real' budget deficit of Rp.91bn, equivalent to 37% of routine receipts. Revenue as a percentage of GDP had remained at around 10% in 1968 and 1969 and increased to 13.2% in 1970, while expenditure continued at approximately 11% (Sundrum, 1973, Table 1).

Credit policy and financial reform

Credit policy had a dual objective – restraining overall credit expansion while extending credit to increase supplies of essential commodities via imports and increased domestic production. Success was contingent in the first instance on fiscal policy and rapid reduction of the fiscal deficit. As Table 3.6 illustrates, in 1966, 68% of the increase in domestic credit had gone to the government. In 1967 the government share in the increment fell to 25% and to 5% in 1968. In 1969 there was actually a slight decline in the absolute level of claims on the government while in 1970 less than 5% of the increment in domestic credit went to the central government. Claims on official entities however accounted for 30–40% of the increase in domestic credit in both 1968 and 1969.

Steps towards restricting overall credit expansion had been taken in May 1966 with a prohibition on overdrafts and new investment credits. The October regulations added further restrictions, including directives that import credits were to be extended only in special cases; export credits were to be strictly controlled; state enterprises were not to be afforded preferential treatment; and the legal minimum reserve requirement of 30% was to be strictly enforced for all banks. Interest rates on loans from state commercial banks were now raised more than three-fold to 6–9% per month.[12] The new rates were still less than one-third of the prevailing 'curb' rates reported to be 20–30% per month (Grenville, 1976). The restrictive credit policy introduced in October 1966 was relaxed in April 1967. The monthly increase in the cost of living had fallen to 4% in March (compared with 30% in March 1966). Given this improvement and in response to complaints from the business community that it was facing a liquidity crisis, interest rates were lowered to 4–7% per month. In July, they were again lowered to 3–5% per month.[13]

Domestic credit almost doubled between December 1966 and December 1967, while the money supply increased by 132% (see Table 3.7). The expansion was particularly marked in the last quarter of 1967. (The rate of growth of domestic credit increased from 14% in the third quarter to 50% in the fourth quarter, while the rate of growth of the money supply increased from 20% to 32%.) Some progress was recorded in redirecting credit towards the private sector (see Table 3.6). Comprehensive data on credit utilisation in 1967 are not available, but Newmann (1974) estimates that between the last quarters of 1966 and 1967 roughly half of the total credit extended was Bank Indonesia credit and that of this, 40% went to agriculture, which had been identified as the priority sector.

The money supply more than doubled in 1968 while domestic credit expanded by 145%. With a December-to-December increase in the

Table 3.6 Indonesia: monetary survey, 1966–74, absolute annual changes (Rp. bn)

	1966	1967	1968	1969	1970	1971	1972	1973	1974
ASSETS									
Net foreign assets	-0.3	2.7	44.6	-4.5	-4.3	-8.8	206.4	74.4	365.7
Domestic credit	18.4	33.0	100.1	118.1	139.5	129.8	163.8	369.0	387.9
of which:									
Claims on government	(12.5)	(8.3)	(5.4)	(-1.7)	(6.5)	(14.1)	(-53.1)	(-24.5)	(-121.1)
Claims on official entities	(. . .)	(. . .)	(37.3)	(36.0)	(-10.3)	(10.5)	(21.6)	(37.1)	(79.3)
Claims on private sector	(5.9)	(24.7)	(57.4)	(83.9)	(143.3)	(105.2)	(195.3)	(356.4)	(429.7)
LIABILITIES									
Money supply	19.6	29.3	64.7	67.2	66.8	69.0	154.8	197.0	271.4
Quasi money	0.2	2.1	9.8	37.7	30.2	68.4	82.9	109.5	204.9
Other items (net)	-1.8	4.3	70.0	8.7	38.3	-17.1	132.6	137.5	277.1

Source: IFS Yearbook, 1980.

Table 3.7 Indonesia: consumer prices, the money supply and domestic credit, 1966–1977 (annual percentage changes)

	Jakarta cost of living index		Money Supply (M2)	Domestic Credit
	Yearly	December to December		
1966	1044.7	635	753.8	103.4
1967	171.0	112	132.0	91.2
1968	128.0	85	125.6	144.6
1969	15.9	10	57.8	69.7
1970	12.3	9	36.4	48.5
1971	4.4	. . . .	27.6	30.4
1972	6.5	. . . .	48.5	29.4
1973	25.8	. . . .	41.6	51.2
1974	40.7	. . . .	40.4	35.6

Source: IFS, various issues and unpublished Fund documents.

Cost of Living Index of 85% in 1968 domestic credit expanded considerably in real terms. This trend continued in 1969 and 1970 (see Table 3.7). A prohibition on credits of more than one year was removed with the introduction of a new medium-term investment credit scheme (providing credit for up to five years) in April 1969.

The authorities' control over credit supply from the commercial banks was imperfect.[14] However, the private banks accounted for only about 20% of bank credit while Bank Indonesia, and the state banks which were more or less under its control, provided 80%.

Turning to the demand for money, it is evident from Table 3.8 that as the rate of inflation declined, confidence in the rupiah was gradually restored. The index of real cash balances (the money supply index divided by the consumer price index) recovered from 85 in 1965 to 191 in 1969.[15] From 1969 restored confidence in the rupiah and the consequent change in liquidity preference made the much reduced inflation rates compatible with large increases in the money supply.

Financial reforms introduced during 1968 were very successful in stimulating the demand for money. The most notable of these reforms was the introduction of time deposits offering positive real rates of interest. These were introduced in October 1968 and offered a nominal interest rate of 6% per month for twelve month deposits. The Jakarta cost of living index showed a 4% rise in the last quarter of 1968 and an 8% increase in the first quarter of 1969. For the first eighteen months of the scheme Bank Indonesia subsidised the interest payments. As inflation moderated the rate of interest was lowered and by January 1970 it was 2% per month on twelve month deposits. As Table 3.9 illustrates, the scheme was very successful in attracting funds to the banks.

Between 1968 and 1969 the share of time deposits in the money supply more than doubled.

Table 3.8   Indonesia: index of real cash balances, 1963–69

	(1) Consumer price index, December figures (Dec. 1966 = 100)	(2) Money supply index, December figures (Dec. 1966 = 100)	Index of real cash balances (2) ÷ (1)
1963	0.8	1.3	163
1964	2.0	3.3	165
1965	13.6	11.6	85
1966	100.0	100.0	100
1967	212.8	231.8	109
1968	393.2	512.9	130
1969	432.3	825.8	191

Sources: Column (1), B.I.E.S., various issues and unpublished Fund documents; column (2) Bank Indonesia Annual Reports and IFS.

The structure of the banking system was also being reformed in these years as part of the general policy of decontrolling the economy. The Banking Act of 1967 repealed the 1965 merger of Bank Indonesia and the state commercial banks as a prelude to re-establishing Bank Indonesia as a genuine central bank divested of its commercial banking operations.[16] Data in Grenville (1976) suggest that during 1960 to 1968 Bank Indonesia provided roughly one-third of total bank credit to the private sector. This declined to 9% in 1969. The state commercial banks, on the other hand, who up to 1965 had provided on average only 4% of credit to the private sector, provided about two-thirds of the total in 1965 to 1970. The responsiveness of the public to the high-interest time deposit scheme greatly facilitated this expansion in the role of the commercial banks.

Table 3.9   Indonesia: the components of the money supply 1965–1970 (Rp. bn)

	1965	1966	1967	1968	1969	1970
Money supply of which:	2.66	22.55	53.67	125.74	233.9	321.07
currency	1.81	14.36	34.05	74.5	114.25	152.79
demand deposits	0.77	7.85	17.37	39.21	68.0	88.27
time deposits	0.08	0.34	2.25	12.03	51.61	80.01

Source: IFS Supplement 1972.

Exhange and trade reforms

A central element in the policy of 'decontrol' was a phased dismantling of the complex multiple exchange rate system and of controls on foreign trade. The rupiah was allowed to float from late 1966 to the end of 1968. The main rate (Export BE) depreciated from Rp.85 per US$ in the last quarter of 1966 to Rp.326 in the last quarter of 1968 (see Table 3.10).

During this period there were two major reforms of the export and import regimes, the first occurring in October 1966. Prior to that time it was mandatory for exporters to exchange at the official Foreign Exchange Fund the product of the volume of their exports and the foreign-currency 'check price' for the product exported set by the Department of Trade. Depending on which of three categories the exports fell into – traditional exports (eg. rubber), primary exports with less established markets (eg. coffee) or non-traditional exports (eg. handicrafts) – the exporter received either 20%, 60%, or 100% of the foreign exchange proceeds in the form of BE certificates and the remainder in rupiah converted at a very unfavourable official rate. The certificates could be used by the exporter to purchase imports on the BE list or sold on the open market. Any excess over the official check price and the price actually obtained by the exporter could be retained. This was known as the over price, or DP. DP could be used to purchase a wider range of imports than could BE, making it somewhat more attractive.

With a view to promoting exports, the October 1966 regulations reduced the proportion of foreign exchange earnings which exporters had to sell to the Foreign Exchange Fund from 80% to 40% for Category I exports and 40% to 15% for Category II. Category III continued to be exempt. However, exporters had to sell 10% of earnings to regional authorities (at the official rate) who could either use it to buy imports or sell it on the open market. Bank Indonesia now began to sell foreign exchange from the Foreign Exchange Fund at a rate that closely followed the free market (BE) rate. In addition, as mentioned above, Bank Indonesia began to sell foreign credits through the BE system, again at a rate determined by the government but following closely the BE rate. Import regulations were liberalised and the 200% surtax on imports was abolished. However, with a view to raising government revenue, the exchange rate used for determining the local currency value of imports on which customs duty was levied was raised from Rp.10 to Rp.75 per US$ and 50% of import duties had to be paid in advance. This latter requirement was removed in March 1967 but the import valuation rate was raised from Rp.75 to Rp.90 per US$.

Thus, following these changes there were four principal exchange rates: the export BE market-determined rate; the credit BE officially determined rate; the DP market-determined rate; and the officially determined rate applied to the mandatory sales by exporters to the Foreign Exchange Fund and the regional authorities, 'essential' government imports, and the foreign exchange transactions of foreign oil companies. The export BE rate was by far the most important, typically covering about 70% of foreign exchange transactions.

Import and export regulations were altered again in July 1967. Thereafter, the central government received 15% of export earnings from former Category I products only. With a view to stimulating domestic production, import duties on raw materials were lowered and sales taxes on some domestically produced, import-competing manufactures were reduced or abolished. In view of its importance to the achievement of a balanced budget, steps were taken in 1967 to promote the sale of foreign assistance on BE credits. For example, the BE list was widened to include capital goods, spare parts and essential food stuffs; credit BE became available from all foreign exchange banks; downpayments on opening letters of credit were reduced from 100% to 50% in the case of consumption goods and 100% to 25% for other imports. The import valuation rate was again raised, from Rp.90 to

Table 3.10   Indonesia: principal exchange rates 1966 quarter IV to 1970 quarter II (quarterly average of month-end figures) Rp. per US$

	BE		DP	Trade weighted real exchange rate, Jan. 1968 = 100
	Export	Credit		(average of monthly figures)
1966 (IV)	85	90	109	. . . .
1967 (I)	102	88	118	. . . .
(II)	139	132	149	. . . .
(III)	143	131	165	. . . .
(IV)	196	137	203	. . . .
1968 (I)	264	238	295	97.9
(II)	296	271	333	83.5
(III)	312		416	92.4
(IV)	326		432	93.7
1969 (I)	326		389	97.1
(II)	326		380	93.4
(III)	326		379	95.0
(IV)	326		378	97.3
1970 (I)	326		378	104.8
(II)	378			

Source: B.I.E.S., various issues; Newmann, 1974, Tables R, K–1 and K–2; and UNCTAD, unpublished figures.

Rp.130 per US$. The exchange rate system was further simplified with the abolition of the Rp.10 to the US$ rate.[17]

In May 1968 the distinction between export BE and credit BE was abolished and the rates unified at Rp.312 to the US$. In view of the continuing foreign exchange shortage further regulations were introduced during June and July 1968 designed to alter the pattern of imports by discouraging less essential items, and to promote the use of foreign credits. During 1969 the authorities intervened to stabilise the BE and DP rates in order to minimise the possible cost-push inflationary effects of further devaluation. (Rosendale, 1981, p. 168). The BE and DP rates were unified at Rp.378 in April 1970. As Table 3.10 illustrates, the real effective exchange rate was virtually unchanged throughout 1969 before depreciating slightly in the first quarter of 1970.[18]

In addition to these exchange and trade reforms, other steps towards decontrol included the abolition of special treatment for public enterprises in the provision of credit, reduction of subsidies to state enterprises and the promulgation of a new Foreign Investment Law in December 1966. The latter provided for tax holidays, the right to transfer profits and to compensation in the event of nationalisation.

How successful were these policies in achieving the aims of the stabilisation and rehabilitation programme? Below we look at their impact on inflation, the balance of payments, growth and income distribution.

III. THE IMPACT OF THE STABILISATION AND REHABILITATION MEASURES

Inflation

Guitian (1982, p. 99) has suggested three possible standards for assessing the success of Fund-supported stabilisation programmes. They are, first, a positive standard which measures performance by comparing the results achieved under adjustment programmes to the situation that prevailed before the policy measures were introduced. This he calls measuring 'what it is' against 'what is was', or for brevity the 'is/was' criterion. The second of Guitian's measures is normative and compares actual results achieved under programmes with the targets specified in those programmes, that is, 'what is' with 'what should be' (the 'is/ought' criterion). The third measure is conjectural, comparing actual performance with the probable outcome in the absence of a programme, that is a comparison of 'what is' with 'what would have been'. How does the Indonesian anti-inflation programme score on these three criteria?

On the 'is/was' criterion the inflation record is impressive. Over the life of the programme the annual average rate of inflation declined from 1045% in 1966 to 12% in 1970 and remained low until 1973. Comparing outcomes with targets (the 'is/ought' criterion) the record is less good. However, Guitian distinguishes between targets and forecasts, pointing out that targets are often formulated with a view to influencing, via expectations, the actual outcome. They may therefore be set at intentionally unrealistic levels. This is certainly likely to have been the case in Indonesia in 1966 when after years of hyperinflation stabilisation depended crucially on lowering expectations. The inflation target was a reduction from 635% in 1966 to 65% in 1967. In the event a substantial reduction was achieved but the target was exceeded by 47 percentage points. As mentioned above, the initial target appeared to be attainable up to September 1967. The monthly inflation figures were following a generally downward trend, but in the last quarter of 1967, a number of factors combined to produce a marked acceleration.

The growth in money supply appears to have been the fundamental cause of this. Grenville (1979), among others, has argued convincingly that this, rather than the impact of higher rice prices, was the critical factor. He contends that since, at the peaks of both the 1967/8 and the later 1972 rice crisis, the non-rice price index flattened out, the impact of the increased rice price was a change in relative prices. He agrees that prior to 1966 rice price increases may have influenced the general price level indirectly through the money supply since, as civil service and military salaries were paid partly in rice, a rise in the rice price would have led to a rise in the budget deficit and therefore in the money supply. However, he argues that since the adoption of the balanced budget policy in 1967, and in the absence of evidence that the money supply rose abnormally during or immediately after the rice crisis, this link no longer exists. However, the practice of paying civil and military salaries partly in the form of rice allowance continued after 1966. The evidence quoted above of considerable extra-budgetary expenditure in 1967 occasioned by the increased cost of the weekly rice rations suggests that the increases in the money supply and the rice price were not totally independent.

More importantly, perhaps, the rice crisis contributed to the apparent loss of confidence in the government's stabilisation policies. The rice price was popularly regarded as 'the touchstone of price stability' (Arndt, 1968, p. 4), and in a still uncertain political and economic climate this factor threatened to put the entire strategy at risk. Rice accounted for 31% of the weight of the Jakarta cost of living index. Between the end of September 1967 and the beginning of February 1968 when rice prices peaked, the cost of a kilo of rice in Jakarta had risen more than threefold.[19] A stable rice price was perceived as crucial to the success of the stabilisation programme and its achievement became the priority for 1968. After the rice crisis ended in February 1968, the monthly changes in the consumer price index ranged between +6% and −6% for the remainder of the year. The December-to-December increase was 85% compared to a target of 55%.

For 1969 the target was to reduce by one-half the rate of price increases of 35% recorded during the twelve months ended January 1969. The rate was reduced during calendar year 1969 to 10%. For 1970, the objective was to contain price increases within the 1970 level and this was achieved, the actual increase being 9%.

These declines in inflation were achieved simultaneously with the pursuit of apparently expansionary monetary and credit policies. As we have seen, the money supply increased by over 100% in both 1967 and 1968 and by 58% and 36% respectively in 1969 and 1970. Domestic credit expanded by 91% in 1967, 145% in 1968, 70% in 1969 and 48% in 1970. Thus the real money stock increased during the programme as the demand for money rose and the level of liquidity in the economy increased from the abnormally low level to which it had fallen during the hyperinflation years. The increasing demand for money was successfully stimulated by the financial reforms. McKinnon (1973) cites Indonesia and Korea as examples of the benefits which can accrue from a rapid shift from financial repression to positive real interest rates. He suggests that the Indonesian financial system was not as efficient as the Korean in directing the lending made possibly by real monetary expansion into high productivity investments. Nevertheless, evidence suggests that the financial reform had a strong positive impact on capital accumulation and output.

What of the third, 'is/would-have-been, criterion'? Guitian suggests that it is perhaps both the most controversial and the most appropriate standard by which to judge programmes. In the Indonesian case it can be used with some confidence since when the programme was launched the existing path was clearly unsustainable. Instability undoubtedly had a negative impact on growth and development. Real per capita growth rates were negative, the investment rate was declining and the country's infrastructure was in disrepair. Negative real interest rates were ineffectual in matching investible funds with investment opportunities. Liquidity preference had been eroded. The very restrictive exchange controls and multiple currency practices combined with growing instability had led to the growth of black markets, capital flight and speculation. The overvalued official exchange rate was a disincentive to exporters. Net foreign reserves were negative and in the twelve months to June 1966 the rate of inflation was more than 1500%. The need for wide-ranging economic reforms and the establishment of a rational system for the allocation of resources was obvious. Thus, the interesting counterfactual in the Indonesian case is less what would have happened without a stabilisation programme than what was the range of alternative policy options open to Indonesia in 1965–66.

Some critics of the path chosen conjecture that had it not been for the successful counter-coup in September 1966, Indonesia might have embarked on a more centrally planned development path, assisted primarily by Eastern bloc rather than Western creditors. This debate does not fall within the compass of this paper. However, it is interesting to note that in 1963, during the last serious attempt to right the economy before the political upheaval of 1966, the economic policy package negotiated by President Sukarno's government with the IMF was similar in all its central features to the programme adopted after 1965. However, it must be seriously doubted whether the government had any serious intention of implementing the 1963 programme. This lack of commitment perhaps reflected a fear that pursuit of economic stabilisation might be politically destabilising, and might threaten the fragile political consensus that underlay 'Guided Democracy'.

Balance of payments

We have seen from Table 3.1 that large balance of payments (BoP) deficits were experienced in the first half of the 1960s. Developments in trade, current account and basic balances over the years of the stabilisation programme are shown in Table 3.11. The trade balance was in deficit only in 1967 and the value of both imports and exports increased rapidly during the programme. The volume of exports increased by 42% between 1966 and 1970. This improved export performance was in large measure due to increased oil exports, which doubled in volume as, encouraged by the new attitude to foreign investment, the oil companies initiated investment programmes. Increased exports were also facilitated by the continuing depreciation of the rupiah, a lowering of taxes on traditional exports in 1968 (from 15% to 5%) and the rehabilitation of the transportation network. Although the terms of trade deteriorated over the first three years of the programme and stabilised thereafter, the purchasing power of exports increased by 78% between 1966 and 1970.

The volume of imports declined from 1961 to 1966 but doubled between 1966 and 1968. From 1967 more than one-third of total imports was financed by aid receipts (see below). The commodity composition of imports altered over these years reflecting the successive phases of the stabilisation and rehabilitation programme. Data in Newmann (1974) show that in 1966 'consumer goods' accounted for 34% of total imports, with 'raw materials and auxiliaries' accounting for 35% and 'capital goods' for the remaining 31%. In 1967 the share of consumer goods increased to 44% as the authorities concentrated on

Table 3.11   *Indonesia: balance of payments 1963–1970* (US$m)

	1963	1964	1965	1966	1967	1968	1969	1970
Exports (fob)	656	631	633	714	771	873	995	1173
of which oil	(269)	(267)	(272)	(203)	(236)	(292)	(336)	(434)
Imports (cif)	–602	–589	–609	–596	–806	–831	–995	–1116
Trade balance	54	42	24	118	–35	42	0	57
Invisibles and transfers	–281	–271	–271	–241	–248	–293	–383	–433
Balance on current account	–227	–229	–247	–123	–283	–251	–383	–376
Direct investment and other long-term capital	123	178	271	71	267	254	314	356
Basic balance	–104	–51	24	–52	–16	3	–69	–20
Memo items								
Purchasing power of exports (1965 = 100)	108	102	100	113	119	135	151	178
Purchasing power of oil exports (1965 = 100)	103	100	100	75	85	105	119	154
Purchasing power of non-oil exports (1965 = 100)	93	86	100	118	120	131	145	163
Terms of trade (1965 = 100)	102	98	100	98	92	88	92	92
Foreign grants and loans ($m)	167	184	88	119	265	265	314	407

Sources: IMF *Balance of Payments Yearbook*, various issues; UNCTAD, *Handbook of International Trade Statistics 1980*, Table 7.2.

increasing the supply of basic commodities. Rice comprised one-quarter of these consumer goods imports and finished textiles one-half. However, in the wake of the rice crisis in late 1967 rice imports in 1968 accounted for almost half of consumer goods imports which increased their share of total imports to 46%. With the achievement of price stability in early 1969, the emphasis of the programme shifted away from stabilisation towards promotion of development. This was reflected in the resurgence of capital goods imports as a proportion of total imports. Having fallen from 21% in 1967 to 14% in 1968 it recovered to 29% in 1969 and 34% in 1970. In line with the policy of trade liberalisation and decontrol, alterations in the commodity composition of imports were achieved by relying on incentives rather than direct controls. During 1968 a number of steps were taken both to reduce the demand for imports (in view of a foreign exchange shortage occasioned in part by much slower than anticipated disbursements of project aid) and to influence commodity composition. Sales taxes were introduced on most imports; duties were raised; and some commodities were moved from the BE to the DP list. In general, the more favourable exchange rate for BE commodities, direction of foreign credits into the BE market, preferential provision of credit for BE imports and relatively lower import duties on BE commodities fostered imports of the basic commodities and capital goods essential to the stabilisation and rehabilitation programme.

Small trade surpluses combined with substantial deficits on services resulted in current account deficits throughout the period. While the more stable economic and political climate gave rise to substantial capital repatriation, the deficits were financed primarily by foreign assistance (see Table 3.11). Negotiations with Indonesia's creditors during the second half of 1966 resulted in the rescheduling of almost all the guaranteed debt incurred prior to July 1966. As a result, debt service in 1966 absorbed less than 12% of the amount that would have been due without rescheduling. Subsequently, arrears and payments due to Western creditors were rescheduled with grace periods of three years and repayment over eleven years. During 1966 bilateral negotiations with the USSR also resulted in a rescheduling of outstanding debts with a grace period until 1969 and later rescheduling agreements were reached with other Eastern bloc creditors. Repayments on long-term debt were to resume in 1970 and to be made over periods ranging from six to thirteen years. Repayment of short-term debt was to resume in 1968 and to be completed over two to five years. A further rescheduling was arranged with the USSR in 1970.

In addition to rescheduling agreements, emergency foreign assistance of $119m was secured during 1966. On the basis of BoP forecasts for 1967 prepared by the Indonesian authorities with the assistance of the IMF, the foreign exchange gap for 1967 was estimated to be of the order of $200m. A request for this amount was made to the IGGI group of Western donors and in bilateral negotiations a total of $173m of programme aid was committed. Including commitments carried over from 1966, a total of $195m of programme and a further $70m of project aid was utilised during 1967. For 1968, $325m of assistance was requested from IGGI on the basis of the predicted foreign exchange gap for that year. Commitments exceeded that amount (by $40m) but utilisation was at the same level as in 1967 since many of the new commitments were made available too late in the year to be utilised in 1968. As a result, the level of imports was lower than anticipated. For

1969 the projected foreign exchange gap was $380m but a total of $500m in new aid commitments was requested from IGGI. This target was again exceeded but utilisation was somewhat lower than antici-pated. At the December 1969 meeting of IGGI the Indonesian author-ities requested aid commitments of $600m for the period ending March 1971. They described the programme as being at the transitional stage between stabilisation and development and progressively larger pro-portions of project aid in the requests from 1969 reflected this.

Growth

The Indonesian programme is often correctly cited as an example of stabilisation with growth. The very low real GDP growth rates experi-enced in the first half of the 1960s continued in 1966 and 1967 (see Table 3.1). During 1968–70 GDP growth averaged 8.6% per annum, or 4.1% in per capita terms. Performance in 1969 and 1970 exceeded the 5% target rate of the first five-year development plan (1969–74). The ratio of gross fixed capital formation to GDP which was only 4.4% in 1966 increased steadily to 13.6% in 1970.

The fastest sectoral annual average rates of growth for 1966–70 were recorded in construction (17%), and mining and quarrying (16%). Transport and communications grew at an average annual rate of 14% and electricity, gas and water supply at 12% (Johnson and Salop, 1979, Table 15). These high growth rates attest to the rapid rehabilitation of infrastructure. Manufacturing grew at 8% and trade finance and ser-vices at 7%. Manufacturing increased its share of GDP by 1% to 9% in 1970. The growth of manufacturing output was facilitated by a number of factors. In the pre-stabilisation period capacity utilisation in industry had declined to 30% due to the shortage of foreign exchange which constrained the supply of spare parts and raw materials. Increased imports of raw materials and capital goods made possible by the liberal-isation of the foreign exchange regime, foreign assistance and the increase in foreign investment, led without delay to increased output as underutilised capacity was brought into operation. Further, the range of industrial goods produced was narrow. Most were processed agricul-tural commodities and basic consumer goods rather than high-tech-nology intermediate goods (McCawley, 1981). Textiles was a priority sector identified in the stabilisation programme. Output of textiles increased by 139% between 1966 and 1970. Tariffs on imports of finished textiles were raised in April 1967 and again in 1968 in response to complaints that local industry was unable to compete. The propor-tion of finished textiles in consumer goods imports fell from 51% in 1967 to 18% in 1968.

Agriculture, forestry and fishing grew less rapidly than the modern sectors, with production of food crops increasing at an average annual rate of 5% and the remainder of the sector at 3%. Within the food producing sector, government policies were concentrated on rice. Rice production increased at 6% p.a. over the stabilisation period, while output of other food crops (maize, cassava, sweet potatoes) decreased on average by 2%. Rice intensification programmes were stepped up in 1966. The following year a food stock authority (BUL) directly responsible to the President was established. When a major new intensification programme was introduced in December 1968 providing fertiliser and credit to farmers, these were supplied by foreign contractors who were paid by BUL. The farmers were to repay BUL in rice after the harvest. This procedure combined with the failure of BUL to recoup the full cost of the inputs had monetary consequences which are discussed in Part IV below.

Income distribution
Income distribution data for the period in question are poor. Such evidence as there is, however, suggests that at least the degree of inequality did not widen during the stabilisation period. Papanek's (1980) analysis of real wages in industry and plantation agriculture found that by the mid-1960s 'wages generally were half or less than half of what they had been eight to ten years earlier' (p. 84). Since the mid-1960s real wages showed a strong upward trend with industrial workers benefiting from a near doubling of both real wages and employment. He points out that this pattern emerged despite the fact that pre-1966 government policy was apparently pro-labour while the increase in real wages occurred at a time when organised labour was being repressed. Nominal wages lagged behind price changes both when inflation was high and accelerating from 1953 to 1966 (leading to a decline in real wages) and when inflation was lower and declining (leading to a rise in real wages). Papanek argues that economic stagnation worsened not only the absolute but also the relative position of wage earners, while during the economic recovery real wages and income increased more than the increase in average per capita income. Moreover, lower income workers lost relatively more during the deterioration and gained more during the recovery. He suggests that income distribution probably became less unequal during the stabilisation period. After 1970 however, he suggests that income distribution probably became more skewed, with disproportionate gains accruing to skilled workers in capital-intensive industries.

The conclusions of work by Hughes and Islam (1981) agree in broad outline with those of Papanek. They suggest that urban inequality in Java showed little change over the 1964 to 1970 period but rose very sharply between 1970 and 1976. For the Outer Islands, they found that urban inequality fell during 1964–70 and remained unchanged during the subsequent six years. For both Java and the Outer Islands they estimated that rural inequality decreased significantly between 1964 and 1976. Work by Johnson and Salop (1979) suggests that the stabilisation policies had only a marginal effect on the existing income distribution. There were, however, substantial shifts in distribution in favour of the urban sector and, within the rural sector, in favour of farmers producing non-food export crops. Evidence of increasing urban inequality in Java during the 1970s is also presented in a 1980 World Bank report and in Booth and Sundrum (1981). The latter point out however that there is much less certainty about trends elsewhere in Indonesia and in particular about trends in the rural areas.

First conclusions

The price stability achieved in 1969 was lost in 1973 as net foreign assets expanded during the commodity boom of 1972 and the subsequent oil price rises.[20] Fiscal policy was not used to neutralise the massive expansion in international reserves and therefore in reserve money and net foreign exchange reserves increased more than five-fold between 1972 and 1974. Rather, the balanced budget policy followed during the previous four years was continued. Reserve requirements proved an inadequate instrument for controlling bank credit and in April 1974 Bank Indonesia imposed credit ceilings on the entire banking system.[21] Reliance on direct ceilings became progressively greater after 1974, so that they became the principal instrument of credit policy (Aghevli *et al.*, 1979, p. 804). In 1975, in a reversal of the monetary reforms introduced in 1966–70, Bank Indonesia was instructed to overstep its central banking function and directly finance huge debts which Petramina, the state oil company, was unable to service. Some of the trade liberalisation achieved during 1966–70 was also undone in the subsequent four years, with a significant increase in the number of prohibited imports designed to protect local manufacturing industry in the context of an import-substituting industrialisation strategy. Dependence on oil for export earnings and government revenue became even more pronounced. In 1974 oil accounted for 70% of export earnings and at least 40% of domestic revenue. Real per capita GDP growth averaged 6% over these years. However, as indicated above, the evidence suggests that the distribution of income was becoming more unequal.

The 1966–70 programme was, nonetheless, a successful anti-inflation programme. Its success was assisted by a number of factors. First, there was little difficulty, at least in the early stages, in unambiguously identifying the immediate cause of the disequilibrium. Reducing the fiscal deficit had clearly to be the top priority. The second factor was a function of the particular political configuration against which economic policy was designed in the immediate post-1965 period. The political upheaval of 1965–66 created a power structure favourable to full implementation of the stabilisation programme. It brought to office a government which successfully consolidated its power between September 1965 and March 1966. Thereafter, Indonesia had a strong government committed to economic stabilisation and rehabilitation. Economic policies encountered minimal opposition, the groups that might have been in opposition having been silenced. The political parties were in disarray and effective pressure groups either did not exist or were regrouping and adjusting to the greatly altered politico-economic environment. The business community was virtually the only interest group outside government which succeeded in exerting any influence on the programme.

Against this background, a small group of Indonesian technocrats sympathetic to the new political direction and enjoying the strong personal support of President Suharto designed and implemented the stabilisation programme with the assistance of the IMF. The crucial difference between the stabilisation programme of 1966–70 and earlier attempts to achieve economic stability, both during the period of 'Guided Democracy' and the prior period of parliamentary democracy, lay in the degree of government commitment to economic stabilisation as a policy goal. Given the size of the disequilibria in 1966 and the need to alter the expectations quickly, a gradualist approach to stabilisation was considered inappropriate. The absence of a political opposition and active interest groups, particularly during the early stages of 'shock treatment', contributed to the government's ability steadfastly to pursue its stabilisation objectives. The degree of commitment exhibited by the Indonesian authorities to the programme designed in co-operation with the Fund was crucial in winning the confidence and support of Western creditors. Their financial support was a third and major factor in the programme' success. Between 1966 and 1970 the IGGI members provided a total of $1200m of aid while approximately $550m of debt repayment originally due to them over these years was postponed. The availability of such large-scale financing contributed to minimising the inevitable short-run adjustment costs. It also assisted the success of the programme. The use of aid counterpart funds as government revenue was vital to the balanced budget policy. The availability of foreign assistance reduced the need for import compression and the acquiescence of the donor countries in the channelling of aid funds through the BE system contributed to the government's goal of directing foreign exchange expenditure into the purchase of essential imports, thereby relieving shortages on the domestic market and contributing to the rapid reduction in the rate of inflation.

IV. THE ROLE OF THE FUND

The IMF's role in the Indonesian stabilisation programme was three-dimensional. In chronological order, it comprised the provision of advice and technical assistance; participation in the meetings of creditors on debt rescheduling and the provision of new aid; and, from 1968, negotiation of six consecutive Stand-by arrangements. Even though Indonesia was not formally a member until February 1967, from mid-1966 Fund personnel worked closely with the authorities in designing and implementing the stabilisation programme. Shortly after Indonesia rejoined, the Fund appointed a resident representative to Jakarta and thereafter a small Fund staff was on hand to advise the Indonesian authorities. In addition, during 1967 at least 14 Fund officials spent periods ranging from three weeks to six months in Jakarta providing technical assistance on such subjects as tax administration and improving the data base.

This close collaboration equipped the Fund to play its second and crucial role as an intermediary between Indonesia and its creditors. The Fund supported the stabilisation programme presented to the September 1966 meeting of the Western creditors and Japan – a programme incorporating most of the elements reportedly recommended by Fund officials. Officials from the Fund participated in all the meetings of the creditor group and made available Fund documents reviewing economic developments in Indonesia and commenting on the stabilisation plans of the Indonesian authorities. At the request of the creditor countries, Fund officials prepared statistics on Indonesia's external debt and its BoP prospects. Fund support was crucial in catalysing assistance from the Western donor group. This was particularly true during late 1966 when rescheduling of Indonesia's debts was proceeding but no new aid commitments had yet been made (apart from some emergency assistance). The importance of Fund support in securing donor agreement to the use of new credits through the BE system at the February 1966 meeting of the IGGI has already been noted. Continued broad support for the stabilisation measures adopted by Indonesia during 1967 and favourable reports to IGGI on the implementation and impact of these measures contributed to the decision to provide further aid for 1968. Fund support was again crucial in early 1968 when accelerating inflation threatened to undermine creditor confidence.

Somewhat paradoxically, it appears that the Fund had greatest influence in IGGI during the early phase of the stabilisation programme, before there were formal agreements between the Indonesians and the Fund. By the time the first Stand-by arrangement took effect emphasis had begun to shift away from provision of programme aid towards development projects. Consistent with this new emphasis, the role of the World Bank became increasingly important. The Bank had declined to take the lead role in IGGI at its inception on the grounds that Indonesia was not at that time receiving aid from the Bank. However, following a visit by its President in early 1968, the Bank's activities in Indonesia increased rapidly. In May, it took the, then unprecedented, step of establishing a permanent Bank mission in Jakarta to advise the Indonesian government. The head of this mission came to be held in very high regard by the Indonesian authorities and played a key role in subsequent deliberations of the IGGI.

The first Stand-by, 1968–69

The first of the six consecutive one-year, upper credit tranche Stand-by arrangements between Indonesia and the Fund came into operation in February 1968. The final arrangement expired in May 1974. Financial flows between Indonesia and the Fund are shown in Table 3.12. There was a net inflow from the Fund to Indonesia up to 1971. Repurchases under the first, second and third Stand-by arrangements were rescheduled at Indonesia's request and were made between 1971 and 1975. As the later Stand-bys were not drawn, this led to a net outflow from Indonesia to the Fund from 1971 to 1974. (The repayments made in 1967–70 were in respect of outstanding drawings held by Indonesia at the time of its withdrawal from the Fund in 1965.) Drawings under the Stand-by arrangements were made in 1968, 1969 and 1970. No drawings were made under the last three arrangements. Two small drawings were made in 1971 and 1972 under the Buffer Stock Financing Facility, but it is the drawings in the previous three years that are of interest here.

Under the terms of the first Stand-by (February 1968 to February 1969) a total of \$51.75m was made available in five instalments, subject to Indonesia meeting the performance criteria. The full amount provided for was drawn. The gross inflow of financial assistance from the Fund during 1968 was \$45.0m. This was equivalent to roughly 14% of the estimated foreign exchange gap in 1968 but the *net* inflow was equivalent to less than 5% of the anticipated gap. The Fund's role in catalysing aid and in facilitating debt rescheduling was much more significant than its own credits.

The Letter of Intent stressed the government's commitment to achieving a balanced routine budget in 1968 from domestic resources. The government intended to use the counterpart funds from foreign assistance to finance the development budget. Cash salaries of civil servants and military personnel would be held at the level sanctioned at the beginning of 1968 while, with regard to wages in kind, cheaper

Table 3.12   Financial flows between Indonesia and the IMF 1968–74 (US$m)[a]

	1968	1969	1970	1971[b]	1972[c]	1973[d]	1974
Gross inflows:							
Credit tranches	45.0	65.8	38.0	—	—	—	—
Buffer Stock Financing Facility	—	—	—	2.8	2.5	—	—
Total gross inflows	45.0	65.8	38.0	2.8	2.5	—	—
Repayments	30.0	17.6	3.2	15.0	18.4	73.0	26.9
Net inflow	15.0	48.2	34.8	–12.2	–15.9	–73.0	–26.9
Use of Fund credit (outstanding balance at year-end)	64.0	112.0	138.0	136.0	116	23	—
Quota (year-end)	207	207	260	261	282	310	313
Credit as % of quota	31	54	53	52	41	7	—

Other receipts as at end-1974
SDR allocations 90.2m

Sources: IMF, *Annual Reports* and *IFS*.

Notes: [a] From 1970 converted from SDRs at the average exchange rate for that year. Indonesia's quota in SDRs
was 260 throughout the period from 1970 to 1974.
[b] In 1971 a one-year Stand-by of $50.0m was agreed but not drawn.
[c] In 1972 a one-year Stand-by of SDR 50.0m was agreed but not drawn.
[d] In 1973 a one-year Stand-by of SDR 50.0m was agreed but not drawn.

grains would be substituted for rice. The practice of quarterly fiscal reviews adopted in 1967 would continue, with expenditure authorisations for each quarter being determined in the light of receipts in the previous quarter. With a view to maintaining the real value of revenue, the valuation of import duties and taxes would be adjusted in line with the BE market rate. Taxation of petroleum products sold domestically would be increased while further steps would be taken to reduce reliance on the taxation of foreign trade.

In view of the rice shortage in late-1967 and early-1968, the Letter stressed the importance of increasing rice production and domestic and foreign procurement. Policies to promote exports and improve further the commodity composition of imports would be implemented. New debt would be contracted only at low interest rates and with long grace and repayment periods. Regulations affecting exports would be simplified and the workings of the BE market improved. It was the government's aim to establish a par value for the rupiah as soon as possible and gradually to reduce the divergences among market exchange rates with a view to establishing a unified foreign exchange market. However, the immediate priority was to stabilise the domestic price level, improve the BoP and introduce new tax measures to replace the revenue currently derived from the spread in the exchange rates. Until price stability was achieved, the government would follow a flexible exchange rate policy. Bank Indonesia would intervene in the market only to smooth out temporary fluctuations and other rates would not be allowed to diverge from the BE market rate by more than 15%.

The programme outlined was in the first instance an anti-inflation one with somewhat less emphasis on the BoP than most Fund-supported programmes. This reflects both the nature of the disequilibria in Indonesia and the fact that the programme predates the break-up of the system of international trade and payments based on fixed exchange rates. At that time, with a view to supporting the fixed parities system, the Fund placed relatively more emphasis on inflation control than it has tended to do since the early 1970s. The programme also contained a substantial supply-side emphasis. In supporting the request for a Stand-by, the Fund staff reported the view of the Indonesian authorities that in order substantially to reduce inflation it was necessary 'to supplement their stronger financial policies by a revival of domestic production'[22] and to use aid counterpart funds to finance production in the textile, sugar and estate sectors, as well as to purchase fertilisers and pesticides. They also reported the view of the Indonesian authorities that 'the current level of international reserves (was) not adequate to guard against unforeseen contingencies' and that the arrangement requested would provide 'a much needed element of flexibility and strengthen public confidence in the implementation of their program'.[23] There was a wide measure of agreement with the Indonesian authorities on the kind of programme required and the Fund was generally satisfied with the progress made during 1967. The staff report on the request noted that 'on all outstanding financial and trade issues, the Indonesian authorities (had) clearly chosen policy alternatives which are consistent with the purposes of the Fund'.[24]

The five performance criteria, related to monetary, exchange rate, and foreign debt policies, were:
- a quarter-by-quarter ceiling on the net domestic assets of Bank Indonesia, limiting the increase to 50% over the life of the agreement;
- a quarter-by-quarter ceiling on the net indebtedness of the government to Bank Indonesia, permitting an increase of 16% over the year;
- a ceiling of $75m on new short-term foreign borrowing;
- a requirement that the net foreign exchange position of the monetary authorities not be lower at end-1968 than it had been one year earlier;
- an undertaking that the legal minimum reserve requirement of state and private commercial banks would not be reduced from the prevailing level of 30%.

In addition there was the standard clause undertaking that no new multiple currency practices, bilateral payments agreements or restrictions on payments or transfers would be introduced.

The ceiling imposed on the net domestic assets of the Central Bank was exceeded in the second half of June 1968. The Indonesians explained that they had increased rice procurement and reduced sales during the harvest season in order to build up reserves. The need to finance this resulted in the domestic credit requirments of BUL exceeding the anticipated level. By the end of June credit to BUL had pre-empted Rp.7bn of the Rp.20bn increase in net domestic assets allowed between January and July. For the year as a whole, net credit to BUL amounted to Rp.19.4bn while the ceiling allowed a total increase of Rp.24.6bn. In view of this, the Indonesian authorities applied to the Fund for a modification of the original agreement excluding rice credits from the calculation of the net domestic assets ceiling until the end of the year. Following protracted negotiations, the Fund, viewing the increase in stocks as 'prudent and desirable', agreed to the modification. Towards the end of the year a request for extension of this modification to the end of the Stand-by period also met with a positive response. The extension was necessary because, given the very good secondary harvest, BUL had not resumed sales of rice and therefore had been unable to reduce its liabilities to the government. Without the modification, the 31 December ceiling of Rp.71.5bn was likely to have been exceeded by Rp.13.5bn. The original ceiling on net domestic assets had allowed for an expansion of 46.2% between January and December 1968 (or 50.3% by the end of the Stand-by period). If one adds the Rp.19.4bn of rice credits to BUL outstanding at the end of December to the December ceiling, the permitted increase during 1968 was Rp.42.4bn or 86.7%.

The second Stand-by, 1969–70

The period covered by the second Stand-by arrangement corresponded almost exactly with the 1969/70 fiscal year. The sum made available to Indonesia was $70.0m in three instalments. Of this amount, $59m was drawn. The gross inflow from the Fund during 1969 amounted to $65.8m, or 17% of the anticipated foreign exchange gap for that year, and the net inflow was equivalent to 13%.

The Letter of Intent outlined the improvements in the economic situation during 1968, particularly stressing the sharp deceleration of inflation and increased production in agriculture, industry (notably textiles) and mining. It was noted, however, that the level of Indonesia's foreign exchange reserves was still very low. The objective for 1969–70 would therefore be 'to strengthen the balance of payments, improve net official foreign exchange reserves, and to foster higher levels of production in conditions of reasonable domestic price stability

. . .'.[25] Food policy would continue to be a cornerstone of the programme. The routine budget for 1969–70 was expected to show a surplus which, together with foreign assistance, would finance the development budget. A substantial increase in the development budget was projected to coincide with the introduction of the Five-year Development Plan, with expenditure directed primarily towards rehabilitation of the existing infrastructure. This second Letter of Intent reads considerably more assertively than the 1968 Letter. The programme is presented as that of the Indonesian authorities, and the various targets and ceilings as emerging from these plans. This may reflect a reported evolution in relations between the Indonesians and the Fund wherein, as inflation moderated, the former exerted progressively more influence on the design of the stabilisation programme and its priorities.

In addition to the standard clauses, the performance criteria again related to monetary, exchange rate and foreign debt variables. There was again a quarter-by-quarter ceiling on the net domestic assets of Bank Indonesia, allowing for an increase of 66% over the life of the programme. Unlike the 1968 agreement, there was no ceiling on the net indebtedness of the government to Bank Indonesia, but credit to BUL was included in the overall ceiling despite modification to the preceding Stand-by to exclude it. There was a floor on the net foreign exchange position of the monetary authorities, permitting a maximum decline of $20m from the end-1968 level. The flexible exchange rate policy was to continue, with Bank Indonesia intervening only to prevent short-run fluctuations and to contain speculative movements. There was a combined ceiling of $125m on external short-term trade and banking credits (maturing in twelve months or less) and medium-term credits (of up to five years). The Letter also included a statement that no change was 'presently contemplated' in the legal minimum reserve requirements of state and private commercial banks.

The performance criteria were met with one exception. The ceiling on the net domestic assets of Bank Indonesia for 4 March, 1970 was exceeded by Rp.24.8bn due to greater than anticipated expansion of credit to BUL for financing rice imports and covering losses incurred in the rice intensification programme (see p. 98). This failure to observe the quarterly ceiling rendered Indonesia ineligible to draw the final tranche of the Stand-by funds ($11m). The actual increase in the net domestic assets of Bank Indonesia was therefore Rp.83.2bn, an increase of 91% since January 1969. As we have seen, rapid credit expansion was compatible with price stability during 1969 owing to the marked increase in voluntary holdings by the public of cash balances. However, the rate of increase during the first quarter of 1970 was considered excessive by the Fund. As a result, the ceiling on net domestic assets of Bank Indonesia in the third Stand-by was considerably more restrictive, allowing for an increase of only 32%.

The third Stand-by, 1970–71

This third arrangement covered April 1970 to April 1971. The amount made available was $46.3m (or less than 10% of the anticipated financing gap) in four instalments, Of this $38.0m was drawn. The Letter of Intent again anticipated a current budget surplus which, combined with foreign credits, would finance the development budget. In addition to the standard clause there were four performance criteria, relating to monetary policy, exchange rate reform, foreign reserves and debt. The ceiling on net domestic assets, *excluding* credit to BUL, permitted an increase of 50% over the fourteen months ending March 1971. A separate ceiling on credit to BUL involved a decrease of 15% over the same period. These combined ceilings allowed for an increase of Rp.54bn in net domestic assets, representing a sharp deceleration by comparison with the previous period. Secondly, there was again a commitment not to reduce the legal minimum reserve requirement for state and private commercial banks. Thirdly, there was again a floor on the net foreign reserve position of the monetary authorities requiring that by March 1971 it be at least $40m higher than its January 1970 level (of minus $61.8m). Finally, there was a ceiling on new short- and medium-term external debt such that new short-term debt would be limited to $70m.

A major feature of the 1970 Letter of Intent was the exchange reform to which the Indonesian authorities committed themselves, merging the BE and DP markets at the higher DP rate, with the unified market to cover all transactions except imports and services paid for with foreign credits. The decision to devalue was the result of a drain on foreign exchange reserves in the last quarter of 1969 and the early months of 1970 due to increased demand for rice and other imports. While the BE rate had been stable at Rp.326 to the $ since October 1968, and the DP rate at Rp.378 since the second quarter of 1969 (see Table 3.11), between September 1969 and February 1970 Bank Indonesia had had to support these rates by sales totalling $88m. While devaluation became a central element of the Letter of Intent, it does not appear that the impetus for that change came from the Fund. An earlier draft of the Letter annexed to a confidential Fund report recommending approval of Indonesia's request for a Stand-by made no mention of the exchange reform. In discussions over the previous eighteen months, the Fund representatives had urged the ultimate adoption of a uniform exchange rate. However, it appears certain that the 1970 Stand-by would have been granted without the introduction of the exchange reform.

The performance criteria set out in the 1970 Stand-by were adhered to up to November 1970, which was the second 'test' date.[26] Thereafter, three of the ceilings were not met. By the end of January the ceiling on the net domestic assets of Bank Indonesia had been exceeded and by 17 March, 1971, the final 'test' date, the ceiling had been exceeded by Rp.6.9bn. Credit to BUL, instead of declining, increased marginally so that on 17 March it totalled Rp.48bn rather than the ceiling of Rp.39.7bn. Thus the actual increase in the net domestic assets of Bank Indonesia during the fourteen months from January 1970 was 41% rather than the 32% increase permitted under the Standby. Thirdly, the Stand-by had envisaged that the net foreign reserve position of Bank Indonesia at the end of the period would be $40m higher than at end-January 1970. In the event, the position was minus $41.2m, or $19.4m below the target. The failure to comply with these ceilings rendered Indonesia ineligible to draw the fourth and final tranche of credit.

Thereafter, Indonesia negotiated a further three Stand-bys but none of these credits were drawn upon. It would appear that they were negotiated because, somewhat in the manner of the commitment to balanced budgets, they had come to have a symbolic significance indicating, both domestically and perhaps to creditor countries, Indonesia's continuing commitment to stabilisation. It is interesting to note the extent to which the ceilings under these later arrangements were adhered to, despite the fact that the credit was not taken up. The credit ceilings were not exceeded during the lives of the fourth (1971–72) and fifth (1972–73) agreements. They were, however, exceeded during the latter half of the final Stand-by period (1973–74). The target for net official international reserves was not reached during the life of the fourth agreement but was greatly exceeded over the fifth and sixth Stand-by periods. The ceilings on borrowing were not exceeded during the fourth or sixth agreements but were exceeded during the intervening period.

The credit ceilings under the first three Stand-by arrangements could be regarded as restrictive. Despite the fact that the ceilings under the second and third Stand-bys were exceeded and those under the first were met only after a modification had been agreed, the actual level of domestic credit expansion was compatible with a rapid deceleration in inflation, a satisfactory fiscal performance and high growth rates. As discussed earlier (p. 87), increases in the money supply were compatible with significantly lower rates of inflation because the usual Polakian assumption of a constant velocity of circulation was not fulfilled. The demand for money increased over the life of the programme and the velocity of circulation declined sharply. In the Fund report on the first Stand-by request it is noted that the credit ceilings were based on the assumption of a constant ratio between the rate of increase of consumer prices and the rate of increase in the money supply; also, should the inflation rate declerate and the liquidity preference of the public alter there would be a case for reviewing the credit ceilings. In agreeing to the Indonesian request for an extension of the modification to the first Stand-by, it was noted that the expansion of credit to BUL had not adversely affected price levels because of increased demand for cash balances. This trend in cash balances became more pronounced from 1968 and contributed significantly to the reduction of inflation levels.

Finally, Fund conditionality played a significant role in the success of the stabilisation programme. Impetus for the programme came from the Indonesian authorities and its full implementation reflected primarily the importance attached to stabilisation domestically. However, the Fund's role in designing the programme of 'shock treatment' was central. It is doubtful whether the Western creditors would have supported the Indonesian authorities without the Fund seal of approval. Particularly during the early stages of the programme, the Fund was able to exert considerable influence on the nature and timing of the stabilisation policies. Its influence was assured by the critical role played by its reports to IGGI in obtaining foreign assistance. Thereafter, Fund conditionality was reflected in the disciplines imposed by the targets and ceilings set in the first three Stand-by arrangements.

V. SUMMARY AND CONCLUSIONS

This chapter has considered some aspects of the Rehabilitation and Stabilisation programme implemented in Indonesia between October 1966 and April 1970.

In Part I the economic and political background to the crisis of 1965–66 was examined. The principal cause of the hyperinflation experienced between 1962 and 1966 was identified as government deficit financing. Some of the social and political pressures for government spending were identified, as were some of the factors depressing government revenue. A major feature of this period, in contrast to 1966–70, was the low priority accorded to stabilisation as a policy objective. While the major causes of disequilibria were identified as domestic, deterioration in the terms of trade over these years also contributed.

Part II described the policy measures included in the 1966 programme: fiscal and credit policies and financial, exchange and trade reforms. A balanced budget policy was adopted in 1967. Its implementation relied on the inclusion of the counterpart of foreign aid funds in government revenue, as well as greatly improved tax collection and restraint on government expenditure. In 1967 foreign aid not only financed development expenditure but also a part of recurrent expenditure. Reliance on taxes raised in the foreign trade sector, which had formerly been a major source of instability, was reduced during the programme but taxes on imports and exports still provided 34% of government revenue in 1969–70. Domestic credit increased more than tenfold in nominal terms between end-1966 and end-1970. Such credit expansion was compatible with greatly reduced inflation rates, however, because as confidence in the rupiah was restored the demand for money increased.

Financial reforms, particularly the introduction during 1968 of time deposits offering attractive real interest rates, were very successful in stimulating the demand for money. The complex multiple exchange rate system was reformed and the import controls which had proliferated during the years of acute disequilibria were liberalised. A dual exchange rate system was, however, maintained until April 1970. As in a number of the Latin American programmes discussed in chapter 2, the Indonesian programme was part of a major re-orientation of economic policy towards free-market principles. However, when compared to the approach adopted for example in Chile in 1975, the Indonesian approach was relatively pragmatic. The objectives included in both instances opening up the economy to the outside world by fostering foreign investment and removing controls. However, the extent of this 'opening up' was less in the Indonesian case, the speed at which it was to be accomplished was slower, and the range of instruments employed was less constrained by the policies of economic re-orientation, including as it did the use of price and exchange controls and increased tariffs as transitional measures.

Part III examined the impact of the stabilisation measures on inflation, the BoP, GDP growth, income distribution and structural adjustment. With the exception of one major setback during late 1967 and early 1968, the rate of inflation decelerated steadily, from 1045% in 1966 to 12% in 1970. Improvement in the trade balance over these years owed much to increased dependence on a single, non-renewable export (oil). Substantial current account deficits were financed by aid inflows and to a much lesser extent by capital repatriation. The level of net foreign exchange reserves remained negative throughout the stabilisation period. The real GDP growth rate, which had averaged less than 2% per annum during 1961–66, averaged 7% between 1967 and 1970, with the highest growth rates in the modern sectors. Evidence suggests that income inequality was not aggravated over the life of the programme, although it subsequently increased in the 1970s.

The programme introduced in 1966 was a successful anti-inflation one. A major reason for its success was the particular political context within which it was implemented, that is, by an authoritarian government firmly committed to full implementation. A second factor was that the immediate cause of the disequilibrium was readily identifiable, and a third reason was the availability of substantial external financing, which eased the burden of adjustment. The IGGI donor countries between them filled the successive foreign exchange gaps estimated by the Fund and the Indonesian authorities. Foreign aid financed on average one-third of Indonesia's imports during the programme. In addition, Indonesia's foreign debt to both Western and Eastern bloc countries was rescheduled. A further factor was the emphasis on supply-side elements. The programme aimed at rehabilitation of the productive structure and stabilisation of prices. Provision of adequate supplies of essential commodities, particularly rice, by means of increased imports and domestic production, was viewed as central to the price stabilisation objective. Simultaneously, rehabilitation of the infrastructure and sectoral policies designed to increase production of essentials and exports contributed to substantially increased output from 1968. The extent of underutilised capacity in manufacturing made possible a rapid increase in output of the narrow range of goods produced, once spare parts and raw materials became available.

Part IV considered the role of the IMF. This was three-dimensional, comprising provision of technical assistance; participation in discussions on debt rescheduling and provision of new aid; and the negotiation of six consecutive Stand-bys arrangements, the first three of which were drawn upon. It was argued that the Fund played a crucial catalytic role in securing new foreign credits from the Western donors and Japan. With regard to the Stand-by, it was noted that only the first could be fully drawn, and even that was possible only after a modification had been agreed – the impact of which was to raise credit ceilings. The credit ceilings were exceeded during the second and third arrangements due to the difficulties experienced by BUL in recouping the cost of the rice intensification programme. (In addition, with the third arrangement, pressure on the exchange rate resulted in a degree of Bank Indonesia intervention in the market that proved incompatible with maintaining the level of net foreign reserves specified in the programme.) It is argued that the credit ceilings specified in the Letters of Intent were restrictive, to the extent that the major objectives of the stabilisation programme, in terms of greatly reduced inflation rates, improved fiscal performance, and strong growth, were achieved despite the failure to keep within the ceilings. It was further argued that steadfast domestic commitment to the stabilisation programme was reinforced by the need to ensure continued Fund support in IGGI.

Notes

1. I am very grateful to the Indonesian Ministry of Finance for supporting this study financially, providing documentation, and facilitating discussions with Indonesian officials.

2. Statistical data from official sources such as *International Financial Statistics* is incomplete for the period covered in this section. As a result it relies heavily on data presented in the *Bulletin of Indonesian Economic Studies (B.I.E.S.)* and an unpublished thesis by Newmann (1974).

3. Between 1960 and 1964 rice imports had averaged a million tons per annum, equivalent on average to roughly 10% of domestic production.

4. Grenville (1976, p. 13) describes the 'monetary reform' as having been primarily designed to centralise the finances needed to launch state enterprises in the hands of the government.

5. The earlier attempts to remove the exchange rate bias against exporters and reduce quantitative restrictions on imports were in 1955 (when the exchange tax on non-essential imports was increased, a tax imposed on essential imports, and the effective rate for exports devalued); 1957 (when exporters were issued with certificates equal to the full value of their exports which were to be sold in a free market with 80% of the proceeds being retained by the seller and the remainder going to the government as a tax); and 1959 (when the basic official rate of exchange was devalued). Kanesa-Thasan (1966, p. 363) describes the exchange rate system immediately prior to the 1963 reform. There were '(1) three different types of exchange certificates valid for different types of foreign exchange payments issued against certain percentages of export earnings; (2) an exchange retention scheme permitting the exporter to retain a small part of his export earnings for use for certain categories of imports; and (3) differential rates of import surcharges applicable to different categories of non-essential imports. There were, as a result, more than 15 separate import rates in operation.'

6. An interesting analysis of why socialist governments appear to be prone to disregarding financial constraints, and of the consequences of such neglect, is contained in Griffith-Jones, 1981.

7. Calculated from data in Newmann 1974, Table 31.

8. The currency reform of December 13 involved replacing old rupiah by new ones with 1 new Rupiah being equivalent to Rp.1000 old. The reason for this 'reform' was reputed to be the inability of the printing press to deal with the announced increased in civil service and armed forces salaries and the payment of bonuses for the Lebaran holiday in late January. 'The decision to introduce the new rupiah . . . made it possible to put into circulation large stocks of Rp.50 and 100 notes printed in 1960 that had been overtaken by the inflation and never used' (*B.I.E.S.*, no. 4, 1966, p. 7).

9. Press statement quoted in *B.I.E.S.*, no. 5, October 1966, p. 4.

10. Although the Indonesians proposed that the certificates be issued for use in a specified country, ie. the donor country, the importers' freedom to purchase any item on the BE list and the preponderance of consumer goods on that list restricted the opportunity for directing the expenditure of the aid funds into particular sectors. The arguments put forward by the donors are fully discussed in Posthumus, 1971, pp. 19–21.

11. This coincided with the rice crop year and was, therefore, better adapted to the seasonal pattern of receipts and expenditure.

12. The new rates varied according to the nature of the activity; for food production and industry it was 6% per month; for export production and transport 7.5%; and for financing the distribution of basic commodities, 9%.

13. Some credits for agricultural production and industrial rehabilitation were made available at rates of 1–1¼% in June.

14. A banking crisis in August 1967 illustrated the weakness of control over the

commercial banks. Twenty-two private banks were found to have ignored the minimum reserve requirements. They were suspended by Bank Indonesia and some of them were barred from resuming banking operations.

15. The income velocity of circulation peaked at 25.5 in 1966 (Sundrum, 1973). It then declined each year until the early 1970s. However, Sundrum argues that from 1968 the decline in the velocity of circulation was due less to re-establishment of confidence in the rupiah than to 'real' factors such as increasing monetisation and structural change resulting in the modern sector becoming relatively more important.

16. In addition to the Central Bank Act, an Act allowing foreign banks to operate in Jakarta was also passed during 1968.

17. From December 1966 government imports had been valued at the full rate and the imports of state enterprises were also valued at this rate after March 1967.

18. The previous BE rate of Rp.326 per $ was maintained for aid funds as an incentive to their greater utilisation until December 1970. In August 1971 the basic exchange rate was altered to Rp.415 per US$ and thereafter remained unchanged until 1978.

19. Cole (1976) argues that the inflation rate could have been reduced to 20–30% in one year had rice supplies been adequate in 1967.

20. For a discussion of the impact of the oil price rises on monetary policy, see Arndt, 1979 and McCawley, 1980.

21. This was part of a package of stabilisation measures which also included a budget for 1974–75 designed to produce a surplus roughly equivalent to the anticipated growth in foreign exchange reserves; the introduction of a new eighteen to twenty-four month time deposit bearing an interest rate of 24% with the banks being subsidised from the government budget as deposit rates now exceeded lending rates; and an increase in reserve requirements on demand deposits (from 10% to 30%), and on time deposits (from 10% to 20%).

22. Unpublished Fund document.

23. Ibid.

24. Ibid.

25. Ibid

26. The April 1970 Stand-by was modified in May 1970 to take account of three minor discrepancies between the exchange reform as outlined in the Letter of Intent and the provisions actually introduced on 17 April.

References

Aghevli, Bijan B. and Khan, Mohsin, S., 'Inflationary finance and the dynamics of inflation: Indonesia, 1951–72'. *The American Economic Review*, June 1977, 67(3), pp. 390–403.

Aghevli, Bijan B., Khan, Mohsin, S., Narvekar, P.R. and Short, Brock K., 'Monetary policy in selected Asian countries', *IMF Staff Papers*, December 1979, p. 804.

Arndt, H.W., 'Survey of recent developments', *Bulletin of Indonesian Economic Studies*, no.10, June 1968, p. 4.

Arndt, H.W., 'Monetary policy instruments in Indonesia', *Bulletin of Indonesian Economic Studies*, XV(3), November 1979, pp. 107–122.

Bank Indonesia, *Report for the Financial Years 1960–1965*, Jakarta, 1968.

Bank Indonesia, *Report for the Financial Year 1969–70*, Jakarta, 1970.

Bank Negara Indonesia (Unit I), *Report for the Financial Years 1966–67*, Jakarta, 1968.

Bank Negara Indonesia (Unit I), *Report for the Financial Year 1968*, Jakarta, 1968.

Booth, Anne and McCawley, Peter, 'Fiscal policy', in Booth and McCawley (eds), *The Indonesian Economy during the Soeharto Era*, Oxford UP, Kuala Lumpur, 1981.

Booth Anne and Sundrum, R.M., 'Income distribution', in Booth and McCawley (eds), *The Indonesian Economy during the Soeharto Era*, Oxford UP, Kuala Lumpur, 1981.

Bulletin of Indonesian Economic Studies, Australian National University Press, Canberra.
(The references in the text are to the 'Survey of recent developments' article which is the first item in each issue but which is not always attributed.)

Cole, David C., 'Concepts, causes and cures of instability in less developed countries', in McKinnon, Donald I. (ed), *Money and Finance in Economic Growth and Development*, New York, Marcel Dekker Inc., 1976.

Glassburner, Bruce, 'Budgets and fiscal policy under the Soeharto regime in Indonesia 1966–78', *Ekonomi dan Keuangan Indonesia* (Economics and Finance in Indonesia), XXVII(3), September 1979, pp. 295–316.

Grenville, Stephen, 'Monetary policy and the formal financial sector', in Booth and McCawley (eds), *The Indonesian Economy during the Soeharto Era*, Oxford UP, Kuala Lumpur, 1981.

Grenville, Stephen, 'The price of rice and inflation', *Ekonomi dan Keuangan Indonesia*, XXVII (3), September 1979, pp. 317–330.

Grenville, Stephen, 'Money, Prices and Finance in Indonesia: 1960–74'; thesis submitted for the degree of Doctor of Philosophy in the Australian National University, December 1976.

Griffith-Jones, Stephany, *The Role of Finance in the Transition to Socialism*, London, Frances Pinter, 1981.

Guitian, Manuel, 'Economic management and Fund conditionality', in Killick (ed), *Adjustment and Financing in the Developing World*, Washington, IMF/ODI, 1982.

Hughes, G.A. and Islam, I., 'Inequality in Indonesia: a decomposition analysis', *Bulletin of Indonesian Economic Studies*, XVII(2), July 1981, pp. 42–71.

Johnson, Omotunde and Salop, Joanne, 'Distributional aspects of stabilisation programs in developing countries', *IMF Staff Papers*, March 1980, pp. 1–23. (The references in the text are to a longer 1979 unpublished version of this paper.)

Kanesa-Thasan, S., 'Multiple exchange rates: the Indonesian experience', *IMF Staff Papers*, XIII(2), July 1966, pp. 354–368.

Mackie, J.A.C., *Problems of the Indonesian Inflation*, Cornell University, New York, Monograph Series, Modern Indonesia Project, Southeast Asia Program, Department of Asian Studies, 1967.

Mackie, J.A.C., 'The Indonesian economy 1950–1963', in Glassburner, Bruce (ed), *The Economy of Indonesia — Selected Readings*, Ithaca and London, Cornell UP, 1971.

McCawley, Peter, 'Indonesia's new balance of payments problem: a surplus to get rid of', *Ekonomi dan Keuangan Indonesia*, XXVIII(1), March 1980, pp. 39–60.

McCawley, Peter, 'The growth of the industrial sector', in Booth and McCawley (eds), *The Indonesian Economy during the Soeharto Era*, Oxford UP, Kuala Lumpur, 1981.

McKinnon, Ronald I, *Money and Capital in Economic Development*, Washington, The Brookings Institution, 1973.

Newmann, John M., 'Inflation in Indonesia: A Case Study of Causes, Stabilisation Policies and Implementation (1966–70)'; thesis presented to the Faculty of the Fletcher School of Law and Diplomacy, in partial fulfilment of the requirements for the degree of Doctor of Philosophy, 1974.

Paauw, Douglas S., 'Frustrated labour – intensive development: the case of Indonesia', in Lee, Eddy (ed), *Export-led Industrialisation and Development*, Geneva, ILO, 1981.

Papanek, Gustav F., 'The effect of economic growth and inflation on workers' income', in Papanek (ed), *The Indonesian Economy*, New York, Praeger, 1980.

Posthumus, G.A., *The Inter-Governmental Group on Indonesia (IGGI)*, Rotterdam UP, 1971.

Rosendale, Phyllis, 'The balance of payments', in Booth and McCawley (eds), *The Indonesian Economy during the Soeharto Era*, Kuala Lumpur, Oxford UP, 1981.

Sundrum, R.M. 'Money supply and prices: a re-interpretation', *Bulletin of Indonesian Economic Studies*, IX(3), November 1973, pp. 73–83.

Thomas, K.D. and Panglaykim, J., *Indonesia — the Effect of Past Policies and President Suharto's Plans for the Future*, Melbourne, Committee for Economic Development of Australia, 1973.

Tomasson, Gunnar, 'Indonesia – economic stabilisation 1966–69', *Finance and Development*, 7(4), December 1970, pp. 46–53.

World Bank, *Indonesia: Employment and Income Distribution in Indonesia*, a World Bank Country Study, July, 1980.

4 Jamaica, 1972–80*
Jennifer Sharpley

I. INTRODUCTION

In the eight years between 1972 and 1980 the overall economic performance of the Jamaican economy deteriorated dramatically compared
with a record of impressive aggregate growth throughout the previous
decade. While the ten years of Jamaica Labour Party (JLP) government
until 1972 had been without any major economic disequilibria, the
underlying structural weaknesses of the economy, including the gap
between rich and poor, were to contribute to the economic stabilisation
difficulties facing the new People's National Party (PNP) government.[1]
When the PNP government took office in February 1972 under the
leadership of Michael Manley, Jamaica was already facing its first
serious balance of payments deficit since independence, and rising
domestic inflation. At the same time, the government was under pressure to raise employment, real wages and government spending, and
reduce social and economic inequalities, in keeping with its election
promises. The responses of the authorities to the situation they inherited in 1972 and subsequent external and domestic events were to
plunge the economy into a prolonged recession and produce disequilibria of major proportions. Some indicators of Jamaica's economic
performance over this period are gathered in Table 4.1.

In the decade 1962–71, real GDP per capita rose on average by more
than 2% annually but in the following years, 1972–80, real GDP per
capita declined at an average annual rate of 4%. Measured in constant
prices, GDP from the manufacturing sector declined on average by
3.3% annually, while GDP from mining fell by 1.3% a year and the
average growth in agricultural GDP was virtually zero over this period.
In sharp contrast to the negative trend in these sectors, the production
of government services, in constant prices, increased by an estimated
8.3% annually. Over the previous decade there were high but fluctuating rates of fixed capital formation which exceeded 18% in every year,
and rose to nearly 30% in 1968–70 during a major cycle of investment in

* My sincere thanks for assistance and advice are due to Asgar Ally of the Bank of
Jamaica and Jan Isaksen of Chr. Michelsen Institute, Norway.

Table 4.1 *Jamaica: economic indicators 1970–80*

	Growth of real GDP %	Growth of real GDP per capita[a] %	Fixed capital formation/GDP %	Final consumption/GDP %	Employees wages/GDP %	Under-employment rate %	Consumer price increase[b] %	Net foreign reserves[c] J$m	Net external debt[c] J$m
1970	12.1	10.6	31.4	72.6	50.1	n.a.	7.7	95.9	80.3
1971	2.9	1.4	27.8	75.2	50.0	n.a.	5.1	132.2	82.0
1972	9.6	8.1	25.5	81.0	52.4	23.0	8.2	88.7	96.0
1973	0.9	-0.6	25.8	78.3	53.8	22.0	28.9	76.1	150.4
1974	-4.1	-5.6	22.0	86.1	54.0	21.2	22.1	130.2	243.3
1975	-0.7	-2.2	23.6	84.8	55.8	20.5	11.4	58.5	353.0
1976	-6.6	-8.1	16.7	90.4	56.6	22.4	8.3	-181.4	421.5
1977	-1.6	-3.1	11.7	89.6	55.6	24.2	16.1	-196.0	452.4
1978	-0.3	-1.8	13.4	83.5	52.2	24.5	47.0	-447.0	1138.4
1979	-2.0	-3.5	17.6	82.6	51.9	27.8	24.3	-758.0	1290.8
1980	-5.4	-6.9	15.7	88.1	51.7	27.4	24.7	-821.2	1544.9

Source: Department of Statistics, *National Income and Product 1980* and *Statistical Abstract of Jamaica 1979*; Bank of Jamaica, *Statistical Digest*, December 1981.

Notes: [a] The average population growth rate of 1.5% annually has been applied throughout to avoid yearly fluctuations in the rate of emigration.
[b] January–January.
[c] Year end figures.

the mining industry. Jamaica also maintained relatively high rates of domestic savings, averaging 21% of GDP in 1962–71, but after 1972 savings and investment rates were lower and fell almost every year.

Despite a rapid growth of the public sector wage bill, officially recorded unemployment was higher than in the previous decade and averaged nearly 23% of the workforce in 1972–80. Inflation had generally been mild in the ten years to 1971 but double-digit inflation occurred frequently throughout the next years. Domestic prices rose particularly fast between 1974–75 and 1978–79, when the average annual increase in the Consumer Price Index was 25% and 47% respectively. Small balance of payments surpluses had generally prevailed until the end of 1971, but thereafter deficits were recorded on basic balance in every year except 1974, and Jamaica's net foreign reserves plummeted sharply and almost continuously from $J88m in 1972 to minus $J821m in 1980. Although net foreign reserves had diminished to zero by early 1976, it was not until mid-1977 that Jamaica entered into a two-year Stand-by agreement with the IMF. Between these dates the Manley government was re-elected with a large majority for a second five-year term of office.

The role of the IMF and economic management have been major factors in domestic politics and conflicts within the ruling party, and were central issues in the 1980 'IMF' general election. Also Jamaica's experience with IMF stabilisation programmes received international prominence at the North–South Conference on 'The International Monetary System and the New International Order', held at Arusha, Tanzania, in June 1980. Both domestically and internationally, the causes, cures and consequences of Jamaica's economic instability have been the subject of much concern. We shall now look in detail at the causes of instability (Parts II and III) and then at the role of the IMF and national attempts to manage the balance of payments and inflation during these two periods (Part IV). Some conclusions are presented in Part V.

II. EXPLAINING THE BALANCE OF PAYMENTS EXPERIENCE: 1972–76

When analysing Jamaica's stabilisation problems in this period, it is convenient to examine the causes of disequilibrium around two types of explanations: (a) *external* trends, fluctuations and shocks; and (b) the underlying *domestic* fiscal and monetary policies and *structural* factors. Selected balance of payments indicators and year-to-year changes in various payments magnitudes are presented in Tables 4.2 and 4.3.

Table 4.2   Jamaica: selected balance of payments indicators 1970–80 (SDRm)

	Merchandise exports f.o.b. (1)	Merchandise imports c.i.f. (2)	Balance on current account (3)	Net long term capital (4)	Basic balance (3) + (4) (5)	Total change in reserves (6)	Exchange rate[a] (J$ per SDR) (7)
1970	341.4	449.0	−152.9	160.7	+7.8	+21.2	0.83
1971	342.6	474.1	−171.7	187.8	+16.1	+25.9	0.85
1972	347.0	486.9	−181.2	116.7	−64.5	−23.0	0.92
1973	328.9	478.5	−207.7	173.0	−34.7	−54.5	1.10
1974	625.5	674.7	−76.4	171.0	+94.6	+55.8	1.11
1975	666.0	798.6	−232.9	164.8	−68.1	−27.6	1.06
1976	568.5	685.6	−262.1	75.3	−186.8	−161.8	1.06
1977	631.9	571.0	−36.0	−7.9	−43.9	−10.3	1.10
1978	663.8	599.1	−40.2	−37.2	−77.4	−44.6	2.21
1979	633.3	690.7	−115.5	−7.1	−122.5	−125.9	2.35
1980	741.1	798.4	−136.0	129.9	−6.1	+57.2	2.27

Source: IMF Balance of Payments Yearbook.

Note: [a] As can be seen from column (7), the Jamaican dollar was devalued substantially in the period 1977–79 and this Table is expressed in SDRs so as to avoid the large discontinuities in balance of payments indicators due to devaluation.

Table 4.3 Year-to-year changes in Jamaica's balance of payments magnitudes (SDRm)

	1970–71	1971–72	1972–73	1973–74	1974–75	1975–76	1976–77	1977–78	1978–79	1979–80
Exports (f.o.b.)	+1.2	+4.4	−18.1	+296.6	+40.5	−97.5	+63.1	+31.9	−30.5	+107.8
Imports (c.i.f)	−25.1	−12.8	+8.4	−196.2	−123.9	+113.0	+114.6	+28.1	+91.6	+107.7
Current account balance	−18.8	−9.5	−26.5	+131.3	−156.5	−29.2	+226.1	−4.2	−75.3	−20.5
Net long term capital movements	+27.1	−71.1	+56.3	−2.0	−6.2	−89.5	−83.2	−29.3	+30.1	+122.8
Basic balance	+8.3	−80.6	+29.8	+129.3	−162.7	−118.7	+142.9	−33.5	−45.1	+116.1

Source: As Table 4.2.

Note: The figures measure changes from one year to the next, with a *minus* sign indicating a change that worsens the balance of payments outcome and a *plus* sign indicating a change that improves it.

(a) External factors

The Jamaican economy is susceptible to disturbances in international trade, for it is heavily reliant upon four export items (bauxite, alumina, tourism and sugar) and is extremely open. In the 1970s the trade ratio (exports plus imports of goods and non-factor services as a share of GDP) fluctuated between 80–65% depending in part upon the availability of foreign exchange. Among the adverse external influences emphasised by the Jamaican authorities and others are oil price increases and declining terms of trade; world recession and falling export demand; increased profit and interest remittances abroad; and smaller net capital inflows.

The rise in crude oil prices in 1973 brought about a sharp increase in Jamaica's oil bill so that in 1974 the cost of petroleum imports was three times the 1973 level and accounted for 20% of all merchandise imports in that year. The oil bill rose only modestly in 1975 and then declined slightly in 1976, remaining around 20% of imports. Non-oil imports added much more than oil to the import bill in these years of deepening balance of payments problems and import price increases were responsible for only part of this increase (chapter M2 above and Bonnick, 1980, Table 5, p. 32). Quantitative import restrictions were introduced on a wide range of consumer goods towards the end of 1972, when it became apparent that liberal bank credit policies and uncertainty about the exchange rate had prompted substantial import speculation and a large increase in inventories. It can be seen from Table 4.4 that in 1973 the volume of imports fell 20% below their pre-1972 level and remained constant in 1974. Jamaica's system of import controls and a constant exchange rate were insufficient to curb non-oil imports in 1975 and the volume of imports increased by 11%, although it was now obvious to the authorities that foreign exchange reserves would be virtually exhausted by the end of the year. By 1976 the volume of imports was 30% less than its peak of 1972.

During the first period of the Manley government, the terms of trade were below their 1972 price level in both 1973 and 1974 following higher oil prices. However, in 1974 the price and volume of bauxite/alumina exports increased and their value rose by 96%, with the result that the deficit on current account declined sharply by SDR 131m (Table 4.3). The terms of trade improved substantially in 1975, partly because of a government decision to force up the supply price of bauxite/alumina, a decision that also curtailed the volume of exports. Although this improvement in the terms of trade was not entirely exogenous, higher world prices for Jamaica's sugar exports also contributed to the recovery. Overall between 1972–76, the terms of trade index averaged 95% of its 1972 level. While certainly contributing factors, neither a permanently larger oil bill nor adverse exogenous fluctuations in the terms of trade were the major cause of Jamaica's huge trade deficits of more than SDR 230m in both 1975 and 1976 (Table 4.2). World recession and declining export demand were far more important external causes of the deepening payments crisis.

The volume of bauxite and alumina exported in 1975 and 1976 fell by nearly 30% compared with the record set in 1974. Bourne (1980a, p. 13) claims that the sharp drop in production was mainly due to falling export demand caused by the North American recession, together with a power-play by the bauxite companies (Alcoa, Alcan, Reynolds, Kaiser) to force a reversal of a $7\frac{1}{2}$% levy on all bauxite exported or processed in Jamaica (imposed by the government in May 1974). Around this time the government also began negotiations with the mining companies to take over majority ownership, and the effects of these domestic actions, coming on top of the world recession, were unfavourable for the volume of production and exports from this sector. Due to higher world prices in 1975, the value of the lower export volume was still 6% above the record earnings of 1974, although by 1976 the value of bauxite and alumina exports had fallen to only 85% of the 1974 level.

The authorities might have anticipated that the response of the multinational companies to the ownership and tax moves would be to cut back production immediately and switch to other sources of supply over the longer term. There is some evidence that the production levy had increased costs so much that Jamaican exports were marginally uncompetitive with those from other sources.[2] Whereas previously Jamaica has a cost advantage over other suppliers in the US market for both bauxite and alumina, after introduction of the production levy, alumina costs in Jamaica rose by about US$33 per ton, which was almost equal to the advantage Jamaica had enjoyed because of its more favourable location and lower transport and mining costs. Moreover, Jamaica's main competitors, Guinea and Australia, did not follow Jamaica's lead in imposing a bauxite levy, and when later Guinea did impose a levy, the rate was much lower. It remains unclear as to,

how much of Jamaica's difficulty was the result of world market conditions, how much a reaction to government pressure on the industry, and how much a result of industrial unrest. Jamaica's proximity to the US market and relative ease of mining operations might have helped sustain production in a falling market, but for the domestic factors (Worrell, 1980a, p. 13).

Tourism is Jamaica's second largest foreign exchange earner after bauxite and alumina, and tourist stop-overs increased rapidly until 1974. The North American recession slightly depressed tourist receipts in 1974, and while other Caribbean destinations showed a strong recovery in 1976, Jamaican tourism failed to respond to the recovery of the North American economy. Widespread domestic violence[3] and

Table 4.4   *Jamaica: volume and terms of trade 1970–80*

	Volume of imports	Volume of exports	Import price index US$	Export price index US$	Terms of trade[a]
1970	90	92	85	98	115
1971	95	101	101	97	95
1972	100	100	100	100	100
1973	80	107	131	108	82
1974	80	114	191	161	84
1975	89	96	222	243	109
1976	69	83	238	240	101
1977	71	91	266	253	95
1978	68	94	268	262	98
1979	70	90	307	301	98
1980	64	93	391	352	90

Source: Bank of Jamaica: *Balance of Payments of Jamaica 1980*; Department of Statistics: *Statistical Yearbook of Jamaica 1979*.
Note: [a] Net barter terms of trade showing the index of export and import prices, measured in US dollars.

ensuing bad publicity contributed to the decline so that travel receipts in 1976 were less than half those of 1974.

At the same time as the world recession adversely affected export demand for bauxite, alumina and tourism, Jamaica's fourth largest export, sugar, enjoyed record high prices in 1975 and sugar export earnings doubled compared with the previous year. Despite favourable external conditions, with a near doubling of world prices and unfilled export quotas, the volume of sugar production declined between 1972 and 1976, largely because of domestic supply difficulties.

Among the other factors affecting the balance of payments in this period were changes in remittances abroad of profits and interest, and reduced inflows of foreign capital. Outflows of net investment income in the five years 1967–71 were almost exactly the same value in current prices as in the five years 1971–76. As Bourne notes (1980a, p. 6) the sizeable increase which did occur after 1975 was mainly for service payments on the foreign public debt incurred by the government to finance the fiscal and trade deficit.[4] Between 1972 and 1976 service payments abroad in connection with central government and government guaranteed debt increased fivefold and the debt service ratio rose from 1.1% to 3.7% of GDP (Table 4.5).

Although increased outflows of investment income were not a major cause of the weakening balance of payments, sharply decreased foreign capital inflows certainly were (Table 4.3). Foreign private capital inflows have always played a key role in Jamaica's balance of payments and capital formation. In the late 1960s and early 1970s, during a major expansion of the bauxite sector, net foreign capital inflows made up 20–25% of all foreign exchange receipts and contributed up to 30% of domestic capital formation. After the completion of these projects in 1971, foreign direct investment declined and by 1975 there was a net outflow. One of the major reasons for the worsening balance of payments in 1975 and 1976 was the precipitous drop in net long-term private capital inflows from J$139m in 1974 to J$30m in 1976. This reduction was only partly offset by the growth in official foreign borrowing on the Eurodollar market in 1973–76. However, Worrell (1980a, p. 11) argues that the decline in foreign financing after 1975 was mainly the result of domestic rather than external factors, insofar as the internal incentives offered to foreign investors were not sufficiently attractive from 1974 onwards, and the social and political climate was a major disincentive. In agreement, Girvan *et al.* (1980, p. 145) also notes that the suspension of direct foreign investment and flight of capital in 1975 and 1976 were largely the result of domestic political developments, and that Jamaica had become a poor credit risk to foreign commercial banks.

In summary, what Jamaica lost from the inflation of oil and non-oil prices was almost gained from higher bauxite, alumina and sugar prices, so that the terms of trade turned only slightly against the country over this period.

Bonnick (1980, Table 5, p. 32) has estimated the net contribution of import and export price changes and other factors affecting export supply. His calculations show that in 1972–76 domestic factors affecting export supply contributed more to these deficits than did the direct costs of Jamaica's fuel bill.

> In other words, problems on the side of export production and sales appear to have played the key role in widening the trade deficit in 1975 and 1976, against the background of continuing import price inflation and a relatively once-and-for-all increase in oil import prices (Girvan *et al.*, 1980, p. 140).

(b) Domestic policies and structural factors

Jamaica's balance of payments crisis appears to have been not so much the result of external forces as of current domestic policies and underlying structural factors affecting the demand for non-oil imports, the supply of exports, and net inflow of foreign finance. Among these domestic factors were quantitative import restrictions, the exchange rate system, the bauxite levy, and fiscal and monetary policy, all of which affected the relative prices of traded and local products as well as the level of aggregate demand and supply.

In the period 1972–76, the country's commercial policy moved from one of tariffs and convertibility to exchange controls. Imports surged in 1972 with the liberal expansion of domestic credit and an accumulation of inventories in anticipation of these shifts to quantitative restrictions. Towards the end of 1972 import restrictions were imposed on a wide range of consumer goods and foreign exchange allowances for holiday travel were reduced. In early 1974 further import restrictions were introduced to cover all imports except those from CARICOM countries. Thereafter, the total value of imports, and of major categories, were subject to ceilings which were adjusted occasionally depending on the projected payments position.[5] When the bauxite levy (paid in foreign exchange) was finalised in May 1974, some freeing of these restrictions was permitted, especially of raw materials and fuel which were to be licensed freely within reasonable limits. Between 1973 and 1976 the share of raw materials rose from 41% to 56% of total imports with the share of consumer and capital goods declining accordingly.

The 1975 import ceilings were promptly exceeded and the volume of imports rose 11% above their 1974 level, partly because of an expanded public works programme. By early 1976 the country had run out of net foreign reserves, and the licensing system was tightened in an effort to enforce very restrictive import targets – a common characteristic of quantitative restriction regimes (Krueger, 1978, chapter 3).

Until 1971 the Jamaican dollar was freely convertible and pegged to sterling, but after 1972 convertibility was restricted and exchange controls were tightened. In December 1971, Jamaica chose to continue to peg her currency to sterling rather than to devalue with the US dollar, but in the second half of 1972 the new authorities allowed the currency to 'float' and in January 1973 the rate was pegged at US$1.10 per Jamaica dollar. This rate was maintained when the US dollar devalued in February 1973. In all, there was a moderate appreciation of the Jamaica dollar in 1971–72, and its value depreciated by 16% relative to the US dollar between mid-1972 and early 1973 (Bonnick, 1980, p. 11). With a rapidly widening payments deficit and declining net foreign reserves, the exchange rate was held unchanged until April 1977. Bonnick (1980, p. 12) notes that this fixed rate was maintained to avoid pressures on the cost of living, especially the domestic prices of imported food items, and the exchange rate was not used to correct disequilibria in the balance of payments. With rising labour and other costs (Table 4.8) and a fixed exchange rate, the profitability of export production declined.

Turning now to fiscal policy, the impact of government expenditure programmes on the level of aggregate demand and production were a major cause of Jamaica's disequilibria. More specifically, the events of 1974 are crucial to understanding the deterioration of the economy and subsequent attitude of the authorities towards curing the balance of payments pressures. In 1974 Jamaica's energy bill tripled and in May of that year the bauxite production levy sharply increased tax revenues. Had the foreign exchange proceeds from this levy been used for building up foreign reserves, and had the domestic value of these tax revenues remained in the Capital Development Fund to promote investment for structural adjustment and growth of physical production in the non-mining sectors, as originally intended, then the prolonged deterioration of the Jamaican economy and living standards might never have happened. Instead, the government spent these revenues on non-investment activities aimed at providing greater social services, increased employment, and further public ownership and control of production. In keeping with the PNP's 1972 election campaign, many new social and economic programmes had already been announced before Democratic Socialism was declared in late 1974 as the official PNP ideology.[6] Nevertheless, this ideological turning point was to influence the priorities attached by the Cabinet to income distribution, inflation and the balance of payments. The attitude of the authorities towards stabilisation is examined in Part IV.

Compared with the previous financial year, government recurrent and capital expenditures increased by 61% in 1974/75 and then by a further 36% in 1975/76 (Table 4.5). Government revenues could not keep pace with the rapid growth in expenditures, even though the bauxite levy receipts were transferred from the Capital Development Fund. The fiscal deficit accelerated at the headlong pace of 108% in 1974/75 and 66% in 1975/76. Foreign bank credits were used to bridge the gap and these both helped to finance the fiscal deficit and provided balance of payments relief. Gross foreign debt outstanding at the end of the year grew from 9% of GDP in 1972 to 18% by 1976 and thereby greatly increased Jamaica's foreign financial dependence. With this foreign borrowing the government sought to improve income distribution and employment, but in the coming years Jamaica's underlying structural and social problems were to be compounded by the shortage of foreign exchange required to service the country's external debts.

Aid loans from multinational agencies and governments decreased as a share of the total foreign debt, as the importance of commercial credit from Eurodollar loans and suppliers increased (Bourne, 1980b, p. 8). Foreign commercial bank loans rose particularly fast after 1973 and peaked at 68% of total foreign debt in 1975, after which it became more difficult for Jamaica to raise bank loans. The maturity structure of Jamaica's debt changed because a growing share of these new loans was for short and medium terms (less than ten years). Whereas in 1972 only 30% of Jamaica's foreign debt consisted of loans for less than ten years, by 1976 this figure had increased to 75%. After 1975 an increasing share of the escalating fiscal debt was financed by domestic borrowing and

Table 4.5 Jamaica: fiscal indicators (in current prices – %)

	1972	1973	1974	1975	1976	1977	1978	1979	1980
Government expenditures/GDP	25	26	33	38	46	41	40	45	44
Overall fiscal deficit/GDP[a]	5	6	10	13	24	19	13	20	18
National external debt/GDP	9	11	13	16	18	18	32	33	30
National internal debt/GDP	18	18	18	18	25	44	44	45	43
External debt service/GDP	1.1	0.9	2.3	2.9	3.7	4.4	9.2	8.7	7.0

Increase over previous financial year	1972/73 –1973/74	1973/74 –1974/75	1974/75 –1975/76	1975/76 –1976/77	1976/77 –1977/78	1966/78 –1978/79	1978/79 –1979/80
a. Central government expenditures	23	61	36	27	–1	23	27
b. Central government revenues and capital development fund	22	48	24	–5	8	58	30
c. Overall fiscal deficit (a – b)	26	108	66	88	–11	–16	77

Source: Ministry of Finance, Financial Statements and Revenue Statements (various years); Department of Statistics, National Income and Product 1979; Bank of Jamaica, Statistical Digest, February 1981.

Note: [a] Expenditures minus domestic recurrent and capital revenues.

this encouraged excess aggregate demand, rapid domestic inflation and declining real incomes.

Fiscal policy, or the rapid growth of government consumption expenditures, was the main cause of Jamaica's trade and payments problems. Worrell (1980a, p. 12) and the analysis of fiscal performance by Girvan *et al*. support this view, although he refuses steadfastly to admit it:

> Government expenditures grew at an extremely high rate, averaging 32% per annum in the five financial years from 1972/73 to 1976/77. . . . The growth in expenditure was partly due to deliberate Keynesian inspired fiscal expansion, the effect of inflation on recurrent expenditure, lack of strict financial accountability in the state bureaucracy and political pressures. Contradictions within the ruling PNP led to a tendency to alleviate the social effects of the crisis by increased expenditure, rather than tackling the underlying structural problems, and the political pressures of an election year contributed to the failure to control public expenditure. However, it is not completely clear that fiscal expansion was the root cause of the deterioration in the balance of payments, or that fiscal restraint in 1976/77 would have prevented the crisis. (Girvan *et al*. 1980, pp. 142–143.)

The excess demand for consumer, intermediate and capital goods that could not be met from local production or imports resulted in higher domestic prices and shortages. Substantially higher real wages added to the costs of production and, together with domestic inflation and a fixed exchange rate, squeezed profit margins, discouraged the production of exports and inflows of foreign investment. Given a constant exchange rate, a growing consumption rate (Table 4.1), and the exemption of government transactions from most import restrictions, excess demand for imports by the private sector is likely to have increased.

Although the deteriorating payments position was dominated by domestic fiscal policy, there were signs of structural weakness underlying the balance of payments in the period prior to 1972. Both Jefferson (1972) and Manley (1974, Part II, Chapter 2) identify the failure to develop forward and backward linkages between the agricultural–traditional sector and the rest of the economy, as one of the major weaknesses underlying Jamaica's economic development in the period prior to 1972. A pattern of capital-intensive import substitution contributed to a growing dependence on foreign private capital inflows to finance current account deficits. There was increasing unemployment and a growing awareness of income inequalities between rich and poor.

In the 1960s growth of GDP was spread unevenly throughout the sectors of production. The manufacturing sector had been stimulated by a variety of industrial incentives designed to encourage private foreign capital. Although a major source of growth in GDP and wage employment, the growth of manufacturing declined towards the end of the 1960s as the opportunities for easy import substitution decreased.

Brown (1969) examined the effects of manufacturing incentives on the structure of production and inputs in the 1960s. He showed that import substitution policies failed to bring about any significant reduction in the sectoral pattern of import coefficients, and failed to develop linkages between import substitution and agricultural processing which could have increased domestic value added. For a more recent study see Ayub (1981).

In the decade before 1972, the agricultural sector, which engages over one-third of the total workforce, grew only half as fast as the rest of the economy. Export agriculture was virtually stagnant as a result of the decline in sugar production, although livestock and crop production for domestic consumption expanded faster. The inadequate overall growth of agriculture in this period gave rise to the rapid expansion of imported agricultural commodities and processed foods, and resulted in declining agricultural self-sufficiency.

In the first two years of the Manley administration the volume of exports increased, but afterwards production of all four major agricultural commodities declined and Jamaica failed to meet its export quotas for sugar and bananas (Table 4.6). Reasons for the lower volume of bauxite and alumina exports after 1974 have already been discussed. As regards agricultural exports, several government policies affecting the agricultural sector were introduced after 1972 and while they were designed to change the ownership of production and share of the private sector, they also had the effect of discouraging agricultural exports. Among these policies were the Land Lease Project which involved the subletting, for only 5–10 years, of idle private land the government had acquired to small inexperienced farmers; the government take-over of the largest private sugar factory, which accounted for nearly 40% of total sugar cane acreage; and the promotion of co-operatives in the management of sugar production.

The sugar industry had been in a state of decline since the mid-1960s as rising unit costs had decreased the profitability of the industry. Owing to the lack of investment, cane yields per acre and the sucrose content of the cane delivered to crushing factories had been declining, and the technological capabilities of the factories needed to be upgraded (Bourne, 1980a, p. 12). The persistent shortfall in the supply of bananas below Jamaica's export quota has been attributed to inefficient spraying, labour shortages and rigid quality controls on bunches for export. As domestic food prices rose rapidly, local sales became more profitable and there was a shift away from exports to the domestic market.

Finally, in the five years after 1972 the structure of Jamaica's exports showed little diversification, and 80% of all merchandise export earnings continued to come from four products (bauxite, alumina, sugar

Table 4.6 *Jamaica: volume of total and principal exports, 1970–80, 1972 = 100*

	Total	Bauxite	Aluminia	Sugar	Bananas	Coffee	Cocoa
1970	92	109	79	110	105	122	88
1971	101	108	81	109	99	120	81
1972	100	100	100	100	100	100	100
1973	107	103	110	94	85	68	103
1974	114	111	128	98	57	21	97
1975	96	77	108	92	53	33	82
1976	83	88	73	84	60	5	153
1977	91	89	92	77	59	153	61
1978	94	90	97	71	58	88	49
1979	90	90	93	68	50	229	38
1980	93	86	107	47	26	143	43

Source: Bank of Jamaica, *Balance of Payments of Jamaica*, 1980, Table 13. Department of Statistics, *Statistical Yearbook of Jamaica*, 1979, Table 2.1, 605.

and bananas) of which 60–70% were from bauxite and alumina. Among the 20% of minor exports, the principal groups were 'other foods', rum and tobacco, oil refining, and small amounts of manufactured goods and chemicals.

In conclusion, Jamaica's balance of payments crisis was not so much the result of external factors (higher oil prices, declining terms of trade, world recession) as of domestic policies and structural factors affecting the demand for non-oil imports, the supply of exports, and net inflow of foreign finance. Among these domestic policies were import restrictions, exchange controls and a fixed exchange rate. Over-expansionary fiscal and monetary policies, financed by the bauxite levy, foreign borrowing and domestic money creation encouraged the rapid growth of government consumption expenditure which led to excess demand for local production and imported supplies. The trade deficit worsened and the country became increasingly dependent on private capital inflows, particularly into mining, to offset the poor performance of exports and growing current account deficit. The decline in import supplies after 1974 was mainly due to domestic policies affecting the ownership and profitability of bauxite and agricultural production. Similarly, the contraction of foreign capital inflows stemmed mainly from adverse reaction to the government's political and economic pressures.

III. EXPLAINING DOMESTIC DISEQUILIBRIA: 1972–76

The overall trends in domestic disequilibria have already been mentioned in Part I, but we shall now examine in more detail the sources of rapid inflation and of declining real GDP in the first term of the Manley administration.

Sources of inflation (a) imported
In the five years 1967–71, import prices rose at an annual rate of less than 5% and the domestic price level increased only slightly faster, by 7% annually. But in the following years import prices and domestic inflation were to accelerate and fluctuate widely, as can be seen from Table 4.7.

Table 4.7   Jamaica: measures of annual price changes 1972–80

	Import price index	Consumer price index	GDP implicit deflator
1972	−1.0	8.2	2.7
1973	31.4	28.9	19.5
1974	45.8	22.1	30.4
1975	11.7	11.4	21.2
1976	5.5	8.3	11.3
1977	13.8	16.1	11.9
1978	2.1	47.0	26.0
1979	14.4	24.3	15.1
1980	27.4	24.7	16.5

Source: Bank of Jamaica, *Balance of Payments of Jamaica*, 1980; Department of Statistics, *Consumer Prices Indices*, 1970–1979; Department of Statistics, *National Income and Product*, 1980.

In 1973 the import price index jumped by 31%. This was mainly due to a 16% devaluation of the Jamaican dollar in January 1973, for it was not until the very end of this year that higher world oil prices were announced. After January 1973 the exchange rate remained unchanged until April 1977, but the impact of higher oil and non-oil prices was felt in 1974 when the import price index rose dramatically by 46%. Data showing the import content of final consumption of input–output coefficients for imported and domestic production costs are not available from which to quantify the impact of import prices on domestic inflation. However, merchandise imports represent about one-third of GDP and in conjunction with the import price index, this indicates that rising import prices may have contributed directly to domestic inflation of 10% in 1973 and 15% in 1974. While admittedly a crude and minimal measure of imported inflation, it suggests that import price rises accounted for perhaps half the increase in the GDP implicit deflator in these years.

Sources of inflation: (b) domestic

Higher real wages also contributed to inflation in this period. Large domestic wage increases preceded the rise in oil prices. Between April 1973 and April 1974, before the full effects of higher oil prices had worked their way through the economy, nominal weekly wages increased by 34–45% (Table 4.8). In 1973 the government itself helped to establish a pattern of large wage increases, when it granted a 30% pay rise to teachers; this was soon followed by large increases in the mining and construction sectors. Wage contracts already in effect were reopened when the actual inflation far exceeded expectations in 1973. Between April 1974 and April 1975 there was a 30–35% increase in the index of median weekly incomes, although the consumer price index increased by 18% over the same period. Of the 131 wage agreements negotiated during 1973–75, 72 were for increases of 30–60% and in 1975 half of all negotiated wage increases were for 60–90%.[7]

Hence import price increases were magnified by domestic wage adjustments which acted as a strong propagating mechanism.

> Jamaica has a highly unionized labour force, and the principle of cost of living adjustments being the minimum wage adjustment has long been the starting point accepted by both sides in labour negotiations. Furthermore, contracts traditionally provide for a retroactive component, so that full compensation for cost of living increases in any one year is feasible even if the contract is settled later in the year. Thus there is a mechanism which ensures that the large increase in prices of imported food and consumer goods triggered a secondary round of price increases as local costs of production were pushed up by rising wages (Bonnick, 1980, p. 20).

These wage adjustments exceeded the rise in consumer prices, and from October 1973 to October 1976 average real wages increased by approximately 30%. The changing pattern of income distribution – between factors, urban–rural sectors, unemployed, self-employed and trade union members – is complex. Although real GDP per capita declined by 15% during 1973–76, the unemployment rate improved slightly and labour's share of GDP recorded a rise. This apparent redistribution of factor shares from capital to labour is misleading, however, for the earnings of workers in co-operatives and those self-employed in farming and petty trading form part of the capital share and are not included in the compensation paid to employees.

The gap between rural and urban incomes (Stone, 1980, p. 247) widened, partly because of higher levels of unionisation in the public service and manufacturing sectors than in agriculture. Government pricing and marketing policies also played a part. While price controls on basic food items and a fixed exchange rate were aimed at protecting the cost of living of the urban poor, they also held down rural incomes and moved the domestic terms of trade against the agricultural sector.

Although data are not available to calculate the domestic terms of trade for agricultural producers over this period, it is clear that the export prices for sugar and especially bananas rose less quickly than the rural cost of living and that increments in export prices were not fully passed on to the growers by the marketing boards. Many of Jamaica's poor are among the one-third involved in agriculture, but social unrest and violence was more likely to stem from the urban areas than from rural poverty. Expenditures on social welfare programmes, such as free education, skill training, food subsidies, and employment creation, were directed more at the urban than rural population and it was those employed in the urban wage sector under trade union agreements who benefited most from rising real wages.

Expansionary fiscal and monetary policies contributed to inflation in this period. It can be seen from Table 4.9 that the annual increase in total domestic credit far exceeded the growth of GDP in current and constant prices and this was mainly the result of rapid growth in public sector credit to finance the widening fiscal deficits. It has already been noted (Table 4.5) that the overall fiscal deficit (excess of domestic recurrent and capital revenues over expenditures) increased from 5% of GDP in 1972 to 24% of GDP by 1976, and that until 1975 much of the deficit was financed by external public borrowing. At the same time, domestic credit to the government sector expanded five-fold in 1971–76, and the share of credit going to the public sector more than doubled, from 14% to 35% of total domestic credit, over the same period. The growth and sectoral composition of these expansionary policies caused aggregate demand to far outstrip the supply of real resources from domestic production and available imports, and added to the inflationary pressures from higher import prices and cost of living adjustments.

The declining level of aggregate supply and the falling rate of investment were due to the absence of an effective production strategy. While government spending expanded dramatically in 1972–76, relatively little of it was for investment that would expand future production. Unpublished estimates of the consumption and investment rates for the public and private sectors (Table 4.10) show that the total public sector expenditures increased from 18.6% to 26.3% of GDP between 1973 and 1976 but that most of this increased share took the form of higher consumption, not investment. Public investment rose duly from 2.7% to 4.3% of GDP but by 1976 the private investment rate had declined to only half that of 1973, a drop which vastly outweighed the small increase in public investment. Although the share of government investment rose from one-tenth to one-third of total investment, aggregate output declined, which suggests that the government's economic strategy had the effect of replacing more productive private activities with less efficient public sector activities (Bourne, 1980b, p. 18). Income

Table 4.8 *Jamaica: real wage indicators 1973–79 (April 1974 = 100)*

	1973 Apr.	1973 Oct.	1974 Apr.	1974 Oct.	1975 Apr.	1975 Oct.	1976 Apr.	1976 Oct.	1977 Apr.	1977 Oct.	1978 Apr.	1978 Oct.	1979 Apr.	1979 Oct.
1. Index of median weekly incomes														
Males	68.9	76.3	100	114.4	135.6	137.2	141.2	152.2	148.9	150.8	166.7	181.6	195.3	218.3
Females	73.5	70.7	100	122.7	130.2	131.2	159.0	174.0	171.8	169.3	177.2	185.0	197.9	228.9
2. Consumer price index	77.9	87.6	100	110.6	118.5	127.0	131.5	138.4	143.2	157.2	168.1	229.4	248.6	275.7
3. Real wage index ($1 \div 2$)														
Males	88.4	87.1	100	103.4	114.4	108.3	107.4	109.9	104.0	95.9	99.1	79.3	78.6	79.2
Females	94.4	80.7	100	110.9	109.8	103.3	120.9	125.7	120.0	107.7	105.4	80.6	79.6	83.0

Sources: National Planning Agency, *Economic and Social Survey* (various issues); Department of Statistics, *Consumer Price Indices: Percentage Movements January 1970–December 1979.*

Table 4.9 *Jamaica: increases in GDP, consumer prices, money supply and domestic credit, 1970–80* (% increase over previous year)

	GDP constant prices	GDP current prices	Consumer price index[a]	Money supply (M_1)	Domestic credit Total	Public sector	Private sector
1970	12.1	18.0	7.7	26.2	21.2	53.1	17.1
1971	2.9	9.3	5.1	7.8	39.9	100.0	27.9
1972	9.6	12.4	8.2	20.5	36.3	-4.6	46.9
1973	0.9	20.6	28.9	23.2	28.5	61.0	22.9
1974	-4.1	25.0	22.1	25.4	33.7	76.3	24.2
1975	-0.7	20.3	11.4	6.9	23.4	81.3	5.0
1976	-6.6	4.0	8.3	48.0	9.8	37.5	-5.5
1977	-1.6	10.0	16.1	8.3	27.3	37.3	19.4
1978	-0.3	25.6	47.0	13.0	19.3	22.3	16.6
1979	-2.0	12.8	24.3	25.1	30.0	43.2	18.1
1980	-5.4	10.3	24.7				

Sources: Department of Statistics, *National Income and Product*, 1980. Department of statistics, *Consumer Price Indices Percentage Movements January 1970–December 1979*. Bank of Jamaica *Statistical Digest*, December 1981.

Note: [a] January to January.

redistribution and short-term employment creation, rather than increased production, dominated government objectives, and the falling investment rate stemmed from adverse private sector reactions to the political and economic policies of the Manley administration (Girvan *et al.*, 1980, p. 144).

Government attitudes towards stabilisation: 1972–76

While the preceding discussion focused on the main causes of instability it should be noted that macro-stabilisation was seldom afforded top priority among the goals of the administration. Social welfare, the living standards of the poor, unemployment, inflation, inadequate growth, and the shortage of foreign exchange were sometimes treated as separate short run problems, although over the longer run they proved to be closely interrelated. The various corrective efforts undertaken by the authorities during this term, including the introduction of tax measures, import controls, wage guidelines and higher commercial bank lending rates, were inadequate to offset the disequilibria largely attributable to the rapid expansion of fiscal spending and domestic and foreign borrowing (Worrell, 1980a, p. 17).

In the first two years of the Manley administration a wide range of social welfare programmes was introduced by the government, including free education, literacy and skill training, land reforms, food subsidies and equal pay for women. After 1974, and the adoption of Democratic Socialism as the offical PNP ideology, the political mood did not encourage fiscal restraint and a desire to live within the country's foreign exchange constraint. In 1974/75 government expenditures exceeded the approved estimates by over 20% but this slippage was financed largely by the new bauxite levy, and the actual overall

Table 4.10 Jamaica: public and private sector expenditures on GDP 1973–77 (percentages)

	1973	1974	1975	1976	1977
Consumption/GDP					
Total	77.4	80.6	82.8	88.9	88.4
Private	61.4	63.5	64.5	66.5	66.3
Public	15.9	17.1	18.3	21.9	22.1
Fixed capital formation/GDP					
Total	25.9	22.1	23.2	16.5	11.6
Private	23.2	17.8	18.6	12.1	7.6
Public	2.7	3.5	4.7	4.3	3.9

Source: Department of Statistics, Bank of Jamaica.

deficit (domestic recurrent and capital revenue minus expenditures) was only 7% higher than the approved estimate.[8] Early in 1975, when it was obvious that foreign resources would be exhausted by 1976, the authorities accelerated their spending programmes, and the slippages between approved estimates and actual budget deficits widened. The actual budget deficit exceeded the approved estimate by 37% in 1975/76 and 75% in 1976/77.

In August 1975 an Economic Stabilisation Committee was set up to advise how the economy should be run after the foreign exchange reserves were exhausted. However, these technical experts differed among themselves in their advice about the nature and urgency of stabilisation measures, and the corrective efforts of the Treasury, Central Bank and Planning Agency were loosely co-ordinated. The PNP administration did not wish to usher in adjustment policies that required a reduction in real incomes to bring aggregate demand and supply back into balance, and the attitude of the authorities towards stabilisation was to delay any major adjustments in domestic demand and foreign exchange costs until after the 1976 elections.

If the general elections had been held early in 1976 and the government returned with a strong mandate, unpopular stabilisation measures might have been introduced soon after net foreign reserves became negative in March 1976. As it turned out, a State of Emergency was called in June 1976 and the elections were postponed until mid-December. In this election year, government spending rose by 20% even though government revenues declined becase of tax arrears and economic stagnation. Around J$300m of additional finance was required to cover the gap between government revenues and expenditures, and this was financed almost entirely by domestic money creation.

In the general elections, the PNP gained an overwhelming mandate but the right and left wings of the party were divided on the policies to be followed and on the need for IMF assistance. This lack of consensus over Jamaica's economic strategy and wavering political commitment to stabilisation were to persist throughout 1977–80.

IV. RELATIONS WITH THE IMF: 1977–80

Although discussions had taken place between the government and the Fund throughout the first term of the Manley administration, the PNP government did not enter into any upper-tranche stabilisation agreement with the IMF until July 1977 – nearly 18 months after net foreign reserves were exhausted. The Jamaican case may therefore be seen as that of a country which allowed conditions to deteriorate dramatically before a last ditch recourse to the Fund. It had difficulty borrowing on the Euro-dollar market because of its poor credit rating and had failed to obtain sufficient alternative sources of finance from foreign governments sympathetic to the Manley administration.

The long delay in going to the Fund stems from the size and conditionality of resources available under IMF upper-tranche programmes. The adequacy of Jamaica's drawings from the Fund may be judged against the projected size of her balance of payments deficits; the number of years over which the Jamaican authorities were required to curb disequilibria and the mix between policies requiring demand restraint and those emphasising supply considerations. Jamaica also provides interesting case material on the flexibility of the Fund's performance criteria in response to the political priorities set by government and the country's changing external circumstances. It is also possible to compare economic strategies and the nature of conditionality under the Stand-by and Extended Facilities. In addition, Jamaica is interesting because it calls into question the theoretical underpinnings of the Fund's advice on the linkages between financial and real sectors, and responsiveness of investment and output.

The financial flows between Jamaica and the Fund are summarised in Table 4.11. Few details are known of the 1973 Stand-by agreement except that after drawing 60% of the agreed funds (SDR18.5m) in the first year, the Jamaican authorities chose not to make any further drawings in 1974 and commenced repayments in 1975.[9]

During the first term of the Manley administration, substantial use was made of the Oil Facility and the Compensatory Finance Facility (CFF), particularly in 1976. In August 1977 Jamaica formally entered into a two-year Stand-by agreement with the IMF that was soon suspended in December 1977. A three-year Extended Fund Facility (EFF) credit was finalised in May 1978 and renegotiated in June 1979 to take advantage of additional drawings under the Supplementary Finance Facility, but this collapsed in December 1979 when the performance tests were failed.

In February 1980, the Prime Minister called for elections to decide the economic path the country should take and the role of the IMF, and in March 1980 negotiations for an interim Stand-by agreement were discontinued. In the general elections held in October 1980, the PNP was heavily defeated and the new JLP government, under Edward Seaga, soon resumed negotiations with the Fund. In April 1981, an agreement was reached for SDR236m under the Extended Facility and this was to be enlarged to SDR448m when the Enlarged Access policy became operational. The discussion in this chapter is focused on the period from 1972–1980 but some details of the 1981 EFF agreement are included for comparison.

Table 4.11 *Financial flows between Jamaica and the IMF: 1972–80 (SDRm)*

	1972	1973	1974	1975	1976	1977	1978	1979	1980
Gross inflows:									
1 Reserve tranche (gold)	13.3	5.5							
2 Credit tranche (Stand-by)		13.2		13.3		19.2			
3 Extended Facility							42.0	35.1	
4 Supplementary Facility								77.9	
5 Oil Facility					29.2				
6 Compensatory Facility			13.3		26.5		15.8	31.7	
7 Buffer Stock Facility								1.1	
8 Total gross inflows	13.3	18.7	13.3	13.3	55.7	19.2	57.8	145.8	nil
9 Repayments	—	5.5	–13.3	–13.3			–7.7	–18.1	–14.6
10 Net inflow	13.3	13.2	—	—	55.7	19.2	50.1	127.1	–14.6
11 Use of Fund credit (outstanding balance at year-end)	—	13.2	13.2	13.2	68.9	88.1	138.2	265.9	251.3
12 Quota (year-end)	53.0	53.0	53.0	53.0	53.0	53.0	74.0	74.0	111.0
13 Credit as % of Quota	—	25%	25%	25%	130%	166%	187%	360%	220%
14 Net drawings/GDP	0.8	0.7	—	—	2.2	0.7	2.4	6.8	0.7

Source: Bank of Jamaica, IMF, *International Financial Statistics.*

Notes: [a] In 1973 a Stand-by agreement for SDR26.5m was agreed.
[b] In 1974 and 1975 Compensatory Facility Funds (CFF) were both effected and paid back.
[c] In 1977 a two-year Stand-by for SDR64m was agreed.
[d] In 1978 a three-year Extended Fund Facility (EFF) of SDR200m was agreed.
[e] In 1979 SDR260m over two years was agreed with SDR33m under the EFF and SDR227m under the Supplementary Finance Facility (SFF).
[f] In March 1980 the Jamaican government decided to discontinue negotiations for an interim Stand-by agreement.

Although Jamaica has borrowed under every IMF facility, it is the economic management of the economy and the size and conditionality of Fund resources under the Stand-by and EFF that are the prime concern in the following sections. Jamaica's relations with the Fund are also analysed in Girvan *et al*. (1980), Bourne (1980a) and Kincaid (1980 and 1981).

The 1977 Stand-by

Before the elections, the government and the Fund had worked out the broad terms of a two-year Stand-by arrangements which included a wage freeze, plans to curb the fiscal deficit, and a devaluation of 20–40%. The closure of the foreign exchange market on 22 December 1976, just after the election, was part of this tentative agreement, the architects of which were technocrats in the Treasury and Central Bank. Although the PNP gained an overwhelming victory, it was felt that this owed much to the efforts of left-wing politicians within the party, who wanted an alternative to an IMF stabilisation programme, and particularly to avoid a major devaluation. In his budget speech of 19 January 1977, the Prime Minister rejected the tentative agreement with the Fund and announced an alternative programme for handling the crisis. There was to be no devaluation. Instead the central features of the programme were a sharp increase in import and exchange controls, strict foreign exchange rationing which included a J$130m reduction in the import target and suspension of foreign loan repayments for 18 months. Demand restraint measures were announced, including a six-month freeze on wages and prices, higher gasoline and income taxes (affecting the middle and upper income groups), the reduction of tax arrears, a slower growth of government spending, and a rise in the liquid asset ratio of commercial banks.

Meanwhile the government sought payments support from foreign governments, including Eastern European countries, Cuba, Venezuela, Trinidad and Tobago, but was unsuccessful in raising sizeable sums. It was firmly advised to settle with the Fund before bilateral assistance would be reconsidered and, in April 1977, Jamaica had little option but to approach the Fund.

The key issues delaying an agreement between April and July were the exchange rate and real wages.

> The powerful argument for the modification of exchange rates was that expansion of employment and resumption of economic growth would only be attained if more foreign exchange was available, and since the ability to borrow appeared near exhaustion, any additional foreign exchange would have to be earned, and this in turn required improved competitiveness of traditional and non-traditional exports both against other sellers in target markets, and against production for consumption at home (Bonnick, 1980, p. 12).

The government argued that devaluation would provide little stimulation to the demand for exports, as bananas and sugar were sold under fairly inflexible negotiated agreements, but that it would reduce the foreign exchange equivalent required to cover the local costs of bauxite/alumina companies. It was not believed that devaluation would stimulate domestic supplies and non-traditional exports. Instead, the higher costs of living of the urban poor, which surely would follow a devaluation, were of far more political concern than the benefits to the rural poor of higher incomes from agricultural exports and a possible switch in demand from imported to locally produced foods.

Devaluation was a pre-condition for the resumption of negotiations. As a compromise between the Fund's insistence on a major overall devaluation and the government's public stance that there should be no change, a dual exchange rate system was adopted in May 1977. The existing exchange rate, or basic rate, was applied to all government transactions, bauxite exports and essential imports of basic foods and medicines, but for all other exports and non-essential imports, a Special Rate was introduced which involved a 37.5% devaluation. Instead of a large overall devaluation, the authorities had undertaken a more limited adjustment and the dual system introduced multiple currency practices commonly outlawed in Fund agreements. Wage guidelines that would limit wage increases to J$10 per week were announced but these were soon rejected by the trade unions and replaced by new guidelines allowing wage increases in excess of J$10 where necessary to maintain real wages at their 1973 level. Hence the exchange rate and wage measures went only part of the way towards meeting IMF requirements.

Following these changes, it then took several months for Jamaica and the Fund to finalise an upper-tranche programme. Although Jamaica went to the Fund as a last resort, during these months the authorities persistently refused any further devaluations and a more restrictive wages policy. Girvan *et al.* (1980, p. 123) claim that the Fund finally settled, and largely on Jamaica's terms about the exchange rate and incomes policy, because of considerable international support for Jamaica from the governments of Britain, Canada and the USA, and growing public criticism of the general nature of Fund adjustment programmes.

Under this agreement, a total of SDR64m was to be made available to Jamaica over a two-year period, with the bulk of the money available in the first nine months. No conditions were attached to the first drawing of SDR19.2m once the agreement had been approved by the Executive Board in August 1977, and further drawings of SDR9.2m each were to become available in December 1977 and March 1978 if Jamaica passed the performance criteria. Each drawing under this Stand-by was to be repaid within three to five years.

The Letter of Intent indicated that strict demand restraint was the underlying strategy, but the policy measures were not spelled out in detail.

> Jamaica's policies will be geared over the next two years to reducing gradually the Government's borrowing requirements and to building up the international reserve position of the Bank of Jamaica. To achieve this, the government plans to increase domestic production, to tighten further its demand management policies, to follow a restrained incomes policy, and to pursue a flexible exchange rate policy (Stand-by Agreement with the IMF Ministry Paper No. 28, August, 1977).

The agreement noted the tax, expenditure and wages policy measures announced in January 1977 and called for a substantial reduction in tax arrears and for expenditure controls to be tightened. Jamaica was required not to introduce any new multiple currency practices or intensify exchange and trade controls, but trade liberalisation measures and devaluation were not included as performance criteria. The dual exchange rate system was accepted as a temporary measure but was to be reviewed if it appeared that the balance of payments targets would not be met.

The performance criteria set out in Table 4.12 required a sharp reversal in economic trends. Virtually no expansion was permitted in the net domestic assets of the Bank of Jamaica and net bank credit to the public sector during the first six months of the agreement whereas domestic credit had increased by 32% in 1976 (Table 4.9). Using the existing trade and exchange rate system, all outstanding arrears in foreign payments were to be eliminated in the first three months and the net foreign assets of the Bank of Jamaica were to be stabilised after declining dramatically in 1976 (Table 4.2). The conditionality required under this agreement seems clearly out of proportion to the size of resources directly available from the Fund (Dell and Lawrence, 1980, p. 10).

The size of these resources from the Fund was far from adequate to cover the actual and projected size of the balance of payments deficit and elimination of arrears. The deficits on basic balance and current account (Table 4.2) far exceeded the resources directly available from the Fund, and net foreign reserves were already negative. The Fund itself projected a current account deficit of J$137m for 1977 and J$92m in 1978, but expected substantial foreign assistance to supplement the resources directly available from the Fund. It was projected that Jamaica would borrow J$175m in foreign funds in 1977/78 and J$130m in 1978/79. An IMF staff member who worked on Jamaica wrote:

> The aim was to attract foreign funds to allow a more gradual adjustment in the balance of payments (BoP) than Jamaica was in fact experiencing and

Table 4.12   *Jamaica: 1977 Stand-by agreement performance criteria and out-turn*[a]

	1977			1978
	June 30	Sept. 30	Dec. 31	March 31
1. *Net foreign assets of BoJ (US$m)*[b]				
ceiling		−162	−138	−138
actual	−164		−227	−317
2. *Outstanding arrears (US$m)*				
ceiling		50.0	0	0
actual	33.0		27	82
3. *Net domestic assets of BoJ (J$m)*				
ceiling		345	355	345
actual	342		384	403
4. *Net bank credit to public sector (J$m)*				
ceiling		745	745	735
actual	730		n.a.	841
5. *Foreign borrowing authorisation (US$m)*				
1–5 years ceiling				75
actual				n.a.
1–15 years ceiling				160
actual				n.a.

Notes: a The agreement was approved by the Fund Board in August 1977 and no conditions were attached to the September ceilings.
b Including outstanding arrears.

thereby to arrest the rapid decline in economic activity. Substantial net foreign assistance (equivalent to 5.5% GDP) was excepted to help finance the budgetary and current account deficits, thus permitting the adjustment process to be spread over time (Kincaid, 1981, p. 19).

In fact the 1977 Stand-by agreement failed to act as a catalyst and the amounts of additional foreign funds did not materialise as expected. In 1977, Jamaica's external borrowings totalled only J$40m, or one quarter of the sum projected by the Fund, and there was a net outflow of long-term capital of J$7m. Directly and indirectly insufficient resources were available to support the expansion of production and imports needed to improve the payments position. Even if substantial foreign funding had been forthcoming, it appears doubtful that the aim of the programme was to spread out the adjustment process. A two-year Stand-by (120% of quota) was negotiated rather than a three-year EFF credit (240% of quota) when by any stretch of the imagination, Jamaica's negative external reserves and declining GDP represented 'fundamental' disequilibria. The short-term demand restraint strategy of this Stand-by was inadequate to cure Jamaica's longer term adjustment problems, and the meagre Fund resources were insufficient to finance the imports needed for export-led growth.

Instead the Fund appears to have viewed the tight fiscal and monetary targets under the Stand-by as a test of the general seriousness of the Jamaican authorities to undertake a stabilisation programme. Although later agreements display much more awareness of the need for political commitment and socially acceptable adjustment costs, such problems were not discussed in connection with the tight fiscal and monetary ceilings of the 1977 Stand-by. Even where the major causes of disequilibria are largely due to domestic policies under the control of the authorities, rather than temporary or permanent external factors, the speed and social costs of adjustment under stabilisation programmes should not be politically impractical, otherwise social chaos may result if the expansion of fiscal spending and domestic credit is sharply and suddenly halted. Although subsequent EFF agreements display greater awareness of the need for socially and politically tolerable adjustment costs and a longer adjustment process, insufficient attention was paid to these matters in 1977.

In December 1977 Jamaica failed the very first test when at least three performance criteria were exceeded: the net foreign assets of the Bank of Jamaica; outstanding foreign arrears; and the net domestic assets of the Bank of Jamaica. The wide margin by which net bank credit to the public sector exceeded the March 1978 ceiling suggests that this ceiling was also exceeded in December 1977. Girvan *et al.* (1980, p. 124) are incorrect in claiming that only the net domestic assets of the Bank of Jamaica exceeded the required ceiling and that Jamaica could have passed this test within a matter of days but for cash flow problems in reconciling new foreign loans and repayments.

The Fund refused a waiver and to re-negotiate the December ceilings, arguing that the Bank of Jamaica and Treasury were unable to hold down government spending. In December 1977 the Prime Minister had announced retroactive wage increases for the police and military, and the technocrats were faced with a choice between refusing to honour the cheques for the additional public spending or failing the IMF tests. They honoured the cheques and expanded the domestic money supply to accommodate this increase in government spending.

The 1977 breakdown illustrates both the lack of independence of the technocrats from their political context, and the lack of flexibility of the Fund in response to changed external circumstances that had made the programme unviable. The Bank of Jamaica and Treasury officials responsible for administering the IMF programme were unable to influence government spending announcements and failed to exert independent control over credit creation. As it had been so difficult for the Fund to negotiate a programme with Jamaica, it is somewhat surprising that the Stand-by was suspended so quickly, without showing more flexibility when net foreign borrowing fell far short of the Fund's projections and additional borrowing was needed to supplement the budgetary deficits. It would appear that the Stand-by was never expected to work.

> In fact both sides regarded the July 1977 agreement as a truce giving time for further manoeuvring. Indeed it was anticipated that negotiations for an Extended Fund Facility would commence in early 1978 for completion by March of that year (Girvan *et al.*, 1980, p. 124).

During 1977 there had been a noticeable improvement in the trade deficit as a result of the intensification of import restrictions and the recovery of world prices for alumina exports. Tighter exchange controls on private capital outflows and the accumulation of outstanding arrears helped temporarily to arrest the decline in international reserves. Real GDP per capita declined more slowly in 1977 (−2.7%) than in 1976 (−8.0%) but the gross investment rate dropped to only 11.7% of GDP because of the tighter import restrictions, a cut in bank credit to the private sector and a lack of investor confidence (Table 4.1). The growth of domestic credit to government was reduced sharply (Table 4.9) and between 1976 and 1977 the overall fiscal deficit declined from 24% to 19% of GDP (Table 4.5). With the introduction of the dual exchange rate system, domestic inflation reached 16% in 1977, twice as fast as in 1975. While the nominal wage index remained constant, real wages declined between October 1976 and October 1977 by around 15% and the unemployment rate increased, despite heavy emigration.

The 1978 EFF credit

The 1978 EFF agreement was signed at a time when Jamaica was in dire need of foreign exchange, a need to which the suspension of the IMF Stand-by agreement had added by holding up other financial assistance already negotiated with the World Bank and foreign banking consortia. The economic strategy and conditionality surrounding the resumption of negotiations and use of resources under this credit reflect the Fund views more fully than did the 1977 Stand-by agreement, but once again the exchange rate and wage restraint were key issues.

> The message which came from the IMF in the first week of 1978 was short and to the point: (a) Jamaica must undertake a total weighted devaluation of 10% as a *precondition* to fresh negotiations; (b) the negotiations would only take place within a framework where Jamaica agreed that, in the first year of

the programme, monthly devaluations would take place equivalent to the difference between the Jamaican rate of wage inflation and that of its main trading partners. The exchange rate was therefore firmly linked to wages policy; the greater the degree of wage increases allowed, the higher the devaluations would have to be; the lower the devaluations the government wanted, the more restrictive the wages policy it would have to impose (Girvan *et al.*, 1980, p. 124).

Accordingly, in January 1978 the basic rate was devalued by 13.6% and there was a depreciation of 5.2% in the special rate, so that the differential between the rates narrowed slightly. While negotiations were in progress, the country's essential foreign exchange requirements were partially met with loans from commercial banks, intergovernment arrangements and lines of credit. Foreign exchange shortages led to arrears in foreign payments, and output and employment were affected by the lack of spare parts and raw materials.

To arrest the downward trend in real GDP and external reserves, the Fund required the government to change radically its policies and to implement the stabilisation measures with political determination. Short run demand restraint targets negotiated by technical experts were clearly inadequate to bring about the political commitment and policy changes required to cure the disequilibria. To underline the great political importance attached to successfully negotiating and implementing an EFF stabilisation programme, the Prime Minister fired his current Minister of Finance (he was also the Deputy Prime Minister and Chairman of the PNP), who was held responsible for the failure of the December test.

When negotiations were finalised in May 1978, the IMF had agreed to provide SDR200m over three years, credit which represented 270% of Jamaica's quota. Repurchases were to be completed within eight years – the maximum period permitted for repayment of an EFF. Unlike the earlier Stand-by arrangement, the Fund now recognise that the size of the resources directly available from the EFF had to permit an increase in imports consistent with the growth objectives of the programme. Furthermore, the Fund more actively assisted the Jamaican authorities in their efforts to mobilise additional external financing from commercial banks, international agencies and foreign governments. The adequacy of Fund and other foreign resources can be viewed in relation to the size of Jamaica's payments problems (Table 4.2). In 1978 the gross inflows from the Fund totalled SDR57.8m (Table 4.1) of which SDR15.8m was under the Compensatory Finance Facility and SDR42.0m under the Extended Facility. These Fund drawings exceeded the deficit on current account but not the deficit on the basic balance of payments. In 1978/79 J$400m was raised in official funding from foreign governments, institutions and commercial banks compared with only J$40m in the previous financial year, but these net inflows of Fund and official foreign resources for balance of payments support were insufficient to cover the net outflow of private capital. In 1978 there was a net long-term capital outflow of SDR37.2m and Jamaica's net international reserves declined by SDR44.6m (Table 4.2).

The Fund and other official resources were to be used in support of a medium-term programme and the conditions involved major changes in the direction of government policies.[10] In a lengthy memorandum attached to the official agreement, the government's commitment to Democratic Socialism was publicly reaffirmed and the general programme outlined. To emphasise commitment to the policy changes, the Prime Minister was required publicly to accept the programme, including the proposed 25–30% cut in real wages. In general terms, the economic strategy envisaged a switch in resources from the public sector towards the private sector; from consumption to investment; and from reliance on administered controls to the greater use of domestic market forces, but import controls were to retain a central role in balance of payments policy during the first year of the programme.

Jamaica's deficits were to be cured in part by a major devaluation, increased taxes and slower growth of government expenditures. Income and price policies aimed to reduce real wages and increase the share of profits in order to stimulate new investment. The speed with which the Jamaican authorities were required to curb fiscal and monetary expansion was reduced, but there was little change in the mix between policies requiring demand restraint and those emphasising supply considerations. The programme reflected a preoccupation with aggregate monetary variables, the prices of traded goods and the balance of payments, but little attention was given to structural constraints and disaggregated policy measures affecting the major sectors of the economy.

The conditions attached to this 1978 agreement included the immediate unification of the exchange rate; overall devaluation of 15% by May 1979 and monthly devaluations amounting to a further 15% over the first 12 months of the programme. Two other conditions of the agreement, but not subject to quarterly performance criteria, were the eventual removal of import controls, trade restrictions and multiple currency practices, and the repayment of arrears in amortisation of private sector debt. The performance criteria (Table 4.13) reflected the Fund's preoccupation with aggregate monetary variables. Under this EFF agreement, in nine months the net domestic assets of the Bank of Jamaica were permitted to increase by 16% (from J$405m to a ceiling of J$473m) and the net bank credit of the public sector was allowed to expand by 20% (from J$856m to J$992m), compared with virtually

zero growth in the first six months of the Stand-by agreement. However, this EFF credit required tight fiscal and monetary policy compared with the period from 1972–1976 when total domestic credit rose
by over 25% annually and net bank credit to the public sector expanded
by around 40% annually.

During the first year of the programme the Jamaican government
carried out every single aspect of the new agreement, an achievement
that was made somewhat easier because of greater consensus and
co-ordination between politicians and technocrats. All performance
tests were passed. The net domestic assets of the Bank of Jamaica were
well within the targets, and commercial banks were faced with excess
liquidity as quantitative import restrictions restrained demand for
credit from the private sector. The balance of payments test (net
foreign assets of the Bank of Jamaica and outstanding arrears in foreign
payments) proved to be the most difficult to pass. Despite the 30%
devaluation, the supply response of investment, output and exports
was sluggish, but import demand kept increasing. In the short run,
devaluation was unlikely to lead to a significant reduction in the import
bill as the major constraint on the volume of imports was the availability
of foreign exchange rather than the Jamaican dollar cost of imports.
Import controls and the lack of foreign exchange had already reduced
demand below the essential minimum.

A switch in aggregate demand from imported to domestic items
depends partly upon the increased availability of domestic supplies, but
the supply response of domestic output was slow and uneven. Bourne
(1980a, p. 24) argues that this was because of low investment rates in
past years and the deterioration of the capital stock. The shortage of
regular supplies of imported inputs and new equipment, plus uncertainties about future profits and the socio-political climate, also curbed
the supply response. Bonnick (1980, p. 13) similarly notes the uncertainty surrounding the size and speed of response of foreign capital
inflows and export earnings. It was to be expected that agricultural
output would be slow to respond because of institutional delays in
passing on higher export prices to farmers, and of lags in land preparation, crop maturation and livestock gestation. Similarly, the demand
responsiveness of traditional exports was delayed because of quota
agreements for sugar and bananas.

Economic performance of the economy during the first year of the
EFF programme was not as good as the Fund had projected or as
Jamaica had hoped for. Given the economy's heavy dependence on
foreign resources, no immediate improvement of any significance was
projected in the balance of payments. Instead of stabilising, the payment deficit on current account and the basic balance widened further
(Table 4.3). It is noteworthy that GDP in the export sectors (bauxite,

Table 4.13   *Jamaica: 1978 EFF performance criteria and out-turn*

	1977	1978			1979
	Dec.	June 30	Sept. 30	Dec. 31	March 31
1. *Net foreign assets of BoJ (US$m)*a					
ceiling		−335.0	−300.0	−300.0	−280.0
actual	(−227)	−318.3	−279.0	−289.5	−258.2
2. *Outstanding arrears (US$m)*					
ceiling		80.0	60.0	40.0	20.0
actual	(27)	79.2	48.8	30.4	18.9
3. *Net domestic assets of BoJ (J$m)*					
ceiling		440.0	445.0	480.0	473.0
actual	(403)	405.2	393.6	424.6	413.1
4. *Net bank credit to public sector (J$m)*					
ceiling		930.0	1,010.0	1,110.0	1,041.0
actual	(841)	856.8	887.0	1,021.5	992.9
5. *Foreign borrowing authorisation*					
1–5 years ceiling		20	20	20	20
actual					n.a.
1–15 years ceiling		100	100	100	100
actual					n.a.

Source: Bank of Jamaica, *Balance of Payments of Jamaica 1978*, p. 22. Ministry Paper No. 34 July 1978.
Note: a Including outstanding arrears.

alumina, agriculture and tourism) recorded some growth in 1978, related in part to the currency depreciations, but manufacturing and construction continued to decline because of shortages of imported materials. Much of the additional foreign support was absorbed by debt service payments and foreign capital outflows, which if not paid, would have undermined further attempts to revive local and foreign investment.

Overall, real GDP did not increase as projected by the Fund, but the decline in 1978 (−1.6%) was less than in 1977 (−2.7%) and 1976 (−8.0%). The failure of the economy to recover as quickly as expected also affected tax receipts and hence fiscal performance. In 1978/79 the recurrent fiscal deficit was 2.5% of GDP whereas the Fund had targeted a *surplus* of 2.8%, although this was not a performance criterion. The size of the fiscal deficit in 1978 is reflected indirectly in the ceiling on net bank credit to the public sector, but this test Jamaica passed. Investment activity remained weak, despite efforts to reduce real wages and increase profits. There was a drop in real wages of 20–25% between April 1978–79 (Table 4.8), partly as a result of the currency depreciations which contributed to a 47% increase in consumer prices during 1978. By October 1978 the real wages of those employed were no higher than they had been in April 1973.

The 1979 EFF credit

In the first year of the 1978 programme Jamaica had carried out every aspect of the agreement, and the success of the EFF programme now became as important to the IMF as to the government. The adjustment costs of inflation, reduced government services and lower levels of income caused immediate hardships, and the sacrifices seemed in vain as the economic benefits of the first year of the programme were discouraging. Public resentment was mounting against the programme and, if not eased, there was a risk of social upheaval (Bourne, 1980a, p. 25). Jamaica needed a more rapid resumption of economic growth, more jobs, less inflation and some gradual improvement in living standards. In an effort to achieve these, the programme was renegotiated and there was a change in the mix of the adjustment policies in the second year of the EFF. The Fund arranged for an expansion of its lending and permitted a stretching out of the adjustment process.

> Among the policies adopted was a suspension of the monthly currency depreciations that was to be combined with greater moderation in both wage demand and price adjustments in order to diminish the upward pressure on prices; there would be no increase in taxes. Program targets were revised to permit higher recurrent and overall fiscal deficits, and a greater current account deficit which would accommodate a further expansion of imports required to foster economic growth. To support the latter effort and to reduce external payments arrears, the Fund doubled its commitment for the remaining two years of the arrangements to about US$330 million (SDR 260 million) (Kincaid, 1981, p. 19).

In the 1978 EFF, wages increases were to be limited to 15% while price controls on basic foods and rents were maintained. In 1979, the Social Contract[11] between the government, private sector and trade unions called for wage increases to be kept to just 10% and a norm for price increases of 10% was established. For the fiscal programme, the authorities sought to improve the efficiency of the tax system and reduce arrears but taxation rates were not raised. Improvement in the recurrent deficit was to be achieved by reducing central government expenditures. Public sector pay increases were to be limited to 10% and current expenditures held at the nominal level of the previous year (*Balance of Payments of Jamaica 1979*, p. 14).

The conditionality and size of drawings under the 1979 EFF credit reflect both a change in the Fund's policy towards Jamaica and a general increase in resources available following the establishment of the Supplementary Financing Facility (SFF) which became operational in February 1979. Under the 1979 agreement, SDR130m was available in each of the two remaining years, and 87% of these resources were provided under the SFF. The SFF was set up for countries in exceptional circumstances with large balance of payments needs relative to their quota who have a problem that requires a relatively long period of adjustment and first obtained an upper-tranche or extended credit. Before this new agreement, Jamaica's total Fund drawings excluding purchases under the CFF and Oil Facility were 221% of quota and following the new agreement it was expected that by June 1980 Jamaica's total drawings would rise to 454% of quota, of which upper tranche drawings would amount to 378%.

> In effect, the IMF opted to substitute direct Fund assistance for the commercial bank inflows which would normally have been expected to take place. The hope was that through the additional resources provided the basis for economic turn around would be created and eventually the commercial banks and foreign and local investors would be induced to support the programme (Girvan *et al.*, 1980, p. 128).

In 1979 gross inflows from the fund were SDR145m (J$340m) of which SDR78m was from the Supplementary Facility and SDR35m from the Extended Facility (Table 4.11). Following this Fund programme Jamaica was able to negotiate with foreign commercial banks an agreement to reschedule seven-eighths of all amortisation payments on the government and government-guaranteed debt falling due before March 1981. While the Fund programme may have helped to trigger pledges of foreign finance, official foreign borrowing in 1979/80 was J$100m less than the year before[12] and the net outflow of private capital continued, although J$80m less than in 1978. Private net capital outflows would have been far greater except that foreign exchange reserves were inadequate to meet debt obligations and arrears. The net inflow of Fund resources in 1979 exceeded the deficit on current account and basic balance, and higher oil prices and higher external debt service payments meant that non-oil imports declined.

Just as under the 1977 Stand-by and the 1978 EFF, the performance criteria for 1979 mirrored the Fund's usual emphasis on monetary variables. The quarterly ceilings and out-turn for the first nine months of the 1979 programme are set out in Table 4.14. When compared with the 1979 performance ceilings (Table 4.13) these are shown to be more generous. In 1978 net domestic assets of the Bank of Jamaica actually increased by only 2% compared with the 16% maximum permitted by the ceilings because demand for private sector credit was curbed by the inability to import raw materials, spare parts and other items. The growth of credit to the private sector was emphasised in the 1979 programme, and the net domestic assets of the Bank of Jamaica were permitted to rise by 32% between March and December 1979. Net foreign assets and arrears of the Bank of Jamaica were required to improve under the 1978 programme, but a further decline of 19% was permitted in the 1979 programme. However, public sector credit was more restrained in 1979. In 1978 the permitted level of credit implies an increase of 16% but this was restricted in 1979 to only 13% above the actual level of March 1979.

It is interesting to contrast the size and conditionality of Fund resources under the 1977 and 1979 agreements. Over a two-year period, the 1977 agreement provided SDR64m whereas the 1979 credit was for SDR260m. The 1977 Stand-by failed to act as a catalyst and additional foreign funds fell short of Fund's projections, but in 1979 the IMF sought to substitute direct Fund assistance for foreign borrowing in order to improve foreign and local investor confidence and finance the additional imports necessary for increased production. Although similar performance criteria were attached to both agreements, the 1977 Stand-by required a quick improvement in the payments position, whereas the 1979 agreement permitted a further decline in the net foreign assets of the Bank of Jamaica. A sudden halt to the rapid growth of domestic credit was required in the 1977 credit, but scant attention was paid to the likely socio-economic consequences if the politicians and technical experts had carried out the Stand-by agreement and sharply reduced aggregate demand. Partly in response to mounting urban unrest, the Fund in 1979 permitted a stretching out of the adjustment process. The EFF emphasised the growth of credit to the private sector and the net domestic assets of the Bank of Jamaica were allowed to rise by 32% in nine months.

Turning to the economic performance of the economy in 1979, commodity exports and tourism increased by J$60m due to the recovery of tourism and growth of minor exports, but severe floods in the middle of the year adversely affected agricultural exports, and in 1979 Jamaica drew J$73m (SDR31.8m) under the Compensatory Facility. Monthly devaluations were stopped and a more disaggregated policy for stimulating exports, the Certified Exporters Scheme, was established. A loan of US$30m was obtained from the Word Bank to establish an Export Development Fund to finance imports of raw materials specifically for the production of non-traditional industrial exports and their domestic suppliers. However, disbursements under

Table 4.14 Jamaica: EFF performance criteria and out-turn

	1978		1979		
	Dec.	March 31 (base)	June 30	Sept. 30	Dec. 31
1. Net foreign assets of BoJ (US$m)					
ceiling	—	—	−425.0	−425.0	−370.0
actual	(−289.5)[a]	−319.1	−318.6	−419.6	−496.7
2. Net domestic assets of BoJ (J$m)					
ceiling	—	—	900.0	925.0	940.0
actual	(424.6)[a]	708.2	866.9	924.5	1,064.1
3. Net banking system credit to the public sector (J$m)					
ceiling	—	—	1,070.0	1,105.0	1,125.0
actual	(1021.0)	992.4	1,059.1	1,072.2	1,265.0
4. Foreign borrowing authorisation (US$m)					
1–5 years ceiling	—	—	60.0	60.0	60.0
actual	—	—	0.9	4.5	12.9
1–12 years ceiling	—	—	110.0	110.0	110.0
actual	—	—	0.9	21.2	41.1

Source: Bank of Jamaica, Balance of Payments of Jamaica 1979, p. 49.
Note: [a] There is a change in definition between Table 4.13 and Table 4.14.

this scheme were slow, and only US$5m had been approved by the end of 1979.

In 1979 Jamaica had to pay substantially higher oil prices and higher interest rates on external debts. Instead of expanding, foreign exchange available for non-oil imports declined in nominal terms from US$407m in 1978 to US$385m in 1979. In real terms, this meant a 13% decline, for the import price index rose by 9%.

As a result of foreign exchange shortages and continuing social and economic uncertainties, the growth objectives of the programme were not met and real GDP per capita declined by −3.5% in 1979 compared with −1.8% in 1978. Partly as a result of the floods, value-added in agriculture declined by nearly 7%, after increasing by 9% in 1978. Manufacturing, mining and construction also declined but to a lesser extent. Real gross fixed capital formation rose by 20% but investment and foreign capital inflows were still far less than anticipated by the Fund. Limited foreign exchange for imports and the poor response of GDP resulted in fewer jobs and by October 1979 unemployment had officially reached 28% of the workforce, against 25% in 1978. After the monthly devaluations were ended, the inflation rate declined from 47% in 1978 to 24% in 1979, and real wages remained roughly the same as in the previous year (Table 4.8).

The continued decline in GDP together with tax arrears reduced government revenues below their projected level. Government recurrent expenditures exceeded their 1978 levels because of higher interest payments on the government debt and public sector wage increases in excess of 10%. Although capital expenditures were within the initial estimates, recurrent expenditures between April–December 1979 were US$50m higher than in the comparable period in 1978 (*Balance of Payments of Jamaica 1979*, p. 38). These trends meant that the fiscal current account showed a deficit of J$177m rather than being in balance. Instead of declining to 9%, the overall budget deficit expanded from 13.5% to 15% of GDP between 1978 and 1979 with some 80% of this expansion in the deficit being financed by the domestic banking system. Meanwhile, private sector demand for credit remained depressed and expanded even less than in 1978.

In December 1979, Jamaica failed to meet three of the major performance criteria (see Table 4.14). The net foreign assets test was failed by US$126m and the ceilings on public sector credit and the net domestic assets of the Bank of Jamaica were also exceeded. Because of Jamaica's poor credit rating, only a quarter of the foreign borrowing authorisation was raised. Girvan *et al.* (1980, p. 128) argues that exogenous factors (higher interest rates, oil prices and floods) were responsible for 60% of the breach in the ceiling on international reserves but he is incorrect in claiming that government expenditures did not exceed their 1978 level or agreed targets. The inability of the authorities to monitor and control expenditures, plus arrears in taxes and recurrent payments, contributed to the failure to comply with the ceiling on the expansion of public sector credit.

In September 1979 the programme had already begun to run into trouble, after references in a speech by the Prime Minister to a non-capitalist development path which effectively precluded foreign private capital inflows. Discussions for new loans and for the refinancing of Jamaica's commercial bank debts falling due in 1980 were promptly suspended, partly because slippages in fiscal targets were now apparent and the government showed no signs of easing up on its spending. The Fund was willing to modify the December performance tests to allow for the effect of floods, higher interest rates and oil price rises. But it also required further tax changes, government expenditure cuts and administrative controls to restrain and monitor the expansion of the fiscal deficit. The lack of consensus within the PNP about the country's economic strategy and need for foreign exchange was reflected in a failure within Cabinet to reach agreement about the requested policy changes. Meanwhile further slippages occurred.

In February 1980, the government and the IMF were unable to agree on budget cuts, and the Jamaican authorities sought to apply directly to the IMF Executive Board for a waiver. The Prime Minister also announced that general elections would be held as soon as feasible:

> I believe that the country needs to settle and decide on its economic strategy and that when that is settled, it will be easy to understand what part the IMF should play; or whether it should play any part at all. What must be brought to an end is the present state of confusion, because the country has to settle down on a path and understand the efforts, the discipline, and the sacrifices that are necessary to that struggle (API, Manley, 3 February, 1980).

It proved impossible for the Jamaican authorities to apply directly to the Board without the endorsement of the Fund's management and negotiating team, and so fresh negotiations began for a Stand-by agreement to tide over the country until the elections were held. These negotiations involved discussions of a further wage freeze and cutbacks in social programmes and the number of government employees; although the Finance Minister reported in March 1980 that Jamaica would certainly fail the performance tests proposed under this interim Stand-by agreement. It was decided to discontinue negotiations but the Prime Minister reaffirmed that Jamaica would remain a member of the IMF and honour its obligations to the Fund (API, Manley, March 1980). As a consequence, there was a net repayment to the Fund of SDR14.6m in 1980.

The role of the IMF and the management of the economy were central issues in the 1980 general election. The PNP campaigned on a platform of rejecting the IMF and its future participation in the economy, proposing the alternative of greater self-reliance. The PNP authorities blamed the economic crisis on external causes largely beyond their control and Party spokesmen condemned the Fund for the economic and social costs of adjustment which the country had suffered since 1977. The JLP, on the other hand, held that domestic policies and not external factors, were the main cause of the economic crisis. It maintained that to cure the country's problems a massive injection of foreign exchange was required and that there was therefore no alternative but to resume negotiations with the Fund.

The 1981 EFF agreement
In the 'IMF general election' held in October 1980, the PNP was heavily defeated and the JLP under Edward Seaga soon resumed negotiations with the Fund. There were political pressures on the Fund to negotiate an early agreement. The size and conditionality attached to

the April 1981 agreement reflects both a substantial change in the Fund's policy towards Jamaica and an increase in resources available under the Enlarged Access Facility. The Fund agreed to drawings of SDR236m over the next three years from the Extended Facility and these resources were to be raised to SDR478m when the Enlarged Access Policy became operational. In addition, SDR37m became available under the Compensatory Finance Facility. The Fund also approved a purchase in the first credit tranche equivalent to SDR21m.

Details are not available of the projected economic performance of the Jamaican economy and it is too soon to evaluate the adequacy of these resources and effectiveness of the programme, but some comparisons can be drawn between the size and conditionality of resources under the 1981 EFF and earlier agreements. In the first year, more resources were made available under the 1981 EFF (SDR179m) than under the 1979 EFF (SDR130m) and 1978 EFF (SDR70m). As with the 1979 agreement, around 60% of the funds in the first year of the 1981 EFF were to come from the more expensive Supplementary Facility, with the remainder financed from the Fund's ordinary resources, which have a lower interest rate.

The economic strategy underlying this agreement emphasised the need to expand output and investment, by relaxing the constraint imposed by foreign exchange shortages for raw materials, spare parts and equipment.

> The strategy falls into two parts: firstly to put unutilized capacity to work with the emphasis on those sectors that will produce quick and substantial incremental foreign exchange earnings, secondly to initiate adjustments in industrial and agricultural policies and so provide a basis for expansion of production capacity with concomitant increases in employment opportunities (Extended Fund Facility Arrangement with the International Monetary Fund, Ministry Paper No. 9, April 1981).

In the 1981 agreement it was recognised that Jamaica's extensive import controls could not be dismantled quickly without exacerbating the foreign exchange shortage, but the eventual liberalisation of the import licensing system was called for. The trade weighted index of Jamaica's real exchange rate was virtually the same in 1978 as 1980/81 (see Table 4.15), yet a 30% devaluation was required in the first 12 months of the 1978 agreement whereas no further devaluation of the official exchange rate was called for under the 1981 agreement. Instead, in 1981, the informal or unofficial foreign exchange market was recognised and import licences financed by these informal (black market) channels were to be exempt from import licensing requirements. In essence, a dual exchange rate system (official and informal) was acknowledged

Table 4.15   Jamaica: real exchange rate index 1970–1981, 1978 = 100

	Total index[a]
1970	89.1
1971	89.0
1972	89.5
1973	94.9
1974	88.6
1975	85.0
1976	83.1
1977	82.8
1978	100.0
1979	110.3
1980	100.7
1981 June	100.0

Source: IBRD, Jamaica: Development Issues and Economic Prospects, January, 1982, Table 8.2 (unpublished).

Note: [a] Weighted average of bilateral indexes based on exchange rates and consumer price indices in Jamaica and each trading partner. The weights were derived as the share of each trading partner in Jamaica's nontraditional exports in 1978.

and strengthened by this Fund programme, notwithstanding the Fund's constitutional and other aversions to this type of arrangement.

The production programme was expected to generate an early increase in foreign exchange from the growth of tourism, bauxite/alumina, sugar and bananas. Steps to deregulate the economy and make greater use of market signals instead of controls were aimed at restoring investor confidence and encouraging private investment. As part of a World Bank Structural Adjustment Programme, a team was to examine Jamaica's industrial and agricultural pricing policies in order to identify changes which may help to promote production and provide greater incentives for investment. Many price controls were to be abolished or relaxed; 'wage ceilings' and wage adjustments based on 'comparability' between sectors were abolished. The new pay policy was to be based on market conditions and wage claims were to be settled on the basis of the ability of the employer to pay. Unlike the 1977 and 1978 agreements, further devaluation and incomes policy measures to restrain real wages were not part of the 1981 programme.

Fiscal policy changes were to constrain the growth of public consumption and shift the emphasis of government expenditures towards capital formation, while a review of the tax system was expected to increase tax buoyancy and reduce tax arrears and evasion. As a result of these expenditure and tax changes, over the three-year programme central government expenditures were to be reduced from around 40%

to not more than 30% of GDP and the overall fiscal deficit reduced from 14% to 10% of GDP.

The performance criteria for the 1981 agreement included the customary ceilings on the net domestic assets of the Bank of Jamaica; net domestic credit to the public sector; and net foreign assets of the Bank of Jamaica. In addition there was a ceiling on foreign debt authorisations, and the standard condition not to introduce any multiple currency practice nor intensify trade and foreign exchange controls. There was one major difference between the 1981 EFF agreement and previous agreements, namely the 1981 criteria on domestic monetary variables and international reserves were subject to automatic adjustments if there was either a shortfall or excess of non-IMF foreign loans and credits above or below the amounts set out in the Letter of Intent. At the end of the first 12 months of the 1981 agreement this amount of foreign finance was US$479m, which was high in comparison with the amount of foreign borrowing in 1979/80. Hence the 1981 ceilings were more flexible and more generous than those under the 1979 agreement. In the first 9–10 months of this programme, the expansion permitted in net public sector credit before adjustment was greater (J$310m) than under the 1979 agreement (J$135m), although less expansion was permitted in the net domestic assets of the Bank of Jamaica and the permitted decline in international reserves was also less than in 1979.

Compared with the 1978 and 1979 agreements, overall the conditionality attached to the 1981 agreement was more flexible in its foreign exchange ceilings and import requirements, and less demanding in terms of exchange rate and wage policies. More emphasis was placed on the government's determination to control public spending and gradually de-control the economy.

V. SUMMARY AND CONCLUSIONS

When examining economic management and the role of the IMF in national attempts to cure instability during the Manley administration, it was convenient to split the eight years into two periods: 1972–1976 and 1977–1980, Broadly speaking, the causes of instability can be identified with the first period, whilst attempts to arrest the decline in the Jamaican economy are associated with the second period. The major conclusions on the causes of instability, analysed in parts II and III were:

(a) Domestic policies and structural factors, rather than external factors beyond the control of the authorities, were largely responsible for the excess demand for foreign exchange and worsening payments position. The main domestic causes were fiscal policy – notably the pattern and growth of government expenditures, the bauxite production levy – and government controls affecting the demand for non-oil imports, and the profitability of export production and foreign investment.

(b) Imported inflation was not found to be a major cause of the deteriorating domestic economy. Large domestic wage increases preceded the rise in oil prices and exceeded cost of living adjustments attributable to higher import prices. While the changing pattern of income distribution is complex to unravel, those employed in the urban wage sector under trade union agreements benefited most from the large rise in average real wages over this period.

(c) Expansionary fiscal and monetary policies caused aggregate demand to far outstrip the supply of real resources and added to the inflationary pressures from higher import prices and cost of living adjustments. Higher costs of production, increased taxes, price controls and a fixed exchange rate all served to squeeze profit margins and reduce production and investment incentives. The sharp decline in private sector investment vastly outweighed the small increase in public investment and although government spending expanded dramatically, most of the increase took the form of higher consumption not investment.

(d) The events of 1974 are crucial to understanding the deterioration of the economy and subsequent attitude of the authorities towards stabilisation. In 1974 Jamaica's energy bill tripled following the announcement of higher oil prices, and the bauxite production levy sharply increased government revenues in order to help finance the programmes announced after the PNP's 1972 election victory. In late 1974 Democratic Socialism was declared the official PNP ideology and this was to influence government attitudes towards the management of imported inflation, growth in government spending, and priorities directly attached to income distribution, short-term employment and macro-stabilisation. In general, the authorities did not wish to usher in unpopular adjustment policies that would have required a decline in real incomes and a curtailment of social welfare programmes.

Economic management and relations with the Fund between 1977–80 were examined in Part IV and a few details of the 1981 EFF agreement, negotiated by the new Seaga–JLP government which succeeded the Manley–PNP administration were included for comparison. Without summarising the details, some major conclusions about attempts to cure instability in this second period and claims levelled against Fund programmes in Jamaica[13] are as follows:

(a) Jamaica's experience surrounding the 1977 Stand-by agreement supports Dell and Lawrence's conclusion (1980, p. 10) that there is a relationship between the ability and willingness of the developing countries to accept Fund conditionality and the amount of resources the Fund is able to make available. While the Jamaican authorities had allowed the economy to deteriorate dramatically before going to the Fund, the conditions required for this credit were out of all proportion to the resources made available. Even if the agreement was seen by the Fund as a test of the government's determination to implement high stabilisation measures, the size and conditionality of Fund resources provided little scope and encouragement to adhere to this goal.

(b) Whether or not factors outside the control of the authorities had been the main cause of Jamaica's stabilisation problems, substantial foreign assistance was required to support a viable stabilisation programme and reduce the social and economic costs of adjustment to a level that was not impractical. Although subsequent agreements displayed an increasing awareness of the need for politically feasible adjustment costs, and a longer period of adjustment, insufficient attention was paid to these matters in 1977.

(c) While in 1977 the Fund's conditionality may have been politically impractical, the 1978 and 1979 EFF agreements illustrate that Fund conditionality was not applied in a rigid fashion, and that there was 'constrained' flexibility in response to mounting social tensions and changed external circumstances. In the 1978 agreement, the speed with which the Jamaican authorities were required to curb fiscal and monetary expansion was reduced compared with the 1977 Stand-by. In 1979 the Fund permitted a stretching out of the adjustment period so as to ease the costs and there was a change in the mix of demand and supply policies, with more emphasis given to structural constraints and disaggregated supply policies aimed at increasing output in key sectors. In December 1979 the performance criteria would have been adjusted to allow for unforeseen external events, such as the damage to export supplies caused by Hurricane Allan, higher foreign interest rates and oil price increases, had an agreement on measures to correct for slippages in domestic fiscal targets been achieved.

(d) Overall, the Fund's programmes reflect a pro-market bias, emphasising the economic efficiency of market forces rather than controls. The eventual liberalisation of the import licensing system was called for in the 1978, 1979 and 1981 agreements, but it was recognised that this could not be done quickly without exacerbating the foreign exchange shortage. Claims of an anti-socialist bias in the Fund are questionable. The 1978 programme did call for a switch in resources from the public to private sectors, but this democratic socialist government, with its left-wing interventionist policies, was the largest recipient of IMF resources on a per capita basis in 1979, when the outstanding balance of

Fund credits to Jamaica was 360% of its quota, against an average of 64% among developing countries.

(e) The Jamaican experience shows clearly that a Fund agreement may help to reschedule old debts and trigger pledges of additional foreign finance but that the IMF seal of approval may not always act as a catalyst providing the desired size of international borrowing. Foreign bank loans are also influenced by evidence of government adherence to the Fund programme and risk of arrears in debt service payments. Recognising this, the performance criteria under the 1981 agreement were automatically adjusted for fluctuations in official external borrowing.

(f) Fund agreements after 1977 could not quickly dispel the uncertainty surrounding the domestic policies of the PNP, which earlier had been the main cause of decline in real GDP and international reserves. The ambivalent attitude of the authorities towards implementation of stabilisation measures persisted throughout 1977–80, and the inadequate and irregular supply of imports continued to restrain the recovery of the domestic economy. Hence, Fund stabilisation programmes proved to be far from sufficient to revive local and foreign investor confidence and promote export-led growth. A sharp change in government policies and attention to stabilisation measures was required to arrest the decline in real incomes and foreign reserves. The experience of the Jamaican economy adds support to the view that there are fundamental laws and constraints for socialist and non-socialist developing countries alike, namely: 'A country that raises wages and vastly increases the Government's budget at a time when productivity and aggregate supply are falling will get itself in a first-class economic mess' (Morawetz, 1980, p. 361).

Footnotes

1. The nature of these structural problems and the economic performance of the Jamaican economy during much of this earlier decade are discussed in Jefferson (1972) and Manley (1974, part II, chapter 2) and referred to later in this chapter. A comparison of the political parties and their public policies can be found in Stone (1980, especially chapters 4, 6 and 11).

2. IBRD, *Market Structure of Bauxite/Alumina/Aluminium and Prospects for Developing Countries*, Commodity Paper No. 24, March 1977.

3. A State of Emergency was declared in June 1976 in an attempt to contain domestic violence and arson.

4. For further discussion of government foreign borrowing, see Bourne (1980b).

5. The import targets and actual out-turn are given in Bonnick (1980, Table 10, p. 37).

6. Democratic Socialism was not mentioned in the 1972 election campaign and is not discussed in Manley (1974) but the key elements of this philosophy are seen as:
   (a) the establishment of control over the economy by government acquisition of utilities; participation in bauxite, sugar and the tourism industry; and price controls;
   (b) concern for social justice and the provision of food, shelter, clothing, education and health care, including a national literacy programme;

free education; a minimum wage; and legislation to protect the rights of women and to strengthen the rights of the trade union movement;

(c)   the deepening of the democratic process by strengthening local government, establishing a system of local community councils; and introducing co-operative ownership of certain large sugar estates and a land reform programme for small farmers.

(Ministry Paper No. 34, July 1978, Extended Fund Arrangements with the International Monetary Fund.)

7. *Economic and Social Survey* 1978, p. 262. The inflationary effects of these large nominal wage increases led the government to strengthen price controls in 1975 and to introduce a form of incomes policy which mainly involved persuasion and voluntary compliance. These income guidelines were introduced in September 1975 by way of Ministry Paper No. 55 and revised in several Ministry papers including: Nos. 8 and 12 of 1976; Nos. 27 and 38 of 1977; and No. 23 of 1979.

8. Ministry of Finance, *Financial Statements and Revenue Estimates* (annual).

9. There is no mention of this 1973 Stand-by in Girvan *et al.* (1980, p. 116).

10. Ministry Paper No. 34, July 1978.

11. API, Manley, broadcast to the Nation on 25 April, 1979: 'The Social Contract'.

12. Ministry of Finance, *Financial Statements and Revenue Estimates*. Between 1978 and 1979, the external debt service ratio declined slightly from 9.2% to 8.7% of GDP (Table 4).

13. 'Message from the Prime Minister of Jamaica,' Hon. Michael Manley to the South–North Conference on the International Monetary System and the New International Economic Order, *Development Dialogue*, 1980: 2. p. 5. 'Solidarity with Jamaica', Resolution adopted by the South–North Conference on the International Monetary System and the New International Economic Order, Arusha, Tanzania, June 30–July 3, 1980, *Development Dialogue*, 1980: 2. p. 24. Girvan *et al.* (1980, pp. 131–132). Kincaid (1981, p. 21).

References

Government publications

Bank of Jamaica, *Balance of Payments of Jamaica* (annual).

Bank of Jamaica, *Statistical Digest* (monthly).

Department of Statistics, *Consumer Price Indices: January 1970–1979*.

Department of Statistics, *National Income and Product 1979*.

Department of Statistics, *Statistical Yearbook of Jamaica 1979*.

Department of Statistics, *Employment, Earnings and Hours in Large Establishments*, 1977, 1978, 1979.

Department of Statistics, *The Labour Force 1979*.

Department of Statistics, *Monetary Statistics 1979*.

Ministry of Finance, *Financial Statements and Revenue Estimates* (annual).

Ministry of Finance, *Memorandum on the Budget*, 1975–76, 1976–77, 1977–78.

National Planning Agency, *Economic and Social Survey* (annual).

Parliament, *Ministry Papers*,

    No. 28, August 1977: Stand-by Agreement with the International Monetary Fund.

    No. 34, July 1978: Extended Fund Facility Arrangement with the International Monetary Fund.

    No.26, June 1979: Extended Fund Facility Arrangement with the International Monetary Fund.

    No.9, April 1981: Extended Fund Facility Arrangement with the International Monetary Fund.

    No.8, February 1976: Prices and Incomes Policy.

    No.12, April 1976: Wage and Salary Guidelines.

    No.27, July 1977: Policy in Income and Prices.

No. 38, 1977: Pay Guidelines.
No.22, May 1978: Pay Guidelines – 1978.
No.23, May 1979: Pay Guidelines 1979/81.
Agency for Public Information (API), Michael Manley (February 1980), 'The need for a new economic path', Broadcast to the Nation, Sunday 3 February, 1980.
Agency for Public Information (API), Michael Manley (March 1980), 'Towards a self-reliant economy: the non-IMF path', Statement by the Prime Minister in Parliament, March 25, 1980.
Agency for Public Information (API), Michael Manley (April 1979), 'The social contract', Broadcast to the Nation on 15 April, 1979: 'The Social Contract'.

Authors

Asgar Ally, 'The potential for autonomous monetary policy in small developing countries', in Percy Selwyn (ed), *Development Policy in Small Countries*, London, Croom Helm, 1975.
Ayub, M.A., *Made in Jamaica*, Washington DC, Johns Hopkins University Press, 1981.
Blackman, Courtney, *The Balance of Payments Crisis in the Caribbean: Which Way Out?* Lecture at the University of West Indies, Cave Hill Campus, Barbados, February 1979, Bridgetown, Central Bank of Barbados, 1979.
Bonnick, Gladstone, 'The experience of Jamaica' in Dell Report, *The Balance of Payments Adjustment Process in Developing Countries*, UNCTAD/MFD/TA/5, 1980. vol. 1.
Bourne, Compton (ed), *Inflation in the Caribbean*, Institute for Social and Economic Research, Kingston, University of West Indies, 1977a.
Bourne, Compton (ed), 'Public finance in the Caribbean', *Social and Economic Studies*, December 1977b.
Bourne, Compton, 'Jamaica and the International Monetary Fund: economics of the 1978 stabilization program', *Studies in Rural Finance*, Department of Agricultural Economics and Rural Sociology, Occasional Paper No.729, Ohio State University, May 1980a.
Bourne, Compton, 'Government and foreign borrowing and economic growth: the Jamaican experience', *Studies in Rural Finance*, Department of Agricultural Economics and Rural Sociology, Occasional Paper No.726, Ohio State University, May 1980b.
Chelliah, R.S., *Tax Effort in Developing Countries*, IMF Staff Papers, vol.XXII, No.1, March 1975.
Dell Report, *The Balance of Payments Adjustment Process in Developing Countries*, UNCTAD/MFD/TA/5, 1980.
Also published in part as:
Dell, Sidney and Lawrence, Roger, *The Balance of Payments Adjustment Process in Developing Countries*, Oxford, Pergamon Press, 1980.
Demas, William, *The Economics of Development in Small Countries*, Montreal, McGill University Press, 1965.
Galbis, Vincent, 'Monetary and Exchange Rate Policies in a Small Open Economy', *IMF Staff Papers*, July 1975.
Girvan, Norman, Bernal, Richard and Hughes, Wesley, 'The IMF and the Third World: the case of Jamaica, 1974–1980', *Development Dialogue*, 1980:2.
Girvan, Norman and Jefferson, Owen, *Readings in the Political Economy of the Caribbean*, Kingston, New World Group, 1971.
International Bank for Reconstruction and Development, *Market Structure of Bauxite/ Alumina/Aluminium and Prospects for Developing Countries*, Commodity Paper No.24, March 1977.
International Bank for Reconstruction and Development, *The Commonwealth Caribbean: The Integration Experience*, Washington DC, Johns Hopkins University Press, 1978.
International Bank for Reconstruction and Development, *Jamaica: Development Issues and Economic Prospects*, (Unpublished report), January 1982.

Jefferson, Owen, *The Post-War Economic Development of Jamaica*, Kingston, Institute of Social and Economic Research, University of the West Indies, 1972.

Khatkhate, Deena and Short, Brock, 'Monetary and central banking problems in mini states', *World Development*, vol.8, December 1980.

Kincaid, G. Russel, 'Fund assistance to Jamaica', *IMF Survey*, December 15, 1980.

Kincaid, G. Russel, 'Conditionality and the use of fund resources: Jamaica', *Finance and Development*, vol. 18, no.12, June 1981.

Krueger, Anne, *Liberalization Attempts and Consequences*, Cambridge, Mass., Ballinger, 1978.

Levitt, Kari and Best, Lloyd, 'Character of Caribbean economy', in Beckford, George, (ed), *Caribbean Economy: Dependence and Backwardness*, Kingston, Institute of Social and Economic Research, University of West Indies, 1975.

Manley, Michael, *The Politics of Change*, London, André Deutsch, 1974.

Morawetz, David, 'Economic lessons from some small socialist developing countries', *World Development*, May/June 1980.

David, 'Economic lessons from some small socialist developing countries', *World Development*, May/June 1980.

Odle, Maurice, *The Significance of Non-Bank Financial Intermediaries in the Caribbean*, Kingston, Institute of Social and Economic Research, University of West Indies, 1972.

Odle, Maurice, 'Public policy' in Beckford, George, (ed), *Caribbean Economy: Dependence and Backwardness*, Kingston, Institute of Social and Economic Research, University of West Indies, 1975.

Palmer, Ransford, W., *Caribbean Dependence on the United States Economy*, New York, Praeger, 1979.

Reid, Stanley, 'Strategy of Resource Bargaining', *Working Paper No, 20*, Kingston, Institute of Social and Economic Research, University of West Indies, 1978.

Stone, Carl, *Democracy and Clientelism in Jamaica*, New Jersey, Transactions Books, 1980.

Taylor, E.S., 'Public finance in Jamaica, 1971–1976', *Social and Economic Studies*, December 1977.

Worrell, DeLisle, 'External influences and domestic policies: the economic fortunes of Jamaica and Barbados in the 1970s'; paper presented at the Caribbean Studies Association, Curaçao, May 1980a, Bridgetown, Central Bank of Barbados.

Worrell, DeLisle, 'The impact of fluctuating exchange rates on Barbados and Jamaica'; paper presented at the San Diego Conference of Western Economics Association, June 1980b, Bridgetown, Central Bank of Barbados.

5 Kenya, 1975–81[1]
Tony Killick

While Kenya is not among the countries whose relationships with the IMF have hit the headlines, there are, as will be seen shortly, factors which make Kenya a particularly interesting case to study. In what follows Part I sketches the performance of the Kenyan economy in recent years and the emergence of major disequilibria; Parts II and III attempt to provide explanations for the emergence of these imbalances; Part IV enquires into the possibilities of short-term economic management; Part V examines the government's relations with the IMF, focusing on a succession of credits beginning in 1975; and Part VI presents a brief evaluation of the sources of difficulty in these relations.

I. ECONOMIC PERFORMANCE AND THE EMERGENCE OF DISEQUILIBRIA

The general orientation of economic policies

To attempt a characterisation of a government's economic objectives in anything more than banalities is a treacherous business. Official statements are invariably couched in general terms and carefully avoid explicit statements of priorities in the face of conflicts between desired goals. There is usually a gulf between the rhetoric and the objectives revealed in day-to-day decisions. So it is with Kenya.

Soon after it won political Independence at the end of 1963 the government issued a seminal statement of its economic objectives and development strategy, *African Socialism and its Application to Planning in Kenya.*[2] The intellectual climate at that time dictated a genuflection to the language of African socialism but, as Stewart (1976, pp. 85–86) has noted, it was a language which obscured rather than clarified the approach of the government:

> The political and economic strategy adopted by the Kenyan government since Independence was self-described as African Socialism. In more conventional terms it may be described as a capitalist strategy, both in domestic policy and in policy towards the world system, modified by the declared

intention . . . of redistributing some of the gains to the poorer sections of the community. While domestic and foreign private ownership has been encouraged, the public sector has simultaneously expanded rapidly, as has government intervention in the economy. In this respect, Kenyan development resembles that of many other economies, in being one of *managed* capitalism, or a mixed economy, as it is sometimes described.

'Managed capitalism' is an apt description. So far as the productive sectors are concerned, the general approach has been to work through the framework of a market system. But there has been no question of laissez faire: a substantial state sector and widespread interventionism were inherited from the colonial government and have since been extended.

In stating its attitude to development the Kenyatta government could scarcely have been more explicit in its acceptance of a 'trickle-down' view (Kenya, 1965, p. 18):

> The ultimate objectives of African Socialism are clear . . . The high priorities placed on political equality, social justice and human dignity mean that these principles will not be compromised in selecting policies designed to alleviate pressing and immediate problems. The most important of these policies is to provide a firm basis for rapid economic growth. Other immediate problems such as Africanization of the economy, education, unemployment, welfare services, and provincial policies must be handled in ways that will not jeopardize growth. The only permanent solution to all of these problems rests on rapid growth. If growth is given up in order to reduce unemployment, a growing population will quickly demonstrate how false that policy is; if Africanization is undertaken at the expense of growth, our reward will be a falling standard of living; if free primary education is achieved by sacrificing growth, no jobs will be available for the school-leavers.

This, however, was written before the upsurge of concern for distributional questions which so marked the literature on development during the 1970s. Heightened sensitivity to this and a dawning suspicion that the growth-maximising strategy might not be working as well as had been hoped led the government to commission what has since become a well-known ILO report on employment, incomes and equality (ILO, 1972). This report drew an apparently favourable public response from the government, and the strategy of 'redistribution with growth' recommended by the ILO had a clear influence on development plans published successively in 1974 and 1979. The actual reorientation of public policies and services in the directions required by the strategy inevitably lagged behind the public pronouncements, however, and while important changes have occurred it is fair to say that there remains more emphasis on overall growth and less on poverty alleviation than the planners intended.[3]

The attitude of the government towards stabilisation will be examined in detail later but, viewing the post-Independence period overall, fiscal and monetary policies have been generally cautious even though they have not been used actively for short-run economic management. As will be shown, the budgetary situation was considerably improved during the 1960s and has remained generally sound since then. Only exceptionally has significant monetary expansion been caused by large-scale deficit financing. And while the government has proved reluctant to vary the exchange rate, it would be impossible to say that at any time the official rate was more than moderately out of line with a notional equilibrium or market rate.

This sketch draws attention to one of the interests of the Kenyan case. As a country with a record of political stability under a rather conservative government and with an essentially market-oriented economy, we might predict that there would be a natural congruence between the type of stabilisation programme favoured by the IMF and the preferences of the Kenya government. Moreover, the government's relationships with the IMF have never been the subject of acute political sensitivity – neither within the government nor with public opinion – in the way that it has been in numerous other countries. There have been no ideological barriers to co-operation with the IMF. It seems, then, that if successful stabilisation and good working relationships with the Fund are not feasible in Kenya, it is unclear where else in Africa they might be achieved.

Economic performance prior to 1973–74

The national product delivered the growth that was sought by official policy after Independence and Kenya gradually built up a reputation as having one of the fastest-growing and most stable economies in Africa.[4] By and large, it was a well-merited reputation. The GDP grew in real terms at about $6\frac{1}{2}$% p.a. in 1964–73 and, even though the population is among the fastest-growing in the world, per capita incomes rose by an average of about 30% in real terms over this period. However, large inequalities and continuing widespread poverty reduce the welfare significance of average income data; many have benefited little from the growth, and income disparities within the African population have probably widened. But it is beyond question that large numbers of Kenyans today enjoy living standards which would have been impossible without a rapidly expanding economy.[5] One guarantee that the benefits of growth were not confined to a small urban elite was that, at least until recently, agriculture played a fairly full part in the growth process, with an increasing share of the output of this sector coming from smallholders. In 1964–73 value-added in agriculture expanded at 4.0% p.a. and the share of marketed output attributed to smallholders (almost certainly an understatement) rose from 41% to 51%.[6] Nevertheless, there was also considerable industrialisation, with manufacturing industry growing at 9.0% p.a. during the same period.

In another aspect, however, the structure remained unchanged – as a very open economy. In 1964 the trade ratio (exports plus imports of goods and non-factor services as a proportion of GDP) stood at 63.4%; in 1973 it was 66.2%; in 1979 it was 66.7% and in 1980 rose to an exceptional 80.4%. Throughout the post-Independence period coffee and tea have remained the dominant export commodities.[7] This heavy reliance on international trade and a few key export crops exposes the economy to exogenous shocks emanating from the outside world.

Given this and the still predominantly rural nature of the economy, it is remarkable that the economy grew in a steady fashion during most of the years under review. As can be seen from Figure 5.1, the annual growth rate fluctuated within the range of about $5\frac{1}{2}$% to $7\frac{1}{2}$% throughout 1968–73. The growth of the 'modern' GDP (i.e. excluding non-monetary and agricultural GDP) was more volatile but in these years remained in the range $5\frac{1}{2}$% to $9\frac{1}{2}$%. Underlying the buoyant growth was an excellent saving and investment record. Starting from 14% in 1964, the gross investment ratio had risen to between 20% and 24% in the early 1970s. Moreover, the bulk of the investment was throughout financed by domestic saving: typically only about a tenth of gross investment was met by capital inflows from the rest of the world. And while there may have been some tendency for the marginal productivity of investment to decline[8] this was only gradual, and it must be rated as an achievement of the economic system that it facilitated productive investment decisions.

The absence of a foreign exchange constraint also contributed importantly to the growth of the economy.[9] Until 1974 deficits on the balance of payments current account were generally modest and little difficulty was encountered in meeting these with inflows of long-term capital. In fact, the basic balance showed a surplus in most years prior to 1974 and from 1966 (when national records of reserves were first compiled) until 1973 the official foreign exchange reserves increased during all except two years. At the end of 1973 reserves were equivalent to about 5 months' imports; the exchange rate had been stable; with certain exceptions, exchange and import controls were either not restrictive or not enforced; and external debt servicing costs were equivalent in 1973 only to about 3% of that year's export earnings. That record was to change dramatically after 1973, however, as also was the growth of the economy.

The first decade of Independence was also remarkable for the virtual absence of inflation. Figure 5.1 also records the annual increase in the Nairobi lower-income index of consumer prices. As can be seen, it shows inflation rates of 0–3% throughout 1966–72 but much higher rates thereafter. The period 1966–72 was remarkable both for the absence of a steeper trend and for the year-to-year stability of the price index.

The performance of the fiscal and monetary systems had much to do with the absence of payments and price disequilibria. During the 1960s and into the early 1970s the government was able simultaneously to greatly expand the services and capital formation undertaken by the central government while improving the budgetary balance and reducing dependence on foreign grants and loans.[10] From being heavily reliant on grants-in-aid from the UK in 1963, the budget was by 1973/4 showing a substantial surplus on current account and use of foreign grants and loans amounted only to 8.5% of total spending, against 20.4% in 1964/5. Throughout almost all this period the state made minimal use of bank borrowing. The financial system developed and expanded, with the real value of total domestic credit increasing two-and-a-half-fold in 1964–72 without, as we have shown, generating significant inflation.[11]

Figure 5.1   Growth rates of constant-price GDP and Nairobi lower-income consumer price index, 1964–80

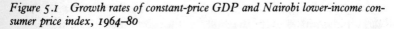

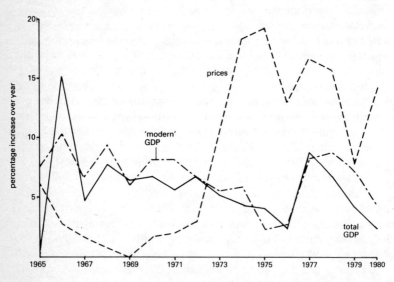

As is immediately apparent from Figure 5.1, and as will shortly be demonstrated for the balance of payments, this picture of stable expansion was radically altered from 1973–74. For present purposes the economic record becomes most interesting from 1973–74 and it is on this period that the remainder of this paper will concentrate.

Economc performance from 1973–74

While there had been a brief alarm in 1971 and some economists had begun to draw attention to underlying weaknesses, no-one could have forecast the abrupt deterioration in the balance of payments that occurred in 1974. The import bill shot up, the current deficit more than doubled to a record size and the basic balance moved from approximate equality into a deficit of K£41 million. Despite substantial use of IMF resources and other short-term borrowings, reserves were run down, so that by the end of 1974 they were equivalent to only 2.7 months of imports, compared with 5.1 months twelve months earlier.

Key payments indicators are marshalled in Table 5.1, showing the worsening in 1973–74 but then a recovery in the following three years. By 1977 the current account was actually in surplus (for the first time in 12 years) and foreign exchange reserves were so large as to be an embarrassment to the government in its requests for continuing development aid. This did not last, however. There was a second dramatic deterioration during 1978, a diminished but still large current deficit in the following year, and a huge one in 1980. Another deficit of about K£275 million was forecast for 1981, with scarcely less bleak prospects for 1982. Exceptionally large inflows of capital in 1978–80 cushioned the impact on the basic and overall balances so that reserves were quite well protected. By September 1981, however, net reserves had become negative and were only restored by utilisation of a Euromarket loan. By

Table 5.1   Kenya: selected balance of payments indicators, 1970–80 (K£ million)

	Balance on Current a/c (1)	Net long-term capital inflows (2)	Basic balance (1 + 2) (3)	External reserves[a] (4)	External debt[c] (5)
1970	−17.5	30.9	+13.4	73.3	n.a.
1971	−39.9	15.2	−24.7	51.8	n.a.
1972	−24.3	30.6	+6.3	66.4	186.9
1973	−46.8	48.1	+1.3	76.3	223.0
1974	−112.0	71.0	−41.0	68.4	258.6
1975	−83.9	57.4	−26.5	70.6	285.1
1976	−51.9	90.7	+38.8	114.0	350.3
1977	+11.4	84.9	+96.3	208.6	458.5
1978	−255.3	168.0	−87.3	133.3	542.6
1979	−178.3	181.0	+2.7	234.5	713.7
1980[b]	−332.8	215.0	−117.8	187.0	835.9

Sources: Kenya, *Economic Surveys and Statistical Abstracts. Debt data from World Bank.*
Notes: [a] Year-end figures. There is a break in the series between 1971 and 1972, so figures for those years are not strictly comparable.
  [b] Provisional.
  [c] Year-end figures. Converted from dollars at K£0.5 = $1.0.

the end of 1981 the country was confronting a full-scale payments crisis.

The inevitable price of increased dependence on capital receipts, of course, was an accelerated accumulation of external debt, all the more serious because the Kenyan government data seriously under-reported the extent of this. According to World Bank data, the foreign-owned public debt rose from K£223 million at end-1973 to K£836 million seven years later (Table 5.1, col.5), while the cost of servicing it rose from £15 million to an estimated K£79 million by 1980. With a debt service ratio in 1980 estimated at nearly 13% and rising fast, the size of the external debt was emerging as a source of major concern.

As can be seen from Figure 5.1, it was not only the payments situation which lost its relative tranquility in these years. Always subject to the imperfections of the statistics, during 1973 the inflation rate suddenly went up into double figures and stayed there for practically the remainder of the decade. There were, moreover, substantial oscillations about the 12–14% norm that established itself in 1973–80, by contrast with the relative absence of major fluctuations in 1964–72. Figure 5.1 also reveals some destabilisation of GDP growth after 1974. There was a major slump in 1974–76, a spectacular recovery in 1976–78 but then a further slowing-down in 1979–80. Taking 1974–80 as a whole, total 'modern' GDP in constant prices expanded at about 5.6% p.a., as against 7.6% in the earlier period. This was not too drastic a deterioration in the circumstances; it was the greater variability about the average which contrasted most with the preceding years. Ominously, perhaps, agriculture almost entirely ran out of steam in the years after 1973, averaging only an 0.7% p.a. growth to 1980. This sharply diminished the country's ability to feed itself and large food imports were necessary in 1979 and 1980. Overall and given a population growing at the startling rate of 3.8% p.a., per capita incomes expanded at only 0.4% p.a. in 1974–80.

So much, then, for this bald statement of the chief developments. We must turn now to look at them more analytically, to seek their causes, starting with the balance of payments.

II. EXPLAINING THE BALANCE OF PAYMENTS EXPERIENCE

In seeking to explain the swings that have occurred in Kenya's payments situation it is convenient, if ultimately artificial, to isolate three types of explanation: (a) those which stress the influence of exogenous shocks; (b) those which emphasise the underlying fiscal and monetary forces; (c) those focusing upon structural factors. It will also be useful to keep in mind some key year-to-year changes in various balance of payments magnitudes summarised in Table 5.2.

(a) Exogenous shocks

It was obviously no coincidence that 1974 was the year in which the current account plunged suddenly into a large deficit, for we have already shown in chapter M2 (Pt. III) that this was a year in which many oil-importing ldcs were thrust heavily into the red. With most energy derived from petroleum but having no mineral oil of her own, Kenya depends heavily upon imported supplies. The quadrupling of oil prices at the end of 1973 therefore had a major impact. Prior to 1974 the country usually had an approximately zero balance in her trade in petroleum products, with the value-added on crude oil which was imported, refined and sold to neighbouring countries roughly meeting the cost of the crude used within the domestic economy. In 1974, however, the petroleum products account swung into a K£35 million deficit (against a deficit of only K£1 million in the previous year), with an average deficit in the following three years of the same magnitude. In 1978 the deficit went up to K£47 million and by 1980 it was K£116 million.[12] Given total export earnings in 1974 of K£218 million, such a large increase in net oil import costs could scarcely fail to have serious consequences.

As is evident from the top left-hand entry in Table 5.2, however, the rising cost of oil could explain only part of the rise in the total import bill (indicated by a negative sign – see note (a) of the table). Associated with this, however, was an acceleration of the already rapid inflation in non-oil import prices, which rose by an average of 31% in 1974. Although there were also increases in the prices of some of the country's exports these were insufficient to prevent a massive deterioration in the commodity terms of trade, which fell from 97 in 1973 to 85 a year later (see Figure 5.2). An admittedly rather crude quantification of the payments effects of changes in the terms of trade in 1973–74 indicated that they explained a total of K£72 million of the K£104 million total deterioration in the balance of trade in that year or more than the entire deterioration in the current account recorded in Table 5.2 (Killick, 1981, Table 5, p. 63).

As can also be inferred from Figure 5.2, the terms of trade continued thereafter to exert a major influence. 1976 and 1977 were dominated by a quite unprecedented boom in the world prices of the country's two chief export commodities, coffee and tea. Following a severe frost in Brazil in July 1975 and difficulties in other producing countries, the world price of coffee escalated from an average of around 65 US cents per pound in 1973–74 to ¢142 in 1976 and ¢229 in 1977.

Table 5.2   *Year-to-year changes in Kenya's Balance of Payments magnitudes*[a] (K£ million)

	1973–74	1974–75	1975–76	1976–77	1977–78	1978–79	1979–80[b]
Imports (cif)	−165.6	+23.8	−28.4	−139.9	−195.6	+59.9	−311.8
Exports (fob)	+61.6	+6.3	+79.7	+155.9	−98.6	+10.9	+80.7
Invisibles and transfers	+38.8	−2.0	−19.3	+47.3	+27.5	+6.2	+76.6
TOTAL CURRENT ACCOUNT	−65.2	+28.1	+32.0	+63.3	−266.7	+77.0	−154.5
Long-term capital	+22.9	−13.6	+33.3	−5.8	+83.1	+13.0	+34.0
BASIC BALANCE	−42.3	+14.5	+65.3	+57.5	−183.6	+90.0	−120.5
Foreign reserves	−7.9	+2.2	+43.4	+94.6	−75.3	+101.2	−47.5

Sources: Kenya, *Economic Surveys* (various issues).

Notes: [a] The figures measure changes from one year to the next, with a *minus* sign indicating a change that worsens the balance of payments outcome and a *plus* sign indicating a change that improves it.
 [b] Provisional.

These traumatic events spilled over into the tea market, where the price went up from ¢65 per pound in 1974–75 to c121 in 1976. With bouyant export volumes as well, the country's export earnings rose dramatically in 1976 and 1977, as can be seen from Table 5.2, resulting in the major improvements on current account, basic balance and external reserves already observed from Table 5.1. An estimate of the payments impact of the higher export prices put the total gain in 1976–77 at K£264 million (Killick, 1981, p. 64). In 1978–80 export prices fell back to more normal levels and combined with further substantial rises in import prices to contribute greatly to the worsening payments situation of those years, which was also aggravated in this case by adverse movements in the quantities of both imports and exports.

Not all the exogenous shocks came from the outside world, however. The vagaries of the weather also played their part. In particular, adverse conditions caused serious food deficiencies in 1980 in a country which normally feeds itself. This added to the already rising trend in basic food imports, with another food deficit predicted for 1981. Changing weather conditions also contributed to the variability of export volumes in these years. Smuggling in and out of Uganda was a further destabilising element.

Clearly, then, Kenya's is an economy exceedingly vulnerable to destabiling influences beyond the control of its government. Note two points, however. First, there are swings as well as roundabouts: if Kenya was the loser from the inflation of oil and other import prices,

Figure 5.2   Commodity terms of trade, 1972–80 (1972 = 100)

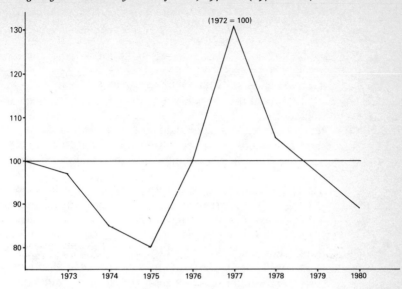

she was massively the gainer from the coffee/tea boom. Second, while reference to the terms of trade provides a strong proximate explanation of trends in the balance of payments they by no means tell all the story. Indeed, monetarist analyses tend instead to attribute the problem to domestic policies so we proceed now to examine this line of explanation.

(b) Monetarist explanations

For the purposes of this volume, not the least interesting aspects of the Kenyan case is the existence of a serious literature placing a monetarist interpretation on payments trends. Although we are here mainly interested in developments from 1974, King's (1979) analysis of the 1967–73 period provides a natural starting point. He is concerned with the relative merits of Keynesian and monetarist models in explaining the macroeconomic behaviour of economies like Kenya's, concluding firmly in favour of the latter. He presents a 'financial flows' model which is a Polak model of the type reviewed in chapter M3. Symbolically, his model is summarised in the following five equations:

(1) $Y = A + \bar{X} - M$
(2) $MO = kY$
(3) $M = mY$
(4) $\Delta MO = \Delta FR + \Delta \bar{D}A$
(5) $\Delta FR = \bar{X} - M + \bar{F}$

where

A   domestic absorption
M   imports of goods and services
X   exports of goods and services
Y   domestic output
F   net foreign capital receipts
FR   foreign reserve assets of the monetary system
DA   domestic assets of the monetary system
MO   the stock of money
k   income velocity of MO, assumed constant at the margin
m   marginal propensity to import, assumed constant

A bar over a variable shows it is assumed to be determined exogen-ously.

Note here the conventional Polakian assumptions of constant mar-ginal values of k and m, with m (the propensity to import) as the only leakage out of the circular flow of income – implying that the marginal propensity to save and the income elasticity of the tax system are sufficiently near to zero that they can be disregarded without a crucial loss of realism. As is well known, the most important policy implication of this model is that, in equilibrium, changes in the value of the foreign exchange reserves (ΔFR) are inversely determined by changes in dom-estic credit (ΔDA), with a £1 increase in DA being associated with a £1 reduction in FR: " . . . in equilibrium, the balance of payments is determined by ΔDA and nothing else" (King, p. 35). As he goes on to point out, however, an economy will not normally be in equilibrium and this readmits the influence of exports and capital flows upon the payments situation.

Applying the model to Kenyan data, King argues that it tracks the actual behaviour of the economy in 1967–73 quite well and that the relationships postulated in the model appear valid. The policy interest of his results is unfortunately limited by the fact that there was a relative absence of major disequilibria in his period. There was, however, a significant, if short-lived, loss of reserves in 1971 which King argues (pp. 80–81) to have been caused by a parallel increase in domestic credit. Given the values derived in his model and a legal requirement for the Central Bank of Kenya to maintain foreign reserves equivalent to at least four months-worth of imports, he concludes (p. 99) that 'the only safe rule for credit expansion to the Kenya government in the long run is that *none should be undertaken*. Any systematic infringement of this rule is bound to lead to balance of payments 'crises'. The focus is upon credit to government because that usually takes forms which add to the liquid asset base of the banking system and thus sustains the system's ability to lend to the private sector. He adds, however, that there would be scope for a 'safe' expansion in credit to the government to the extent that this was offset by reductions in private credit.

Before proceeding to examine analyses of the post-1973 period we can note that IMF staff members were also drawing attention to the strong connections between domestic credit and the balance of payments during the period analysed by King, and have continued to do so since. However, their work is not derived from a thorough-going monetarist model of the type just described, their contention being the more 'partial' one that in Kenya bank credit affects the payments situation essentially through a strong positive correlation between credit to and imports by the private sector, with most other payments items relatively independent of credit changes. The correlation is strong because much credit to private borrowers is to finance importing, with changes in lending having a particularly strong impact on inventory holdings. They derive the following demand function for private sector non-oil imports:[13]

$$IM = 12.78 + .067 \, CR + .214Y$$
$$R^2 = 0.99 \quad DW = 1.7$$

(where IM = private non-oil imports; CR = private commercial bank credit; Y = monetary GDP). An earlier IMF paper also noted that the payments crisis of 1971 was association with a large upsurge in domestic credit.

Later work by Grubel and Ryan (1979 – hereafter G&R) is of even greater interest because it places an explicitly monetarist interpretation on payments trends up to 1978. While their work is clearly in the same tradition as King's and also focuses particularly on credit to the government, their model differs from his in isolating the domestic component of the high powered money base as the key variable. They present a conventional demand function for money and a money supply function of the form:

$$MO = bH$$

(where MO is as before, b = a money multiplier and H = high-powered money, i.e. the reserve base of the monetary authority). For computational purposes, however, the money supply function was estimated in the form

$$MO = Ae^{\alpha t} H^{\beta}$$

where A is a constant, β is a constant elasticity and α is a constant growth rate. H in turn is given by the identity:

$$H = FR + D$$

(where FR is as before and D = the net domestic asset component of the high-powered money base of the monetary authority). Reading from the balance sheet of the Central Bank of Kenya, D appears to be made up of the items set out in Table 5.3.

Table 5.3   The composition of 'D', as at end-June, 1981 (K£ million)

1. Securities issued or guaranteed by the government	42.4
2. Direct central bank advances to the government	90.7
3. Treasury bills	3.5
4. Advances and discounts	1.6
5. Uncleared effects	34.7
6. Other assets	19.9
less	
7. Government share of central bank profits	−12.0
8. Other liabilities and provisions	−9.5
9. Capital	−1.3
10. General reserve fund	−7.2
11. Revaluation account	−22.7
12. NET TOTAL (D)	140.1

Clearly, D is not an operationally simple concept, although its most important components are all forms of central bank lending to the government (items 1–4). According to G&R (p. 23) 'The crucial point' is that the central bank has D 'under its deliberate control through open market operations' which determine its holding of government paper. Solving their model mathematically, G&R obtain the result that ΔFR is inversely related to ΔD, which is very similar to the chief policy inference of the Polak model (p. 24):

> . . . the weighted growth rate of reserves is a decreasing function of the weighted growth rate in the domestic component of the high-powered money base, after adjustment for the exogenous growth in the other variables influencing the transactions demand for money: real income, prices and interest rates, and for changes in the money multiplier.

Testing the model with Kenyan data, they obtain the predicted negative correlation between ΔFR and ΔD, significant at the 99% level despite a small number of observations. Reference to Figure 5.3, however, provides only limited support for a monetarist position, with changes in the foreign assets of the banking system ('foreign reserves') inversely related to changes in the credit variables in only some years. G&R find their model to be quite successful in tracking the actual behaviour of foreign exchange reserves and contrast their results with those of Maitha *et al.* (1978). These they criticise as leaving 'the overwhelming impression' that payments imbalances 'are the result of very many forces beyond the control of policy makers' (p. 14), against G&R's conclusion that 'Kenya's balance of payments has been determined primarily by the deliberate monetary policy actions of the Central Bank of Kenya' (p. 29).

Given the prima facie evidence presented earlier of powerful exogenous forces operating on balance of payments outcomes from 1974 onwards, a conclusion which 'attributes most payments imbalances to influences fully under the control of government' (G&R, p. 14) is radical to the point of straining credulity. It is worth devoting some space to a critical evaluation of this, not least because of the apparent influence of monetarist explanations on the policy recommendations of the IMF.

First, note how G&R (and also King) use 'changes in reserves' and 'changes in the balance of payments' as synonymous. This, indeed, is characteristic of the monetary school and implies rejection of the type of definition of a payments equilibrium of the type proposed in chapter M2 (p. 17). Comparison of line 7 with the other entries of Table 5.2 reveals immediately that changes in reserves are an undependable indicator of changes on current account, with long- and short-term capital movements in some years dampening (1974, 1975, 1978, 1980) and in others magnifying (1976 and 1979) the impact of the current account on monetary account. If we accept the definition of a payments equilibrium presented in chapter M2, it is clearly inadequate for policy purposes to take changes in reserves as the sole (or even the chief) indicator of the payments situation, not least because the later 1970s saw a worryingly rapid increase in Kenya's external debt. It is better to study a

Figure 5.3   Year-to-year changes in monetary aggregates (K£ million)

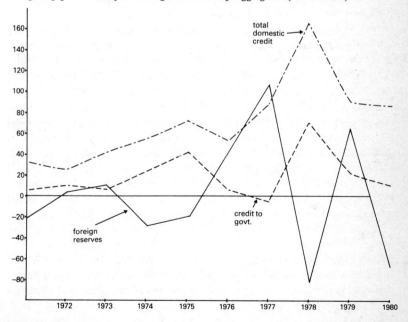

range of indicators and there must be doubts about the policy value of an analysis which takes a single-indicator view.

Second, it is evident from close examination of the results that G&R's analysis predicts best for 1968–72 and 1977–78, breaking down rather badly in 1973 and 1976 (G&R, Fig.7). Had there been enough observations to confine the test to the period of major disequilibria, beginning 1974, it is not at all clear that it would have yielded statistically acceptable results. Their analysis, and also the predicted relationships in Figure 5.3, tend to break down in 1975, with a smaller volume of imports and a larger stock of reserves than would be predicted. Maitha *et al.* (p. 10) explain the small volume of imports in terms of lagged price-elasticity responses to higher relative import prices, the income effects of the depressed state of the domestic economy, a once-for-all inventory adjustment and the effects of tightened import licence allocations.

This leads to a third line of criticism, that the rather exclusively monetarist interpretations placed by King and G&R on their results underplay the 'real' forces featured in their own models. Chapter M3 has, for example, suggested that the Polak model is an amalgam of monetary and Keynesian theory; and in the model employed by G&R real income must be expected to have a strong influence on the demand for money, so that the performance of the export and import-substituting sectors will have an impact on how the economy reacts to a given monetary impulse. Insistence on a purely monetarist interpretation leads G&R apparently to dismiss the relevance of variables other than D in a way which is difficult to defend. For example, writing of the pre-1974 period Maitha *et al.* (1978, p. 14) had drawn attention to an underlying tendency for the payments position to worsen because export volumes had been growing more slowly than the remainder of the economy. G&R criticised this, arguing that the payments position in this period 'simply was due to excess growth in the money base' (p. 20). Does this mean that they regard export performance, and the structure of incentives underlying it, to be irrelevant? Surely not. Interestingly, although the exchange rate does not feature in G&R's model and their emphasis on the potency of D seems to leave no room for an active exchange rate policy, one of the authors was a well-known advocate of a devaluation in the late 1970s, which suggests that his views were not as purely monetarist as might be thought.[14]

There are, in fact, difficulties about the policy inferences drawn by G&R. We have already shown that, in accounting terms, their variable D is complex and includes items ('uncleared effects', 'revaluation account', 'other' assets and liabilities, etc.) which probably could not be easily manipulated for the purposes of short-run economic managment but which do, in fact, change quite substantially from one year to the next. It is true that central bank credit to the government is the most important ingredient of D and this does appear to be a magnitude that could be manipulated. Bolnick (1975a) has argued, however, that the magnitude of deficit financing is determined by the Treasury (although we suggest later that this is not the case in any other than a very approximate way) and is not under the control of the monetary authority. Of course, this leaves open the possibility that the Treasury, working with the central bank, could vary its own deficit financing as a way of managing the balance of payments, but we will see that there are formidable difficulties in the way of doing this (Table 5.7). In any case, G&R reject Bolnick's view. They suggest (p. 23) that, even though deficit financing may be beyond its direct control, the central bank could regulate its holdings of government paper 'primarily through open market operations . . .' To this one must ask, what open market? To the extent that there exists in Nairobi any non-bank market for government paper it is extremely slender. An active policy of market intervention by the central bank (which has never yet been attempted), buying and selling large values of securities so as to maintain a desired level of D, would be liable to have wildly destabilising effects on interest rates and would probably be quite unfeasible.

But while the monetarist interpretations are open to criticism they nevertheless do contribute importantly to an understanding of Kenya's payments problems. The models are right to stress the constraints imposed by the balance of payments in an economy like Kenya's on the speed of credit expansion. They are right too in drawing particular attention to credit to the government (deficit financing), for this normally takes forms which maintain or augment the high-powered money base and hence the banks' ability simultaneously to lend to the private sector.

King has successfully demonstrated the influence of credit expansion on the reserve crisis of 1971 and there were later years in the 1970s when the monetary factor was strongly in evidence. This was most obviously the case in the commodity boom period of 1976–77. In terms of economic management, there was an overwhelming case for preventing all the windfall gains created by the extraordinarily high world coffee and tea prices from accruing to the farmers. These were purely fortuitous profits, is no sense a return on past investments, and they were large in relation to total domestic demand. Alone among the major coffee producing countries, Kenya did not tax coffee revenues, either directly or through a marketing board arrangement (Davis, 1980, Table 4). The obvious response, therefore, was to introduce a tax to cream off much of the windfall, putting the proceeds into a stabilisation fund which could be used to support the farmers in leaner times (but not using the proceeds to finance an equivalent increase in government spending!). The central bank proposed such a measure and IMF staff also urged the desirability of action along these lines but the government effectively vetoed this and decided that the gains should go to the farmers. The word 'effectively' is used here because the government did introduce a nominal export tax in the 1977 budget but this was (a) too late and (b) designed to leave most of the gains in the hands of the farmers and raised only derisory revenues.[15] It was, in fact, a personal decision of the late President Kenyatta that virtually all proceeds should be passed on to the farmers; Finance Minister Kibaki was faced with important party elections at the time and was content to go along with that decision.

This decision led directly to the unsustainable upsurge in imports of 1977–78 revealed in Table 5.2 and fathered the payments crisis of 1978. While it is true that the government did not increase its own bank borrowing in this period, it actually took measures to stimulate the expansion of bank credit to the private sector in 1977, instead of raising banks' reserve ratios to minimise the impact of the swollen incomes of the coffee and tea farmers on aggregate demand. Thus, between end-1976 and end-1978, while the foreign assets of the banking system went up by nearly half, total domestic credit was also allowed to rise by 67%. Lacking experience in such matters and caught off-balance by the speed and size of the world price rises, the government during this period neglected the basic tenets of economic management and compounded the difficulties emanating from the world economy. As the Central Bank of Kenya (1981, p. 34) has since stated, the lesson of this episode is that 'next time a bonanza of the 1976 and 1977 magnitude occurs, the authorities would be well advised to pay out the resulting incomes to society gradually in an orderly manner rather than in one season as was the case at that time'.

(c) The influence of structure

While we have chosen to concentrate largely on the period of most acute difficulties, beginning 1974, even before then there were signs of a gradual deterioration. The World Bank (1975) drew attention to these and made projections showing a large and probably unsustainable financing gap for the second half of the 1970s. Underlying this trend was the indifferent performance of the export sector. While the total value of exports tended to rise more rapidly for Kenya than for ldcs as a whole, this was entirely due to favourable prices and the volume of exports scarcely grew at all (Ibrahim, 1980). The official index of export volumes stood in 1980 at 119 with 1970 = 100, which implies an annual growth of 1.7% and may be compared with the 4.4% growth rate of GDP over the same period. The export sector hence contributed a diminishing share of total GDP during the 1970s.

Similarly little success was achieved with the long-standing government policy of export diversification. Since the oil refinery came on stream in the mid-1960s there has been no major addition to the country's exports and Ikiara (1981, Table 14) has shown that an index of export concentration has shown no sign of declining since Independence and may have been rising.

We should also pay attention to the performance of the agricultural and industrial sectors as they also have a potent influence on the longer-term payments situation. In fact, the ability of agriculture to participate rather fully in overall growth during the first decade or so of Independence meant that Kenya, unlike several of her neighbours, had little normal need to import staple foodstuffs and, indeed, was usually a net exporter (Maitha *et al.* 1978, p. 3). Since 1974, however, agriculture has been growing only slowly (value added actually meant down in 1979 and 1980) and food imports have assumed increasing importance. To a considerable extent (especially in 1974–75 and 1979–80), this deterioration was caused by adverse weather but, even so, it is clear that the underlying trend is not strongly upward.

The industrialisation that has occurred since Independence has also influenced the payments situation. It has reduced Kenya's dependence on imported consumer goods (Hazlewood, 1979, pp. 71–76) although many of these import-substituting industries are themselves heavily reliant upon imported inputs and capital equipment – a reliance that may even be growing over time (Ikiara, 1981, Table 7). While a significant part of total exports is of manufactures and a good deal of industrial output is exported, the statistics on this are dominated, perhaps distorted, by sales of an oil refinery which processes imported crude and generates only modest local value-added. If petroleum products are excluded, a little under 8% of total maufacturing output was exported in 1979.[16] To some extent, this small proportion was caused by the collapse of the East African Community in 1977 and Tanzania's closure of her frontier with Kenya, but analysts have pointed to the dangers of inefficiency created by the often generous provision of protection from competing imports and have expressed doubts, therefore, about the international competitive potential of the country's manufacturing industries (Hopcraft, 1972). Both the IMF and World Bank have been particularly forceful in pointing to the inefficiencies created by a rather undiscriminating use of import controls as a way of providing protection to local industry. Underlying these aspects of productive performance, of course, is a structure of incentives. The sluggish export performance suggests that the relative rigidity of the exchange rate has not been sufficiently compensated by export subsidies. Agricultural performance has been affected by the generally adverse trend in the domestic terms of trade between the agricultural and non-agricultural sectors and by the large-scale outflow of investible resources from the former to the latter (Sharpley, 1981). Industrial efficiency has been particularly affected by the excesses and arbitrariness of the system of protection (Westcott, 1981).

But while it is clear that the structural factors just summarised cannot fail to influence the balance of payments they have probably played a minor role in the wild swings that have occurred since 1974. Structure helps us understand the underlying trend but not the fluctuations, which have been dominated by the exogenous and monetary factors already surveyed.

III. EXPLAINING DOMESTIC DISEQUILIBRIA

As was shown in Part I, there was a destabilisation of domestic activity from about 1973 so we turn now to examine the cause of this. While concentrating largely on the inflation of this period, we commence with a summary examination of the sources of fluctuations in the growth of GDP.

Fluctuations in the growth of GDP

Under this heading, the greatest interest centres on the slump of 1974–76 (when the GDP growth rate fell to about $3\frac{1}{2}$% p.a., implying static per capita incomes) and the rather remarkable recovery of 1977– 78 (when growth rate averaged nearly 8% p.a.). There was another downturn in 1979–80, during which years there was a small decline in average per capita incomes. Most of these events have already been analysed by Maitha *et al.* (1978, pp. 31–34), with the present writer as one of the authors, and it may therefore suffice to summarise their main conclusions, modified in the light of more recent information. It is suggested that:

(a) The 1975–76 slump was partly the time-lagged effect of greatly increased import surpluses, which absorbed a large amount of domestic demand.

(b) This was reinforced by the lagged monetary effects of the deterioration in the balance of payments, with an expansion in domestic credit being substantially offset by losses in the foreign assets of the banking system, resulting in an expansion of money supply well below the expansion of current-price monetary GDP in 1974–75.

(c) These depressants originating in the world economy coincided in 1974 and 1976 with drought conditions at home. This seriously held back the expansion of agriculture, independently of the slump in the remainder of the economy.

(d) The recovery of 1977–78 was also much affected by trends on the world economy, in particular the boom in world coffee and tea prices. As we have already seen, the export boom much improved the balance of payments on current account, although a very large deficit reappeared in 1978. The improvements of 1976–77 reduced the deflationary drag exerted by the former import surpluses and, with domestic credit still expanding, was associated with a rapid monetary expansion which, whatever its negative effects, did release the economy from any monetary constraint that may have existed.

(e) These sources of recovery were reinforced in 1976–77 by renewed but short-lived agricultural expansion, largely in response to better rainfall.

(f) Given the deflationary effects of the large payments deficits, a resulting slow-down in monetary expansion and actual reductions in real agricultural value-added, it is surprising that the economy as a whole did not decline more steeply into recession in 1979–80. Modern sector growth held up quite well. Nevertheless, overall GDP growth in 1980 was well below the expansion rate of the population.

The fluctuations of these years are thus seen as resulting from a combination of the income and monetary effects of external world forces, combined with domestic credit policies and the random effects of changing weather conditions.

Sources of inflation: (a) imported inflation

As was shown in Figure 5.1, consumer prices, after a long period of relative stability, moved abruptly into double-figure inflation during 1973 and remained there for virtually all the remainder of the period. While not denying the presence of domestic factors, the government has consistently emphasised rising import prices as the chief causes of inflation, so we may begin by examining the likely impact of this factor. Here again we build upon the methodology employed in Maitha *et al*. (1978, p. 37).

In seeking to establish the impact of import prices on the lower-income consumer price index the key fact is that this index has a small import content.[17] Use of the inverted matrix of an input–output table for Kenya in 1971 yields the result that the weight of direct *and indirect* imports in this index is only 0.14. Multiplying the official index of import prices by this coefficient gives an approximate estimate of the contribution of rising import prices to general inflation, summarised in Table 4. Not surprisingly, 1974–75 emerges as the period in which imports had the strongest effect, although even then they accounted for only a little over a quarter of the total. In several years of rather rapid inflation (1976–78) the influence of rising import prices was only minor, implying that we must look to other factors as our chief explanatory variables. These results are consistent with those of Adongo (1975). Using the GDP deflator as his measure of inflation he found for 1971–77 that import prices did not yield a statistically significant explanation of domestic inflation, although it had been significant during the low-inflation 1960s.

It could reasonably be objected that calculations of this kind greatly underestimate the influence of imports by neglecting the dynamic forces at work. If there were a strong propagation mechanism, for example trade unions and other pressure groups powerful enough to protect their members from the effects of higher import prices by securing larger incomes in compensation, the initial impulse from the outside world would be magnified and could lead to a self-sustaining inflation. There is little evidence of any such process in Kenya at this time, however. Partly as an anti-inflationary device and partly to create new employment, the government embarked upon a policy of wage restraint which was so effective that the real value of average wage-earnings was cut by 8% in 1973–75, the period in which import prices were rising most rapidly (Killick, 1981, Fig. 1, p. 15). Even in 1980 real earnings were still nearly 6% below the 1973 level. If there was a propagation mechanism at work in Kenya it certainly was not operating through the labour market. There may, however, have been some such effect as a result of expenditure switching away from imports in favour of local goods and services.

Table 5.4   Contribution of Import Prices to Consumer Price Inflation in Kenya, 1973–80

	Increase in CPI (%)[a] (1)	Increase in import prices, lagged (%)[b] (2)	col. (2) multiplied by .14 (3)	col. (3) as % of col. (1) (4)
1973	10.2	15.7	2.2	22
1974	18.4	34.3	4.8	26
1975	19.3	36.6	5.1	27
1976	13.0	15.9	2.2	17
1977	16.7	11.8	1.7	10
1978	15.7	6.7	0.9	6
1979	7.9	10.8	1.5	19
1980	14.0	24.0	3.4	14

Sources: Kenya, *Economic Surveys* and *Statistical Abstracts*.

Notes: a Changes in Nairobi lower-income consumer price index, calculated from averages of quarterly data.
  b Lagged by approximately six months by taking the mean value of the import price index in the current and previous years.

The obvious next step is to explore the behaviour of monetary variables. Indeed, many monetarists would deny the legitimacy of the exercise illustrated in Table 5.4 on the grounds that higher import prices would be compensated by falls in other prices if the supply of money were restricted to a sufficient extent. Even if we reject this on the grounds that prices are sticky downwards and that so restrictive a policy was neither feasible nor desirable, it is still worth investigating whether the large residual of inflation not directly explained by import prices was caused by excessive monetary expansion at home.

Sources of inflation: (b) monetary factors

First, there is the question of how a monetary explanation of the inflation might be reconciled with the monetarist interpretations of the balance of payments discussed earlier. According to the monetary theory of the balance of payments, excess money balances result in additional imports rather than higher domestic prices. An increase in domestic credit (or in the high-powered money base) is expected to lead to corresponding reductions in foreign reserves, leaving total money supply at approximately its trend value. This is the rationale for concentrating on domestic credit, rather than total money supply, as the key policy variable for the management of the balance of payments. In practice, however, imported goods are only imperfect substitutes for locally-produced goods and services, so that unwanted money balances are likely to operate jointly on the volume of imports and domestic prices. Moreover, while the Kenyan experience has shown a clear inverse relationship between changes in reserves and domestic credit (or the domestic component of the money base), this has not been of a one-for-one nature. In all years in which foreign assets diminished, domestic credit rose by a larger amount and in some of the years in which foreign assets increased, domestic credit increased too, leading to large increases in money supply. It is therefore appropriate to investigate the behaviour of the money supply in our attempts to explain the inflation of those years.

Table 5.5 summarises data on the growth of GDP and money supply during the period under investigation. In addition to the direct influence of import prices, we hypothesise that the rate of inflation will be inversely related to the real growth of the economy[18] and positively related to the growth of money supply (which is lagged six months in Table 5.5). We thus expect inflation to be greatest when the expansion of money supply much exceeds the real growth of GDP. Column 5 of the table shows there to have been particularly large excess increases in money supply in 1973, 1976 and 1977, with substantial excesses also in 1974 and 1978. 1973 was the year in which inflation first emerged as a problem, which this evidence suggests was initiated by a combination

Table 5.5   Increases in GDP, consumer prices and money supply in Kenya, 1973–80 (% increase over previous year)

	Constant-price GDP (1)	Current-price GDP (2)	Consumer price index (3)	Money supply lagged[a] (4)	col. 4 minus col. 1 (5)
1973	6.5	16.0	10.2	25.5	19.0
1974	4.8	20.4	18.4	16.2	11.4
1975	1.2	11.6	19.3	6.4	5.2
1976	5.7	23.1	13.0	22.3	16.7
1977	9.0	28.4	16.7	47.4	38.4
1978	6.6	9.0	15.7	19.0	12.4
1979	4.1	10.7	7.9	11.1	7.0
1980	2.4	12.2	14.0	9.7	7.3

Sources: Kenya, *Economic Surveys* and *Statistical Abstracts*; Central Bank of Kenya, *Economic and Financial Review*.
Note: [a] Lagged by six months, e.g. 1973 entry refers to increase between June 1972 and June 1973.

of excess money creation (Table 5.5) and the influence of rising import prices (Table 5.4).[19] The influence of import prices was also apparent in 1974 but the further rapid expansion in money supply was probably the major source of the continuing inflation. In 1975, however, the increase in money supply was much more moderate but proportionately less demand was absorbed by imports and this plus the impact of import prices prevented inflation from falling. The years 1976–78 are those in which the monetary expansion was at its peak and they were also years of further rapid price rises. However, in 1977–78 a substantial part of the inflationary potential of the excess money creation was absorbed by the balance of payments, as was seen earlier, with Table 5.2 recording massive increases in the import bill in both years. A moderation in monetary expansion during 1979 was accompanied by slowing inflation despite a reduced import bill; and the acceleration of 1980 is particularly baffling, given both the continuing moderation in money supply growth and the huge import surplus of that year. The work by Adongo (1978) cited earlier confirmed the general importance of monetary factors. For 1971–77 changes in money supply, lagged two years, provided his strongest explanatory variables, significant at the 99% level. However, our work does not support a two-year lag, possibly because we are seeking to explain a different price index.

We saw earlier that G&R's monetary analysis of the balance of payments placed heavy emphasis on domestic sources of monetary expansion, especially credit to the government, so we should enquire into the sources of the monetary growth recorded in Table 5.5. In fact, during the three years of the most rapid money creation (1973, 1976 and

1977) the foreign assets of the banking system increased, so the balance of payments added an important monetary impulse of its own. This was particularly the case, of course, during the coffee/tea boom. But this does not mean that domestic credit was blameless. From 1974 onwards there were major increases in domestic credit. There was a case for credit expansion in 1974–75 to offset the deflationary influences then in operation, and in September 1974 an IMF report expressed concern that credit policies had become too restrictive. During 1976–77, however, there was no attempt to cut back on credit in a counter-cyclical manner to offset the monetary effects of the commodity boom. In 1976 a monetary contraction emanating from reductions in international reserves was swamped by a very large rise in domestic credit; the same was true to a lesser extent in 1980.

As can be seen from Table 5.5, three-quarters of the total increase in domestic credit went to the private sector with the other quarter being borrowed by the central government. Only in the 1974/75, 1978/79 and 1980/81 fiscal years were there large amounts of deficit financing. On the other hand, the statistics in Table 5.6 do tend to understate the importance of government borrowing because, unlike that of the private sector, much of it took forms which added to the reserve asset base of the banking system and thus had a potential money-multiplier effect. This was most obviously so with borrowings from the central bank which accounted for the bulk of the increase in lending to government. It can also be seen, from column (4), that lending to the government grew more rapidly by comparison with the private sector. Even so, it would clearly be easy to exaggerate the contribution of deficit financing to the monetary expansion of these years.

Table 5.6   Composition of increases in domestic bank credit in Kenya, 1973–80 (K£ million and % p.a.)

Borrowers	Amount of credit as at: end-1973 (1)	end-1980 (2)	Increase over period (3)	Growth rate (4)
1. Central government (net) of which:	23.90	165.97	142.07	31.9%
(a) from central bank	(–4.80)	(101.15)	(105.95)	—
(b) from commercial banks	(28.70)	(64.82)	(36.12)	—
2. Other public sector	18.77	26.02	7.25	4.8%
3. Private sector	150.23	587.93	437.70	21.5%
4. TOTALS	192.90	779.92	587.02	22.1%

Source: Central Bank of Kenya, *Annual Report*, 1981.

Sources of inflation (c) structural factors
We should finally examine the influence of the productive structure on
the inflationary process. The chief influence of this has, in fact, already
been discussed under the heading of imported inflation. Had it been
less open and less reliant upon imported energy it is no doubt true that
the economy would have been less vulnerable to the effects of world
inflation. On the other hand, it was shown in chapter M2 that there is
nothing intrinsically inflationary about trade dependence and this is
supported by the absence of significant inflation in Kenya prior to
1973.

More generally, it can be said of the productive structure that during
the 1960s and into the 1970s it demonstrated an impressive ability to
combine rapid and sustained economic growth with price stability.
Leaving aside the element of imported inflation, it would be implaus-
ible to hold that the sudden emergence of an inflationary problem in
1973 could be explained by the nature of the productive structure, for
that changes only slowly. The relatively good agricultural performance
of the first decade after Independence was a major factor in the stability
of the earlier years. Even since 1974, when agriculture has grown
slowly, food prices have not set the inflationary pace for more than brief
periods. With December 1972 = 100, the food price component of the
Nairobi lower-income consumer price index stood at 297 in June 1981,
against 301 for all items taken together.

Conclusions on domestic disequilibria
As in the earlier analysis of the balance of payments, the foregoing
implicitly rejects the idea that Kenya's domestic disequilibria can be
satisfactorily explained by any single cause. The income and monetary
effects of transactions with the outside world and trends in domestic
credit creation have emerged as important explanatory variables, as was
also the case with the balance of payments. The vagaries of the weather
and other more temporary factors also played their part from time to
time.

To those who are tempted, as the government is, to blame most of the
problems on the outside world, we have shown that government deficit
financing and large increases in credit to the private sector were almost
certainly of greater importance in the inflation of 1973–78. But to those
who might take a strict monetarist line and argue that the influence of
imported inflation, as well as the more domestic factors, could have
been neutralised by a more effective monetary policy, we would reply
that fiscal and monetary policies so severely deflationary as to offset
completely the effect of rising import prices would surely have imposed
economic costs larger than the costs of the inflation itself. It is thus
unlikely that such a policy would have been politically feasible. Partly

for reasons to be provided shortly, there would also have been formidable technical difficulties in the way of effective monetary action. Nevertheless, policies certainly could have been improved. The mishandling of the 1976–77 commodity boom, in particular, revealed serious weaknesses in the management of both the balance of payments and inflation.

IV. THE POSSIBILITIES OF SHORT-TERM ECONOMIC MANAGEMENT

Government attitudes to stabilisation

The criticism of the last sentence may be misplaced, however, in its implicit assumption that stabilisation was among the government's prime objectives. In fact, if we attend to actions rather than public statements it is not at all clear that the government gave much priority to short-term economic management during the 1970s. One could interpret the post-1973 period as revealing a failure to come to terms with the new policy challenges posed by the emergence of financial constraints.

It is useful in this context to draw a distinction between fiscal and monetary policies which are conservative in their general thrust and policies of active economic management. King (1979, pp. 60–62) has shown, for example, that the Finance Minister of 1962–69, James Gichuru, pursued conservative policies designed to reduce the government's dependence on outside budgetary support, which involved tight restraints on the spending ministries and substantial increases in taxation, but that the corollary of these policies was that 'aggregate fiscal policy could not be and was not used for short term stabilisation measures' (p. 62). In 1969 Gichuru gave way as Finance Minister to Mwai Kibaki, who held the post until 1982 (also becoming Vice-President in 1979). Kibaki proved more expansionist and King (pp. 65–67) blames the 1971 budget for causing the foreign exchange crisis of that year by opting for expansion when reserves were already falling, prices had begun to rise, domestic credit was already expanding fast and there was little Keynesian-type excess capacity in the economy. The adverse consequences of this led to more cautious budgets in 1972–74, giving greater emphasis to control over government expenditure. During this period the Treasury widened the tax base and, despite the increasing difficulty of controlling the spending ministries (resulting in substantial over-runs against budget estimates), it made only modest use of borrowing from the banking system.

The first half of 1975 saw a potentially important landmark in the history of economic management with the publication of *Sessional*

Paper No. 4 of 1975 : On Economic Prospects and Policies. This was issued in response to the worsened world economic climate that had emerged with the oil crisis and attempted to state how the government intended to adjust. It could be described as the first serious public attempt to reconcile the objectives of long-run development and short-term stability, and contained explicit recognition of the desirability of using fiscal policy as an instrument of stabilisation. Unfortunately, in this as in other respects, the implementation of the admirable policies set out in that document left much to be desired.[21] The budget of 1975, announced a few months after the issuance of the sessional paper, was sensible but by the 1976/77 fiscal year the beneficial effects of the coffee/tea boom were already large and the Treasury chose to exceed the credit ceilings agreed with the IMF, forfeiting access to the extended facility credit that had been negotiated in the previous year, in favour of a more expansionary budget. The result was a record budget deficit on current account, although other forms of borrowing limited the government's recourse to the banking system.

If the 1976 budget gave forewarning that the government was not serious in its statements about the use of fiscal policy for stabilisation the next one proved the point to the hilt. When it was obviously only a matter of time before world coffee and tea prices fell back to more normal levels, when the turnaround in the balance of payments was already leading to large increases in the domestic money supply and when the economy was already awash with the spending power resulting from the export boom (which the government refused to tax), the 1977 budget opted for large increases in government spending and a record amount of deficit financing.[22] The 1978 and 1979 budgets were more moderate but both could be – and were – criticised for accurately identifying the re-emergence of a balance of payments problem without proposing any solutions.[23] The new development plan issued in 1979 was criticised on the same grounds.[24] In short, if during the 1970s the government ever was serious about the importance of stabilisation it abandoned this priority as soon as the commodity boom allowed it off the hook.

There were signs, however, that the 1980s might usher in a more genuine change of attitude. In the first half of 1980 a new sessional paper was issued (Kenya, 1980) for purposes exactly analogous to the 1975 paper. Like its predecessor, it included a strong assertion of the need for more effective economic management, for measures to adjust the economy in the face of a payments constraint and other sensible things. Its specifics included the replacement of quantitative import restrictions by tariff equivalents, and the standardisation and reduction in levels of industrial protection – all designed to strengthen the ability of the manufacturing sector to achieve a better export record. A higher interest rate structure was promised, although not for the first time. The crucial question, of course, was whether these good intentions would be carried into effect and the 1980 and 1981 budgets made a good start to their implementation.[25] The programme of import liberalisation and of rationalising protection was being carried out and the interest rate structure was indeed being raised.[26] On the other hand, the government was having more modest success in carrying out its stated income policies, it was reluctant to introduce major new tax measures and, as we will see, no end was in sight to the difficulties of containing government spending.

There were other signs of change, too, for example on exchange rate policy. Since Independence and until 1980 the central bank had consistently acted as if it agreed with the first managing director of the IMF that devaluation was a form of confiscation, and had sought to 'maintain the integrity of the Kenya shilling', This it interpreted as entailing a fixed exchange rate (but not, curiously, as entailing the control of domestic credit as a safeguard against domestic inflation). There was, it is true, a 14% devaluation in October 1975, undertaken in collaboration with the Tanzanian and Ugandan governments (the three currencies were at that time fixed at par with each other as part of the East African Community arrangements) under pressure from the IMF.[27] Thereafter, by word and deed, the government set its face against the overt use of the exchange rate, even though the effect of the 1975 change was gradually eroded by differential inflation,[28] and despite the fact that the government tacitly admitted the existence of over-valuation by fiscal measures – an import duty surcharge, and export subsidy etc – which had the effects of partial devaluations.

The logic of the 1980 Sessional Paper pointed clearly to a devaluation and while in 1979–80 the government explicitly declined to employ this policy instrument, a change occurred in 1981 when there were two devaluations with a combined effect of raising the shilling price of SDRs by nearly 24%. Whether these changes reflected a fundamental change in government thinking is unclear, however, for they almost all were undertaken at the prompting of the IMF and World Bank. This was true of the second, larger, devaluation of 1981; of the interest rate changes; of import liberalisation; and of the rationalisation of industrial protection. It remained unclear, for instance, whether there would be a more active use of monetary policy in economic management than had previously been the case; and whether the commitment to stabilisation would weigh heavily enough when the government was faced with specific spending decisions attractive on their own merits but tending to widen the budgetary gap.

But whatever weaknesses there may have been in the past, it is important to keep them in proper perspective. For example, while there has been a case for currency depreciation, the official rate of exchange has never been allowed to move hugely out of line with a notional 'equilibrium' rate, as has occurred in other ldcs. Similarly, while the budget has not been used effectively as an instrument of short-run management, in other respects the fiscal record has been good.[29] While there has been a massive increase in state spending since Independence, current revenues have generally kept pace and in almost all years (including the most recent) have financed 75–80% of total spending. Budgetary reliance on external grants and loans is much below the immediate post-independence situation and in recent years has generally fluctuated around 10% of total spending (although this went up to an average of 15% in the 1978/79–1980/1981 fiscal years). As already shown, large-scale financing of deficits by bank borrowing has been confined to a few years (mainly the mid-1970s, 1978/79 and 1980/81). International comparisons of tax effort among ldcs show Kenya with an above-average and improving record,[30] and another comparison shows the overall budgetary deficit to have been slightly better in recent years than the African average.[31] Kenya could not be accused of the fiscal irresponsibility which has marked some other countries.

Similarly, while we have criticised the weak implementation of the 1975 sessional paper, it would be wrong to leave the impression that nothing has been done to adjust the economy to the post-1973 economic realities. There has been useful improvements in the structure of price incentives, taxation, government spending and industrial protection. The government has proved itself more willing than some to increase its taxation of petroleum products, and the indications are that its policies are resulting in some diminution of the economy's dependence on oil-based energy sources. Moreover, the signs are of a better implementation record on the 1980 sessional paper.

The main criticism, therefore, is not that the government has acted irresponsibly but rather that the fiscal and monetary authorities have failed to adapt to the need for more effective short-run economic management necessitated by the financial constraints which first emerged in the earlier 1970s and re-emerged a few years later. The stabilisation of an economy such as Kenya's is bound to be most difficult, however, so we turn next to examine some of the technical difficulties which the authorities would encounter in attempting this task.

Problems of stabilisation
The earlier analyses of the causes of the inflationary and balance of payments disequilibria placed considerable stress on the influence of unpredictable changes in world prices, as well as the more secondary

influence of weather conditions, with the strength of external factors particularly large on the balance of payments in 1974–77 and again in 1979–80. Were these exogenous forces to remain as unruly in the future as they were then, it must be doubted whether stabilisation would be an attainable objective, although the relative stability of an extended period prior to 1973–74 indicates that exogenous disturbances are not inevitably unmanageable. Nevertheless, to maintain equilibrium in such an economy must be a demanding task necessitating the use of powerful policy instruments with which to counter the exogenous forces. How potent are the conventional fiscal and monetary instruments of economic management in Kenya?

As a first approach we can enquire into the extent to which fiscal variables are sufficiently predictable to be capable of short-run manipulation. A study was undertaken of the eight budgets of 1973/74 to 1980/81, comparing actual outcomes with the values that were predicted in the budgets, with the results summarised in Table 5.7. Column (1) provides a measure of the extent to which actual outcomes differed from the budgeted amounts and columns (2) and (3) together reveal the direction of bias in the budgets.

Take variability first. All the items show significant average deviations of actual from budgeted values. As might be expected, the residual balances (entries 3, 6 and 7) display the largest deviations from budgeted estimates. Strong systematic biases are also revealed. On current account both revenue and expenditure is generally under-estimated, but the absolute difference is largest with expenditures, so that there is a persistent tendency to over-estimate the current account surplus (line 3). External aid almost always falls short of budgeted amounts, but the potential for non-bank domestic borrowing tends to be under-estimated, as can be inferred from a comparison of lines 6 and 7. Interestingly, there is no particular bias in the estimates of bank borrowing, although the proportionate extent of deviation from budgeted values is very large.

Particular interest attaches to this last fact, for bank borrowing by the government is generally regarded as the chief fiscal variable available to be manipulated for short-term management, and is the main ingredient of the domestic component (D) of the high-powered money base (H) featured in the G&R model (see page 175). But since it is a residual, meeting whatever deficit (or absorbing whatever surplus) happens to result when all the other entries in the budget have been completed, can it rightly be treated as a *policy instrument* at all? As one Kenyan adviser complained it is a 'residual of a residual', ie, that part of residual item 6 which is left over after the Treasury has made its decisions about non-bank borrowing. Since the total deficit to be filled by domestic borrowing has a coefficient of variation of 259% and bank

Table 5.7   *Variability and bias in Kenyan budgets, 1973/74–1980/81*

| | Coefficient of variation[a] (1) | direction of bias[b] | |
		Over estimate (2)	Under estimate (3)
1. Current revenue	13.2	1	7
2. Recurrent expenditure	12.5	0	8
3. Current account surplus	119.3	6	2
4. Capital expenditure	39.6	5	3
5. Receipts of external grants and loans	28.6	6	2
6. Remaining deficit for domestic financing	258.7	2	6
7. Deficit for financing by bank borrowing	152.5	4	4

Sources: Central Bank of Kenya, *Annual Reports*; Kenya, *Economic Surveys*.

Notes: [a] In percentages of original budget estimates.
         [b] Number of observations.

borrowing of 153%, it is not at all clear that manipulation of deficit financing is a practical way of trying to maintain the macro balance of the economy.

To this it can reasonably be retorted, on the other hand, that it should be possible to improve the accuracy of budget forecasting, as the IMF staff has urged. A reduction in the eccentricity of the tax on company profits, which yields almost all its revenue in the fourth quarter of the fiscal year, would ease the task of prediction and reduce the present large degree of seasonality in government revenues. Imperfect information inevitably means that there will be some – possibly quite large – deviations from budget forecasts but the biases revealed in Table 5.7 are presumably capable of reduction because other African governments have managed to avoid the severe sources of unpredictability which characterise Kenya. It should be possible for the Treasury to adjust for the tendency to under-estimate revenues and current spending; and to correct for the over-estimation of current savings, capital spending and aid receipts. Were this achieved, it would undoubtedly bring greater predictability to items 6 and 7 of the table. Whether there would be sufficient improvement for deficit financing to become a practical instrument of stabilisation policy must nevertheless remain in question, although this has been the chief item upon which the IMF has focused in Stand-by negotiations.

There are further difficulties, concerning the transmission mechanism between deficit financing on the one hand and the performance indicators it is intended to influence, on the other: the GDP growth rate, the balance of payments and the price level. For one thing, variations in government indebtedness to the banks may be offset by contra-variations in credit to the private sector, as tended to happen in 1974, 1975 and 1978. It is thus necessary to look at the total credit scene. There is also the question of the magnitude of the impact and of time lags. King (1979, p. 100) expresses doubts about the practicability of a workable contra-cyclical stabilisation policy (a) because his financial flows model indicated that 'budgetary policy has a relatively small effect upon economic activity at the best of times' and (b) because of 'the eighteen months delay between the Kenyan authorities' decision to borrow in 1970 and the impact of this decision on the economy'. In this context, we should also remember Adongo's finding of a two-year time-lag between changes in money supply and the price level.

When we turn from fiscal to more purely monetary factors, there are further technical complications, of a type already examined generally in chapter M3. As was noted earlier, the Polak-type model utilised by King treats the marginal propensity to import (m) and the marginal income-velocity of circulation (k) as constants. The G&R model analogously required stable relationships between the money supply, on the one hand, and time (as a proxy for income?) and high-powered money on the other, as well as stable elasticities of demand for money with respect to prices and interest rates. Calculations of the coefficient of variation of m and k yield the following results (as % of the mean values for each period):

	m	k
1968–71	8.3	4.7
1972–80	12.1	10.6

The estimate for k can be compared with a similar calculation by Park (1970, Table 1, col. V_3) for 14 ldcs which had an average coefficient of variation of 7.1% in 1953–68. On the basis of his estimates Park was pessimistic about the practicability of monetary models for short-term forecasting and management, yet the Kenyan figure for the 1972–80 period is half as large again. The variability of m is even greater, of course.[32] It is true that the above calculations are for the *average* propensity and velocity, whereas King merely assumes constant *marginal* values, but it is surely the case that the variability revealed above is also inconsistent with assumptions of constant marginal values.

This leaves us to examine the stability of the money-multiplier, b. This was investigated by Bolnick (1975a) for 1967–73 who concluded that:

(1) Variations in the 'money multiplier' on a quarter-to-quarter basis have been relatively large, implying instability of the behavioural parameters affecting the money stock.

(2) The major source of variation in the money multiplier has been com-

mercial bank liquidity behaviour. Our analysis suggests that the liquid asset ratio is neither fully predictable nor fully controllable . . ..

Bolnick's analysis thus casts doubt on the feasibility of effective monetary policy but G&R (1979, p. 27) obtain less negative results. Utilising annual (as against quarterly) data they derive a money supply function which provides a good statistical explanation, with the high-powered money base and a time trend as the independent variables (R^2 = 0.98). They think their result is consistent with Bolnick's because, by using annual data, they abstract from intra-year variations and 'it is well known that in most countries the money multiplier is much more unstable in the short than in the long run. But relevant for policy is the long-run stability observed in our data.' This latter point is questionable however. In the context of economic management (and negotiations with the IMF!) it is most important to be able to predict for the short-run.

We must conclude this section, therefore, on a note of scepticism concerning the feasibility of effective short-term stabilisation. Against the potentially large exogenous destabilising forces are arrayed a set of fiscal and monetary instruments of dubious reliability. It is unclear:

- whether the government could be in a position to manipulate the volume of its deficit financing for stabilisation purposes in more than a very approximate manner;
- how much impact deficit financing will have on total domestic credit and/or money supply;
- whether the key parameters are sufficiently well behaved to permit the short-run forecasting accuracy needed for stabilisation policy;
- whether the time lags are short and predictable enough to allow the manipulation of instrument variables to achieve desired, short-run macroeconomic results.

It seems clear that there can be little hope of effective 'fine tuning' in such circumstances and that the most that can be hoped for is a rough-and-ready avoidance of the worst extremes of economic fluctuations.

Having thus laid an analytical foundation we turn next to examine the role of the International Monetary Fund in the quest for stabilisation in Kenya.

V. RELATIONS WITH THE INTERNATIONAL MONETARY FUND

A number of considerations make a study of Kenya's relations with the IMF of more than normal interest. First, being wholly dependent on imported supplies Kenya has been one of the countries most seriously affected by the large relative rise in crude oil prices and by the oscillations in world economic conditions associated with that.[33] Second, even though the economic philosophy of the government is closer to that of the Fund than is true of many ldcs, being essentially pragmatic, conservative and market-oriented, Kenya–IMF relations have had a troubled recent history and it is thus particularly interesting to enquire into the reasons for this. Third, while we have seen that Kenya has had major payments difficulties since 1974, it is not a country which has allowed economic conditions to deteriorate dramatically before a last-ditch recourse to the Fund, as demonstrated by its good Euromarket credit rating. In general, the government has been fairly prompt in commencing negotiations and might therefore expect to have received more favourable policy conditions than the late-appliers. Finally, Kenya has been the subject of collaboration between the IMF and the World Bank, and was the first country to reach an agreement under the Fund's extended facility (EFF) which came into operation in 1975.

Financial flows between Kenya and the Fund are summarised in Table 5.8. As can be observed, credits were used under the 1974 and 1975 Oil Facilities and substantial use was made of the Compensatory Financing Facility in 1976 and 1979. There were also credits from the higher-conditionality facilities recorded in lines 2–4 of the table in 1975 and 1979–81 and it is on these that we focus below. Line 9 reveals significant net inflows from the Fund in 1974–76 and 1979–81, with a relatively large net return flow in 1977. Lines 13–15 record the balance of certain other receipts as at mid-1980, not included in the remainder of the table.

What follows will concentrate on the higher-conditionality credits of 1975–76 and 1979–81, most notably the EFF credit of SDR67.2 million (equivalent at that time to K£29 million) intended to be drawn down during 1975–78, and two-year upper-tranche Stand-by credits negotiated successively in 1979 and 1980. These were of SDR122.45 million and SDR241.5 million (K£59 and K£117 millions) respectively, which latter amount was equivalent to approximately 350% of Kenya's IMF quota. We choose this focus because these are the credits which raise the issues of economic management and Fund conditionality which are the prime concern of this study.

The 1975 Extended Facility Agreement
The EFF was established in September 1974 to give medium-term assistance to countries in 'special circumstances of balance of payments difficulty' whose solution would require a longer period than that for which normal credit tranche facilities are available.[34] Requests for EFF credits may be approved 'in support of comprehensive programmes

Table 5.8   Financial flows between Kenya and the IMF, 1974–81[a] (K£ million)

	1974	1975	1976	1977	1978	1979	1980	1981
Gross inflows:								
1. Reserve tranche	5.4	—	—	—	3.2	—	—	—
2. Credit tranches	—	5.8[b]	—	—	—	8.4	8.1	8.1
3. Supplementary facility	—	—	—	—	—	—	20.8	9.8
4. Extended facility	—	3.7[c]	—	—	—	—	—	—
5. Oil facility	14.0	13.9	1.5	—	—	—	—	—
6. Compensatory facility	—	—	11.6	—	—	33.3	—	—
7. TOTAL GROSS INFLOWS	19.4	23.4	13.1	—	3.2	41.7	29.0	17.9
8. REPAYMENTS (repurchases)	—	–5.8[b]	–5.1	–18.1	–1.2	–14.8	–3.4	–4.2
9. NET INFLOW	19.4	17.6	8.0	–18.1	2.0	26.9	25.6	13.7
10. Use of Fund credit (outstanding balance at year-end)[d]	14	33	41	23	25	52	74	104
11. Quota (year-end)	21	23	23	23	33	33	50	62
12. Credit as % of quota	67%	144%	177%	100%	75%	157%	148%	169%

Other receipts as at mid-1980

13. SDR allocations	14.5
14. Profits from gold sales	2.8
15. Loans from Trust Fund (gross)	22.6

Sources: IMF, *Annual Reports* and *International Financial Statistics.*

Notes: a Converted from SDRs at the year-end exchange rate. There were no transactions of the type recorded in lines 1–6 prior to 1974.

b A net credit tranche drawing of K£5.8 million was both effected and paid back during 1975.

c During this year an Extended Fund credit totalling K£29 million was agreed, intended to be drawn during 1975–78.

d Year-by-year changes in this line do not necessarily agree with line 9 due to exchange rate changes and minor adjuctments.

that include policies . . . required to correct structural imbalances . . .'
Credits may be drawn over a 3-year period. They were originally
repayable over a maximum of 8 years, since extended to 10 years.

Kenya's request for assistance was the first to be received and
approved (in July 1975) under this scheme and was thus regarded as of
particular interest. The credit was approved on the grounds that the

economy was 'suffering serious payments imbalances relating to structural maladjustments in production and trade and where price and cost distortions have been widespread'. The request was in support of a three-year programme covering the 1975/76 to 1977/78 fiscal years, spelled out in the sessional paper on economic prospects and policies referred to earlier (Kenya, 1975). According to Bhatia and Rothman (1975, p. 40 – hereafter B&R). 'The program reflects, in part, extensive discussions by the Kenyan Government with staff members of the Fund and of the World Bank who have made coordinated policy recommendations to the Government.' The credit was payable in six half-yearly instalments, with the bulk of the money becoming available during 1976 and 1977, subject to six monthly reviews of progress. It was repayable over a maximum of eight years. Performance criteria were established, satisfaction of which would govern the government's continued access to the credit. The total value of the credit of SDR67.2 million was then equivalent to 140% of Kenya's IMF quota. At approximately the same time, the World Bank approved a programme loan for $30 million (K£11 million).

Given that this was the first use of the EFF, particular interest attaches to the extent to which the policy conditions for this credit differed from those associated with conventional Stand-by credits. Unfortunately, different answers are provided, according to the source of information. Two facts can be asserted with some assurance, however. First, the existence of a medium term adjustment programme, of the type set out in the 1975 sessional paper, was a pre-condition for agreement on an EFF credit. The Fund essay describing the agreement (B&R) includes an account of the longer-term factors contributing to the payments difficulties (although it rather remarkably fails to mention the payments impact of higher oil prices and other exogenous factors analysed above) and gave prominence to the programme set out in the sessional paper. The paper sent by the IMF staff to the Executive Board recommending the credit similarly spent 16 pages on medium-term developments and policies, against only 3 on the financial programme.

Second, however, it appears to be the case that the Fund staff were content to play a largely passive role in the formulation of the sessional paper's policies for structural adjustment, although they did press for a tariff reform in support of a restructuring of the manufacturing sector, for more credit to agriculture and some other measures. The World Bank made most of the running, however, initiating the idea that the government should prepare a paper in support of its application for a programme loan. The Bank particularly pushed for the inclusion of measures that would limit the (previously very rapid) growth of spending on education, increase the share of government spending on agriculture, and introduce a more active use of interest rates (although in the event the paper was notably non-committal on this latter point). The IMF and World Bank co-ordinated their respective contributions and the Bank's decision to approve the programme loan was influenced by the government's willingness also to comply with the additional conditions accompanying the EFF credit.

It is more difficult to provide a firm judgement about the extent to which the substance of the conditionality for this credit differed from the policy conditions normally attached to short-term Stand-bys. While it probably incorporated a less abrupt (and hence lower cost) adjustment, at a formal level the similarities appear greater than the differences. As explained in the companion volume, letters of intent from member governments to the Fund identity certain 'performance criteria', satisfaction of which governs continuing access to the credit. The performance criteria written into Kenya's 1975 EFF agreement related only to government borrowing from the banking system and to total domestic credit, both of which were restricted to specified ceilings. In these respects, the agreement was identical to an ordinary Stand-by. And, on at least some descriptions, when it came to the crunch of detailed negotiations it was as if the government were negotiating a Stand-by: demand management primarily through credit restrictions with the usual provisions concerning performance criteria, six-monthly reviews, and so forth – although admittedly set within a 3-year framework – and with the detailed discussions largely focusing on the rival merits of government and Fund forecasts for the 1975/76 budget and the resulting requirements for deficit financing. The Fund was thus apparently emphasising policies of short-run demand management to deal with problems which the Fund itself identified as longer-term structural weaknesses. As shown earlier, they were also problems substantially created by external forces entirely beyond the control of the Kenyan authorities.

However, these criticisms should be qualified by two other considerations. This credit, it must be remembered, was the first to be negotiated under the EFF arrangements and it was understandable that the Fund should tread carefully in consenting to major innovations in its conditionality. Further, the nature of the negotiations was no doubt conditioned by the fact that an acceptable medium term adjustment programme was already in place. Had this not been the case, discussions between the Fund and the government would probably have been taken up more with putting such a programme together and would hence have appeared rather less like a Stand-by negotiation. The fact stands, however, that the performance criteria were the strictly conventional ones of credit control and we should also bear in mind the view within the Fund itself, reported in chapter M6 that the EFF generally has not in fact represented any large change in the substance of conditionality.

Although it seems that the Fund took limited interest in the contents of the sessional paper, had it done so and if the EFF credit would not have been agreed in the absence of some such medium-term policy commitments, it follows that any such conditions were *additional* to the Fund's conventional short-term monetary conditions. Careful reading of the Board decision setting up the EFF confirms this because,

> a member making a request for an extended arrangement must, *in addition to* presenting a program 'setting forth the objectives and policies for the whole medium-term period . . .' present 'a detailed statement of the policies and measures for the first twelve months . . . of the program' (B & R, p. 41, our italics).

This new form of support provided by the EFF, while undoubtedly valuable, thus provided an occasion for increasing the scope of Fund conditionality and by retaining the conventional demand management programmes for which the Fund is well known it places an exceedingly ambiguous gloss on the extent to which the Fund's policies were adapted to take account of structural or supply-side considerations, or of externally caused disequilibria.

Whether the actual credit ceilings written into the agreement were reasonable is a question taken up shortly but we should also ask about the adequacy of the EFF credit in relation to the size of Kenya's payments imbalances of that time. Relevant data are summarised in Table 5.9, from which it appears that the value of the credit was substantial in relation to past and expected future payments deficits, especially when viewed as part of a package which also included the World Bank loan, possibly increased aid from bilateral sources (which did, in fact, increase – see Maitha *et al.*, 1978, p. 45) and any additional private inflows which might result from agreement with the Fund. In

Table 5.9   Financing gaps and Kenya's EFF credit, 1974–76 (K£ million)

	Sums available from EFF[c] (1)	Actual deficit on basic balance (2)	Expected financing gap[a] (3)	EFF target[b] (4)
1974	—	41	35	—
1975	3.7	27	50	37
1976	13.0	n. app.	60	17

Sources: Kenya, 1975, p. 4 and other official sources.

Notes: [a] Expected gap after 'normal' inflows of aid and other capital.
   [b] Targeted deficit on overall balance.
   [c] A further amount of K£15.7 was scheduled to become available during 1977.

the event the EFF targets and the value of the credit itself were quickly rendered obsolete by the coffee/tea boom but what is important for present purposes is the size of the assistance in relation to the payments deficits experienced in the immediate past and anticipated at that time for the immediate future. Even taken by itself, the EFF credit would in 1976 have been equal to about half the actual previous year's deficit on basic balance, about a quarter of the government's estimate of the financing gap and nearly all of the targeted deficit on the overall balance.

As things turned out, coffee export prices began a fairly rapid rise in the second half of 1975, standing at the end of the year 69% above the June level, although it was not until April 1977 that the price peaked and it was not until 1977 that tea export prices were strongly influenced. The favourable movement in the commodity terms of trade (see Figure 5.2) took pressure off the government and probably explains why it quickly borrowed from the banks in excess of the ceiling agreed with the Fund, forfeiting continued access to the credit. This failure by the government to observe the terms of the agreement was not allowed to stand in the way of reaching new understandings at the time of the 1976 budget but by then much of the rationale for the loan had disappeared and the ceilings were again breached. This first experiment in the use of the EFF thus fizzled out. Only the initial instalment of K£3.7 million was drawn and the actual impact of the demand management package associated with it was negligible, although that was scarcely the fault of the IMF.

The 1979–81 Stand-bys

As was shown in Part I, major improvements occurred on the balance of payments in 1976–77 followed by a drastic deterioration in 1978. Towards the end of that year, the government applied for a Stand-by loan within the first credit tranche, to which, of course, it had nearly automatic access. This credit of K£8.4 million was drawn down in the first half of 1979, as recorded in Table 5.8. The government anticipated financing needs additional to this sum and thus initiated a number of further moves. First, it approached commercial banks and agreed a Eurodollar loan of $200 million (K£74 million). This was arranged prior to the budget in June 1979, although it was not signed until July, and a substantial part of it was almost immediately utilised. No policy strings were attached but the commercial terms ($1\frac{1}{2}$% above the libor rate, repayable over 7 years) were expensive.

This loan gave the government an assurance that it would not be forced into a devaluation during the politically sensitive period of a presidential election and the settling-in of the President's new Cabinet. Simultaneously, however, the government began negotiations for a two-year upper-tranche Stand-by credit of SDR122.5 million (K£59.2 million) and agreement was finalised in August 1979. Finally, negotiations were also commenced with the World Bank for loan under its new 'structural adjustment' facility, totalling $70 million (K£28 million),[35] agreement on which was finalised in February 1980. We are particularly concerned here, of course, with the Stand-by, especially because it was negotiated after the Fund had reviewed its guidelines on conditionality in March 1979 (see chapter M5). Since this review was heralded as ushering in some relaxation in the stringency of the Fund's policy conditions, it is instructive to enquire whether as a result the conditions put to the Kenyan government showed signs of a greater liberality.

It would be difficult to assert that they did. In fact, they were arguably tougher than in 1975. The programme presented by the goverment for the two-year period of the loan included provisions for improvements in tax revenues; real reductions in government recurrent and development spending in 1979/80; a 15% expansion in bank credit to the private sector; a study of the potential value of interest rate adjustments as a policy instrument (again!); a policy of wage restraint which would reduce real wages; and careful control over new additions to the external public debt. As always, however, what was of greatest importance were the items included as performance criteria. These were (a) ceilings on the net domestic assets of the central bank; (b) ceilings on net government borrowing from the banking system; (c) an 'understanding' with the Fund on exchange rate policy, to be reached by the end of 1979; and (d) another 'understanding' by the same date on the early elimination of an advance import deposit scheme which had been introduced at the end of 1978 and had proved highly effective as a means of achieving a once-for-all reduction in the volume of imports.

The import deposits scheme was, in fact, relaxed in November 1979 (which contributed to the large volume of imports experienced in 1980), and no difficulties were experienced with the agreed ceilings on the domestic assets of the central bank. An IMF report recommending a devaluation was quietly pigeonholed and the official exchange rate remained unchanged. However, the ceilings on bank credit to government proved unworkable. These were greatly exceeded during July–December 1979 and, although the government was able to reduce its indebtedness to the banks in the final three months, it was only at the very end of the fiscal year that the amount came within the agreed ceiling and the government seemingly became eligible to draw upon the credit. In retrospect, Kenya government and IMF officials recognise that the intra-year ceiling was excessively restrictive.

When in mid-1980 its bank borrowing eventually fell within the ceiling and the government sought to draw upon the credit it was astonished to be told that it was ineligible on technical grounds. The letter of intent had contained the standard undertaking not to introduce multiple currency arrangements. In his 1980 budget, however, the Minister of Finance announced certain changes intended to make the long-standing export subsidy scheme more effective. The rate of subsidy was doubled and, to speed up payments of the subsidies, its administration was to be transferred from the Customs Department to the Central Bank. The Fund was notified of the intention to make these changes and offered no objection. After they had been announced in the budget, however, the Fund's lawyers ruled that this administrative transfer (which in the event was never implemented) converted the scheme into a multiple currency arrangement and that the government thus stood in breach of its undertaking. This left a hapless Fund mission to break the news to annoyed Kenyan officials and to advise them that the best course was now to scrap the 1979 agreement and negotiate a new one. Strong views are still held by some about what was regarded as the malign influence of remote lawyers whose inflexibility revealed scant sensitivity to local problems but those opinions on this issue prevailed in Washington over the objections of the Fund mission.

The end result of these events was that the credit negotiated in 1979 was never utilised, even though there is no question that the country was faced with major payments difficulties, monetary expansion was fairly moderate and bank credit to government by the end of the fiscal year was actually lower than at the beginning. In compensation for the difficulties created by the break-down of the 1979 agreement, however, a new two-year Stand-by was quickly agreed, worth considerably more than would have been due under the 1979 agreement. The new credit was for SDR241.5 million (K£117 million) and received IMF approval in October 1980.

It was believed in official Kenyan circles that the ceilings agreed for government bank borrowing in 1980/81 were less draconian in amount and form than those for 1979/80 and, more generally, that the Fund mission displayed flexibility during negotiations, departing substantially from their initial brief in response to the case presented by Kenyan representatives. In fact, Kenyan officials suspected that the IMF mission chief was under instructions to reach an agreement at any reasonable cost: the 1980 Fund–World Bank annual meeting was imminent and it was desired to minimise allegations of Fund harshness and rigidity on policy conditions. Whether or not this is the case, members of the Executive Board in Washington expressed disquiet about what was regarded as the laxity of the policy conditions in the agreement, although it was eventually approved.

In one respect, however, the 1980 agreement incorporated a widening of the scope of conditionality, for it required the government to reach agreements with the Fund on import policy *as a performance criterion*. Specifically, this was intended to ensure the implementation of the government's policy of replacing quantitative import restrictions by tariff equivalents and represented a most interesting innovation because it is rare for the Fund to include unquantified policy commitments as performance criteria. This could be seen, perhaps, as a move in the direction of paying greater attention to medium term structural adjustment, because the import policy was seen as an important aspect of the strategy of industrial restructuring. This strategy was, in turn, the hard core of the policy conditions attached to the World Bank's February 1980 structural adjustment loan and, viewed as complementary to the Bank's conditions, the new IMF credit terms could be seen as paying greater attention to medium-term adjustment. The IMF press release announcing the 1980 credit emphasised this aspect.[36] On the other hand, in the nitty-gritty of detailed negotiations the focus was again largely on short-run credit ceilings and the underlying fiscal projections.

As regards the adequacy of these credits, what can be said is that the amounts agreed upon in 1979 and (especially) 1980 were quite large in relation to the country's payments magnitudes. Had they been fully utilised, the 1979 agreement would have provided K£59 million over two years and the 1980 agreement was for K£117 million, also over two years. These sums may be compared with the deficits recorded in columns (2) and (3) of Table 5.1 and with the government's expectation of an overall financing gap of K£139 million in the twelve months beginning July 1980. Although the increase in Kenya's quota was modest as between 1975 and the times of the 1979 and 1980 negotiations (see Table 5.8, line 11) and indeed diminished in real terms (when deflated by an index of the country's import prices), policy changes allowed the IMF to grant larger credits relative to quotas, so that the amount of assistance agreed in 1979 and 1980 was substantial relative to the likely size of the payments deficits. The assistance was still relatively short-term, however, being repayable over a maximum of five years.

In the event, the 1980 agreement proved even less workable than its 1979 forerunner. With considerable difficulty, the Kenyan Treasury managed to remain within the agreed ceiling on its bank borrowing until the first benchmark date of 31 December 1980, thus entitling it to utilise the second instalment of the credit but thereafter the amount of deficit financing far exceeded the agreed total, as can be judged from Table 5.10. That the actual level of government bank borrowing was more than double the agreed ceiling for the fiscal year as a whole was, as is candidly admitted by the Treasury, due to unforeseen government spending rather than to any intrinsic unreasonableness in the height of the ceiling. There was an unbudgeted 30% increase in civil service salaries – an increase which only partially restored a past erosion in the real value of salaries but which nevertheless was not anticipated in the 1980 budget. There were also unexpected calls on the revenues resulting from the food shortages of that year; and there were a number of other spending increases, some of which reflected inadequate expenditure control by the Treasury over other ministries.

Attempts by the government and Fund staff during the second half of 1981 to rescue the remainder of the two-year programme and to agree ceilings for 1981/82 ran into a number of difficulties and in the end it was decided to abandon that programme and to put in its place a 12-month stand-by for SDR151.5 million (K£90.5 million). This was finally approved in January 1982. It was a tougher agreement than that of 1980. The Fund was anxious to safeguard against a repetition of the 1980/81 failure. It had had similar recent experiences of agreements breaking down in several other African states and this further increased its determination to close any remaining loopholes. And the cold wind blowing from the Reagan administration, which was first felt at the 1981 IMF/World Bank annual meeting added greatly to the pressures on the Fund mission not to come back with an agreement which could be branded as 'soft'. In consequence, the Kenyans, with a major balance of payments crisis on their hands, found themselves obliged to enter into a wider range of commitments than in 1979 and 1980 – on external debt, on government spending and on import liberalisation. Moreover, the largest instalment of this credit was reserved to the end, until satisfaction of the performance criteria at the conclusion of the agreement period, thus raising the Fund's effective leverage during the full span of the agreement. It remained to be seen whether this agreement would work better than its predecessors but there seemed to this observer a probability that the government would once again be unable to stay within the agreed ceiling on government bank borrowing. The government was reluctant to introduce major revenue-raising measures so all the burden of an improved fiscal balance was falling on a limitation of expenditure that was bound to prove most difficult for the Treasury to enforce. (*Postscript*: Kenya's access to this credit was suspended by the IMF in mid-1982 partly, if not wholly, because bank credit to the government had exceeded the agreed ceiling.)

Evaluation of the credit ceilings

We have seen that bank credit to the government was a key – *the* key – performance criterion in all the higher-conditionality credits negotiated.[37] Evaluation of the policy conditions attached to these credits therefore involves forming a judgement about whether the credit ceilings were reasonable. Evidence on this issue is summarised in

Table 5.10   Targeted and actual bank credit to Kenyan government, selected years [a]

	1975/76 (1)	1976/77 (2)	1979/80 (3)	1980/81 (4)
1. Amount of additional credit during year[b] (K£m)				
(a) ceiling	17.5	30.8	45.0	53.5
(b) actual	26.6	9.5	–6.3	114.7
Ceiling as percentage of:				
2. Amount of government credit at year-beginning[c]	32	38	31	41
3. Money supply at year-beginning[c]	5.8	8.3	6.2	6.7
4. Domestic credit at year-beginning[c]	6.3	9.7	7.2	7.5
5. Total budgeted government spending	4.9	8.0	6.2	3.4
6. Monetary GDP[d]	1.9	3.1	2.7	2.7

Source: Own computations.

Notes: [a] The years selected are those for which upper-tranche or EFF credits were negotiated. The figures do not agree with published data because of differences in the definition of credit to government.
  [b] On a June-to-June comparison. Ceilings were also agreed for various dates within the fiscal year, which are not shown above.
  [c] 'Year-beginning' refers to the balance as at end-June 1975, 1976, 1979 and 1980 respectively.
  [d] As a percentage of monetary GDP at factor cost and in current prices, in the last calendar year before commencement of the fiscal year in question.

Table 5.10 for each of the fiscal years for which higher-conditionality agreements were negotiated up to 1980/81. These statistics are based on June-to-June comparisons (the fiscal year runs from July to June) and thus ignore the additional ceilings for intermediate dates within the year.

On the basis of the evidence in Table 5.10 it would be impossible to characterise the ceilings as very restrictive. They generally envisage total government borrowing increasing annually by between 31% and 41% (line 2) which, when compounded, are rapid rates of increase. Lines 3 and 4 record the amount of the ceilings as percentages of money supply and total domestic credit but this understates the monetary expansion that would result because much state borrowing from the banking system takes forms that increase the high-powered money base, thus permitting a secondary round of credit expansion to other borrowers. Bolnick (1975a, Table 1) found a money multiplier with an average value of 2.3 so the figures in lines 3 and 4 might be roughly doubled to obtain a better grasp of the degree of expansion implicit in the deficit financing ceiling. (In fact, the letters of intent also contained explicit or implicit targets for the expansion of total domestic credit, which were 19% for 1975/76, 21% for 1976/77, 19% for 1979/80 and 23% for 1980/81.)

In the light of information then available and reasonable forecasts of the immediate future, there was a case for some monetary expansion in mid-1975, to offset the deflationary forces then emanating from the outside world, even though the government had set itself the objective of reducing inflation to 'no more than half of the increase in import prices' (Kenya, 1975, p. 7) and the emergence of the coffee boom in the second half of 1975 soon changed the situation. But any case for expansion had disappeared by the time of the 1976 budget and the ceiling for that year could be criticised as *too high* for the purposes of economic management; 1979/80 was perhaps an intermediate case but given the underlying weakness of the balance of payments situation it would be difficult to argue that a ceiling permitting a 31% increase in government bank borrowing (and a 19% increase in total credit) was excessively restrictive. The same general judgement also holds for the 1980/81 ceiling, which actually envisaged a 41% increase in credit to government (and a 23% increase in total credit). The fact is, of course, that in two of the four years actual deficit financing was well below the agreed ceiling (but see page 205 on the 1979/80 situation), which increases the difficulty of viewing the ceilings as too low.

The matter no doubt looked different to Treasury officials, concerned more with the fiscal situation and how to balance the accounts. Line 5 of the table shows the ceilings as proportions of total budgeted government spending. These were relatively modest, especially in 1980/81. The Treasury was being buffeted by competing pressures – from the IMF to limit the deficit, from the public not to raise taxes and from the spending ministries to raise their budget allocations. Its authority over the spending ministries was also far from unquestioned and was tending to weaken over time. The ceilings were also modest in relation to GDP (line 6). It was through the monetary system, rather than through its direct impact on aggregate spending, that the deficit financing would have its main impact on the economy. But, to repeat, it is difficult to think that the monetary impact of the ceilings would have been deflationary.

VI. MATTERS ARISING

We have analysed three higher-conditionality agreements between the Kenyan government and the IMF, all of which quickly broke down. Generally, the relationship has not worked smoothly. It was the Kenyan government (and the improving payments position) which was responsible for the break-down of the 1975 agreement, although the government may have been less inclined to go its own way had it not perceived the Fund terms as onerous. In 1979/80, however, intra-year credit ceilings proved unworkably tight so that the government was unable to use this credit, for which it was finally declared ineligible in mid-1980 on a legal technicality. This was immediately followed by another Stand-by that was more generous both in value and policy conditions, but this too broke down, largely because of unplanned increases in government spending.

These difficulties must be seen in the context of an economy which has rarely been grossly mismanaged – no hyper-inflation, no hugely over-valued currency – with a rather conservative, pragmatic and generally market-oriented government. The government's dealings with the IMF have not been of any great political sensitivity and there has been no great ideological divide. Ministers and senior officials in the Treasury and central bank are by no means heedless of the importance of economic stability and the Treasury does not disagree with the thrust of the IMF's policies. The principle of conditionality is not contested by them and they see the Fund staff as potentially useful allies in strengthening the hands of the Treasury and bank in their efforts to impose financial discipline. It is thus worth repeating what was said earlier: if successful stabilisation and good working relationships with the Fund are not feasible in Kenya, it is unclear where else in Africa they might be achieved.

It is all the more significant, therefore, that things have worked badly, even though personal relationships have been generally cordial. While they are by no means hostile to the basic task of the Fund, Kenyan officials dislike the way in which that role is played. They contemplate an application for an IMF credit with reluctance and regard negotiations with it as unnecessarily taxing. They also point to the considerable costs of a Fund credit (a) because the interest charges are not now very far below commercial rates and (b) because of what is regarded as the excessive amount of high-level manpower tied up in the preparation of a credit application, the subsequent negotiations and the monitoring of results.

One reason for their reservations about the Fund is that they view it as being too concerned with the short-term, too anxious to achieve quick results. We have shown earlier that, in addition to short run monetary factors, Kenya's payments difficulties stem from basic structural weaknesses and from the effects of rising oil and other import prices. In truth, the increase in real oil prices will not be fully reversed and Kenya must adjust to it. But such adjustment cannot be expected quickly and in the interim there will remain large financing needs. One of the most interesting results to emerge from our research has been the uncertain importance attached by the IMF to medium-term restructuring, even in the context of the EFF, with negotiations and performance criteria being largely confined to conventional, short-term concerns. When Kenyan negotiators urge the need to take a longer-term view and to go beyond the scope of demand management the response from Fund missions is to the effect that they are personally sympathetic but that Washington is looking for a conventional financial programme and that longer-term adjustment is more a concern of the World Bank. On the Kenyan evidence, the EFF makes few concessions to the case for structural adjustment when it comes to detailed policy conditions and to the extent that 'structural' measures are included they are additional to the usual Fund performance criteria. This not only opens the Fund to the criticism that the limitation of aggregate demand is far from being a sufficient condition for adjustment to major disequilibria but also leave it appearing always to require rapid action when a gradual approach might achieve an equal result at a smaller cost.

Comparison with the World Bank invites itself because Kenya was among the first countries to obtain a 'structural adjustment' loan, early in 1980, with another agreed in 1982. The Bank's conditionality for the 1980 loan was quite stringent, involving a rather wide range of specific commitments, largely on industrial protection, and a detailed programme of action, progress with which would influence access to further Bank project and programme loans. The loan signed in 1982 widened the range of conditionality to agricultural and energy policies. In no sense did the Bank's conditions represent a soft option but they differed from those of the Fund both in taking the form of agreed policy actions (rather than numerical outcomes) and in relating to longer-term variables. What is more, the 1980 agreement was regarded as working fairly well, with the Bank reportedly satisfied with implementation and the Kenyan authorities apparently more comfortable in their policy commitments to the Bank than to the Fund.

Another point of interest in the Kenyan case is that there is no evidence that Kenya has obtained an easier deal from the IMF than other member governments because it has asked for assistance at relatively early stages of its crises. It was also difficult to perceive any softening in conditionality as a result of the guidelines review of March 1979. The general scope of the conditions in August 1979 was no less extensive than in 1975. The Fund ceilings on government borrowing at various dates within the 1979/80 fiscal year were regarded in Kenya as harsh and, in the event, proved unworkable. Consistent with more general changes which were occurring in Fund policies at that time, there were signs of some relaxation in 1980 but this was turned sharply around in 1981, again as a reflection of policy changes in Washington.

This said, however, we should bear in mind the conclusion drawn from Table 5.10 that, year-on-year, the ceilings on governments' credit were not generally deflationary, nor particularly restrictive.

But even though they were not excessively restrictive and we have shown that domestic credit is among the important influences on the balance of payments, the credit ceilings are open to the criticism of being highly imperfect and insufficient instruments of macroeconomic management. For reasons given earlier and also as argued more generally in chapter M3 we suggest that:

- monetary forces are only partly responsible for the payments difficulties and inflation;
- the relevant parameters are not sufficiently stable and the time lags not sufficiently understood for the outcome of any given credit restriction to be predicted with reasonable confidence;
- the uncertainties surrounding budget planning are too large and the diffusion of political authority too great for the deficit financing residual to be readily manipulated as an instrument of macro-management.[38]

Deficit financing is important, of course, and, as we suggest shortly, the government could certainly improve its policies in this regard. But the precise quantities of deficit financing and of private credit are weak reeds upon which to place so much of the burden of macroeconomic management. A Fund response to this complaint would be that these ceilings should be viewed as monitoring devices rather than as policy instruments. Suffice it here to refer back to the discussion of this view in chapter M6, which draws attention to a number of difficulties with it.

Not the least of the practical drawbacks of a focus on deficit financing ceilings is the attention bias it causes in negotiations between the government and Fund missions. Much time and effort is spent arguing about the merits of rival forecasts of government spending and revenue, how best to define credit to government and other concepts,[39] and other minutiae of far from central importance to balance of payments adjustment. The arguments tend to be about numbers and may thus be a distraction from a serious discussion of the nature of the problems and how best to solve them. Government officials tend to find this particularly irksome and to make adverse comparisons with what they see as the more fundamentally relevant policy negotiations for World Bank structural adjustment loans.

This type of attention bias adds force to the common ldc complaint that the Fund has a doctrinaire tendency to focus narrowly on a small number of monetary variables. This is particularly unfortunate because, however falteringly, the Fund has sought to adopt a wider, longer-term approach in recent years. Depending on the personality and interests of the mission chief (an important factor in Fund-country relations), staff reports on Kenya have reflected this change. We have already cited the 1974 report which suggested a relaxation of credit policies; this report also urged the government to begin to give thought to the medium-term adjustment problem. Over the years, other reports have concerned themselves with tariff reform, agricultural policies, energy conservation and so forth. We have found it more difficult to tie down the extent to which such longer-term, supply-side concerns have influenced the course and content of concrete credit negotiations – a factor made elusive because of the concurrent existence of agreements or negotiations with the World Bank based upon policies of structural adjustment which may otherwise have featured more prominently in agreements with the Fund. What remains undoubtedly true is that (with an interesting exception in 1980 noted on page 205) the hard core of the EFF and Stand-by agreements – the performance criteria – have retained the Fund's traditional concern with demand management. Had the Fund been able and willing to substitute improved supply-side policies for credit ceilings in its performance criteria the relationship may have been more successful. However, such a suggestion raises questions extending much further than the specifics of the Kenyan case and are dealt with elsewhere in this study.

It would, in any case, be wrong to conclude on a note which suggests that all the difficulties have stemmed from the Fund's approach. This is not at all the case. The Kenyan government has yet to demonstrate a *steady* adherance to the objective of economic stability, especially when it would necessitate politically unpopular measures. It is important here not to confuse the conservatism and responsibility which has generally characterised government policies with the conscious pursuit of policies for short- and medium-term economic management. It has not yet set in place the data base and reporting procedures necessary for monitoring short-run economic trends.[40] There is need for further studies of key macroeconomic relationships and for the development of an econometric model designed to meet the needs of economic management. Experiences in 1980/81 revealed serious weaknesses in the Treasury's ability to monitor the ongoing budgetary situation and in its knowledge of the true extent of external debt. The poor record of fiscal forecasting shown in Table 5.7 could and should be improved. Although we have drawn attention to the limitations of monetary policy, we would add that monetary policy has been weak in Kenya, partly because the central bank has usually interpreted its role in ways which have been incompatible with the increasingly urgent need for effective economic management.

Above all, it seems that during the period surveyed the government had not fully come to terms with the unwelcome implications for its economic policies of a world environment which worsened drastically in 1973 and shows every sign of remaining sharply adverse. Left to itself, a simple inability to import would impose its own payments solution but one that would levy a heavy cost upon the economy and, perhaps, on the country's political fabric. There were encouraging signs in the early 1980s that the government was increasingly coming to the conclusion that the adoption of a more planned approach to payments adjustment was an urgent necessity.

Footnotes

1. My greatest debt is to the Kenyan and IMF officials who assisted me both with information and with comments on an earlier draft but who would prefer to remain unnamed. In addition, I am grateful for helpful comments to Gerry Helleiner, John King, John Roberts, Terry Ryan, Jennifer Sharpley and John Williamson. However, the usual caveat that those who have helped do not necessarily agree with the final product applies with particular force in this case. The following is based upon research conducted in 1980–81 and on information available up to the end of 1981.
2. Kenya, 1965. Other official documents of particular importance include the third and fourth development plans, sessional papers on economic prospects and policies (Kenya, 1975 and 1980), the annual budget speeches, and economic surveys.
3. Papers by the present writer have examined this issue in some detail – see Killick, 1976; a detailed examination of the fourth development plan and joint essays with Kinyua and House, all in Killick, 1981. See also Stewart, 1976; and Hazlewood, 1979.
4. Killick, 1981, provides an extensive introduction to Kenya's economic performance, problems and policies, with the first two chapters providing a general survey of post-Independence performance. Hazlewood, 1979, offers a concise general introduction to economic performance and policies.
5. The distributional aspect of the country's economic record is examined in some detail in Part IV of Killick, 1981.
6. Heyer *et al.*, 1976, provide an excellent treatment of the development of the agricultural sector.
7. See Ikiara, 1981, Tables 14 and 15. The 1979 and 1980 figures were calculated from Kenya, *Economic Surveys*. Strictly speaking petroleum products are the second-most important export earner but this is misleading because it is based on the refining of imported crude oil.
8. See World Bank, 1975, pp. 93–94 and passim.
9. The most detailed examination of the balance of payments is provided in Maitha, Killick and Ikiara, 1978. See also Grubel and Ryan, 1979; and Killick, 1981, paper II-3.
10. See Brough and Curtin, 1981, on this.
11. In 1968 prices, domestic credit went up from £37m in 1964 to £132m in 1972, a growth rate of nearly 16% p.a. (c.f. Killick, 1981, Table 4, p. 7).
12. These figures are taken from Kenya, *Economic Survey, 1981*, Table 10.1 and similar tables in earlier *Surveys*.
13. From an IMF paper of August 1980. The regression reported is the one which gave the highest R^2 and is based on 1966–78 data. The results reported are after the regression had been re-run correcting for autocorrelation using the Cochran-Orcutt method. The significance of the results was much reduced, however, when 1979 data were included.
14. Herbert G. Grubel, 'Why the Kenyan shilling should be devalued', *Sunday Nation*, Nairobi, 11 February 1979.
15. In the 1977/78 and 1978/79 fiscal years revenue from this tax amounted to just K£10.8 million, against export proceeds from these crops in 1977–78 of K£464.2 million. It is only fair to add, though, that governments in other coffee producing

countries also failed to resist the temptation of windfall gains. While they typically creamed off far more of the gains through formal or informal export taxation they also typically used it to finance an unsustainable burst of government spending; see Davis, 1980 and also Struckmeyer 1977.

16. Computed from Kenya, *Economic Survey, 1980* and *Statistical Abstract 1979*.

17. In principle the GDP deflator would be a preferable price index. In the case of Kenya, however, many of the 'indices' used to deflate the national accounts are very crude and unreliable. The Nairobi CPI, while much more limited in scope, is at least reasonably reliable and there is evidence that rural prices have moved in a similar manner. We have chosen the lower-income index as being the most relevant to the majority of Kenyans.

18. There is much evidence from other countries for such an inverse relation, as shown in chapter M2, page 44.

19. The 10.2% inflation recorded for 1973 in Table 5.5, which is based on comparisons of averaged quarterly data, disguises the acceleration which occurred during that year On a December-to-December basis, the inflation rate was 16.0%.

20. One complicating factor here is that during 1978–79 credit by non-bank financial institutions expanded rapidly, so that the 1978–80 figures in col. (4) probably understate the relevant trend. This may help us a little to explain the 1980 inflation but it adds a further complication to the 1979 experience.

21. See Killick, 1981 pp. 113–14, for a brief general evaluation of the implementation of the sessional paper; also Killick, 1980, pp. 41–42.

22. In a newspaper article at the time of the budget the present writer criticised it as ill-advised, based on a mis-reading of the economic situation and adding fuel to an already over-heated situation, cf. Tony Killick, 'Kenya's budget: expansion or inflation', *Sunday Nation*, Nairobi, 19 June 1977. In the event, an unforseen upsurge in tax revenues resulted in a much improved budgetary out-turn, but what is most relevant for present purposes is that in its fiscal planning the government should favour what it intended as an expansionary budget in circumstances where short-run management clearly indicated the desirability of moderation.

23. On these budgets see articles by Killick in the *Sunday Nation*, Nairobi, 18 June 1978 and 17 June 1979.

24. Killick, 1981, pp. 104–5, criticises the plan for the weakness of its balance of payments policies, especially its silence on exchange rate policy and its failure to offer adequate incentives for improved export performance.

25. See Rupley and Finucane, 1980, for a detailed examination of the 1980 budget.

26. By October 1981 the interest rate on bank savings deposits was up to 10% against only 5% at end-1979; and maximum bank lending rates were up from 10% to 14%.

27. See Maitha *et al.*, 1978, pp. 50–51, for a discussion of this.

28. Estimates by UNCTAD show the real exchange rate, after adjustment for differential rates of inflation, to have reverted to the pre-1975 devaluation level by early 1978.

29. See Brough and Curtin, 1981, for a general review. Also Killick, 1981, pp. 6–7, Table 3 and text.

30. Tait *et al.*, 1979, compute international tax comparison indices for 47 ldcs for 1969–71 and 1972–76. By this comparison Kenya ranked 18th and 11th for the two periods respectively. Chelliah *et al.*, 1975, also rank Kenya with above-average tax effort indices in 1966–71.

31. Data in *IMF Survey*, 7 September 1981, p. 276, show an average overall deficit for 1973–78 equal to 19% of expenditures for Kenya, against 20% for Africa as a whole.

32. The variability of both parameters is much smaller for the 1968–71 period, which may explain why King obtained reasonable predictions from his model.

33. According to the World Bank, 1981, p. 148, petroleum imports represented 95% of total Kenyan commercial energy consumption in 1978, which was among the highest recorded in Africa.

34. This and the following paragraph are based upon Bhatia and Rothman, 1975, which provides a useful account of Kenya's EFF credit. See also chapter M5.

35. Of this sum $55 million was to come from the World Bank's IDA window, to be supplemented by a $15 million EEC Special Action Credit.

36.   The relevant part of the press release read as follows (*IMF Survey* 27 October 1980, p. 339).

The Government has formulated a set of medium-term policies designed to strengthen the balance of payments and establish a high rate of growth of output and employment. These policies address the restructuring of the economy, with greater emphasis on agricultural growth and a reorientation of the manufacturing sector away from import substitution and towards exports. This medium term strategy will be complemented by short-term demand management policies designed to contain inflationary pressures and the external deficit while the reallocation of resources in the economy is taking place. The Government also intends to take firm action to restrain the consumption of petroleum-based energy by making optimal use of imported fuels and by accelerating the development of alternative energy sources.

37.   The ceilings on the net domestic assets of the central bank never created any difficulties and this item was dropped as a performance criterion in 1980, when total domestic credit was added.

38.   The 1975 EFF agreement provides a revealing illustration of the uncertainties and the resulting difficulties of treating government bank borrowing as a variable to be consciously manipulated as a policy instrument. This set a ceiling on bank lending to the government in the July 1976/June 1977 fiscal year of K£30.75 million. In a draft communication to the Fund of 11 May 1977 (i.e. only about 7 weeks before the end of the fiscal year) the government wrote that it now expected government borrowing to exceed the ceiling by the end of the year and to amount to K£42.5 million: 'It appears that the budgetary situation has become more intractable than we had anticipated.' In the end, however, there was a large reduction in government indebtedness in the last weeks of the year and the net increase in government borrowing was only K£9.5 million. A year later a Fund staff evaluation wrote of 'growing uncertainties surrounding budgetary prospects which have led the authorities to produce varying estimates of likely budget deficits and, correspondingly, their requirements of bank financing'.

39.   There was, for example, much concern in 1976–77 within the Fund and the Treasury about precisely what item should be included in calculations of net credit to the government from the banking system, and there appears to have been considerable confusion about the application of this.

40.   See Murugu, 1978, for a survey of short-run economic indicators in Kenya and suggestions for improvement.

References

Adongo, J.I., *Inflation in Kenya, 1964–77*, M.A. Research Paper, University of Nairobi, June 1978.

Bhatia, Rhattan J. and Rothman, Saul L., 'Introducing the extended Fund facility: the Kenyan case', *Finance and Development*, December 1975.

Bolnick, Bruce R., 'Behaviour of the determinants of money supply in Kenya', *Eastern Africa Economic Review*, 7(1), June 1975.

Brough, A.T. and Curtin, T.R.C., 'Growth and stability: an account of fiscal and monetary policy', in Killick (ed), 1981.

Central Bank of Kenya, *Sources and Uses of Foreign Exchange in Kenya, 1974–79*, Nairobi, 1981.

Chelliah, R.J., Bass, H.J. and Kelly, M.R., 'Tax ratios and tax effort in developing countries, 1969–71', *IMF Staff Papers*, 22(1), March 1975.

Davis, Jeffrey M., 'The economic effects of windfall gains in export earnings, 1975–78', Washington, *IMF Unpublished paper*, February 1980.

Grubel, Herbert G., and Ryan, T.C.I., 'A monetary model of Kenya's balance of payments', University of Nairobi (mimeo), n.d. ca 1979.

Hazlewood, Arthur, *The Economy of Kenya: the Kenyatta Era*. Oxford University Press, 1979.

Heyer, Judith, Maitha, J.K., Senga, W.M. (eds), *Agricultural Development in Kenya*, Nairobi, Oxford University Press, 1976.

Hopcraft, P.N., 'Outward-looking industrialisation: the promotion of manufactured exports from Kenya, *Discussion Paper No. 141*. Institute for Development Studies, University of Nairobi, September 1972.

Ibrahim, Tigani E., 'Prospects for export growth in an African economy: the Kenya case', *Viertelsjahresberichte*, No.80, June 1980.

International Labour Office (ILO), *Employment, Incomes and Equality: a Strategy for Increasing Productive Employment in Kenya*, Geneva, ILO, 1972.

Ikiara, G.K., 'Structural changes in the Kenyan economy', in Killick (ed), 1981.

Kenya, Republic of, *African Socialism and its Application to Planning in Kenya*. Nairobi, Government Printer, 1965.

——, *Sessional Paper No.4 of 1975: On Economic Prospects and Policies*, Nairobi, 1975.

——, *Sessional Paper No.4 of 1980: On Economic Prospects and Policies*, Nairobi, Government Printer, 1980.

Killick, Tony, 'Strengthening Kenya's development strategy: opportunities and constraints', *Eastern Africa Economic Review*, 8(2), December 1976.

——, 'On implementing development plans: a case study', *ODI Review*, 1980, No. 1 (with J.K. Kinyua), also published in Killick, 1981a.

——, (ed), *Papers on the Kenyan Economy: Performance, Problems and Policies*, Nairobi and London, Heinemann Educational Books, 1981a.

——, ' "By their fruits ye shall know them": the fourth development plan', in Killick, 1981a–1981b.

——, 'Inequality and poverty in the rural economy, and the influence of some aspects of policy' (with W.J. House) in Killick, 1981a–1981c.

——, 'Problems of an open economy: the balance of payments in the 1970s (with M. Thorne), in Killick, 1981a–1981d.

——, 'The performance of the economy since Independence' (with G.K. Ikiara), in Killick, 1981a–1981e.

King, J.R., *Stabilization Policy in an African Setting: Kenya, 1963–73*. London Heinemann Educational Books, 1979.

Maitha, J.K., Killick, Tony, and Idiara, G.K., *The Balance of Payments Adjustment Process in Developing Countries: Kenya*, University of Nairobi, 1978.

Murugu, John K. *Requirements for Short-Term Economic Management in Kenya*. M.A. research paper, University of Nairobi, January 1981.

Newlyn, W.T., 'Monetary analysis and policy in financially dependent economies', in I.G. Stewart (ed.), *Economic Development and Structural Change*, Edinburgh University Press, 1969.

Park, Yung Chul, 'The variability of velocity: an international comparison', *IMF Staff Papers*, XVII (3), November 1970.

Rupley, Lawrence A. and Finucane, Brendan P., 'Kenya's 1980 budget', International Bureau of Fiscal Documentation, *Bulletin*, January 1981.

Sharpley, Jennifer, 'Resource transfers between the agricultural and nonagricultural sectors, 1964–77', in Killick (ed), 1981a.

Stewart, Frances, 'Kenya: strategies for development', in U.K. Damachi, G. Routh and A-R E. Ali taha (eds), *Development Paths in Africa and China*, London, Macmillan Press, 1976 (also reproduced in Killick, 1981a).

Struckmeyer, Horst J., 'Coffee prices and Central America', *Finance and Development*, 14(3); September 1977.

Tait, A.A., Grätz, W.L.M. and Eichengreen, B.J., 'International comparisons of taxation for selected developing countries, 1972–76', *IMF Staff Papers*, 26(1), March 1979.

Wescott, Clay G., 'Industrial policy: a case study of incentives for industrial dispersion', in Killick (ed), 1981a.

World Bank, *Kenya: Into the Second Decade*, Baltimore, John Hopkins, 1975.